PRAISE FOR
WAKING *the* WITCH

"Pam Grossman has written a flowing history that I scarfed down like an éclair. She reminds us that witches are not monsters so much as *possibilities*. The archetypal, swirling symbol of 'witch' is a guide to remind us that we are allowed to act on our desires AND congratulate ourselves for choosing to. I hope this book makes everyone who reads it ask themselves 'What do I deny myself and why?' I started this book all in, but when I read the sentence 'Show me your witches, and I'll show you your feelings about women,' I knew I was done for."

—Neko Case, singer-songwriter

"Deftly illuminating the past while beckoning us towards the future, *Waking the Witch* has all the makings of a feminist classic. Wise, relatable, and real, Pam Grossman is the witch we need for our times."

—Ami McKay, author of *The Witches of New York*

"A masterful and moving meditation on female power and persecution, *Waking the Witch* deftly lifts the veil between fact and fiction, indulging joyfully and critically in the distortions and delectations that have surrounded magical women for millennia. Pam Grossman is a beacon in the world of contemporary witchcraft and neo-paganism, and this comprehensive work grounded in scholarship and cultural criticism is brought to life through intimate stories from her own life and spiritual practice. *Waking the*

Witch is an artful gateway into a history that is both profoundly and painfully relevant today. Whether you're intrigued by or deeply committed to the who, what, when, where, and why of the witch, this book is for you."

—Kristen J. Sollée, author of *Witches, Sluts, Feminists:*
Conjuring the Sex Positive

"The wonderful Pam Grossman takes us on a whirlwind tour of witches in history, literature, and the cinematic and visual arts, serving up much food for thought along the way. Her exploration of alchemical artists Leonora Carrington and Remedios Varo is no less than brilliant. But my own favorite parts of *Waking the Witch* are Pam's generously shared descriptions of her own personal journey to magic and power. Recommended!"

—Judika Illes, author of *Encyclopedia of Witchcraft*,
The Encyclopedia of 5000 Spells, and other books of magic

"With this brilliant offering, Pam untangles the web of the witch and invites us to explore all the aspects of ourselves that linger in the shadows. *Waking the Witch* weaves us into the mystery of the witch, reminding us of her familiarity through stories, symbols, and the subconscious, inviting us into her world with a wink and the promise of an apple. Pam reminds us of the resilience of the witch, of all we have to learn from her, and of what she has to offer us. Through both her words and practice, Pam exemplifies that now more than ever, we need to wake the witch in her magick. This book is an indispensable addition to anyone's altar or bookshelf, witch or not."

—Gabriela Herstik, author of *Inner Witch:*
A Modern Guide to the Ancient Craft

"Elegant, grounded, and warm, Pam Grossman is the perfect guide for initiation into the mysteries of the witch. Pam conjures witches from their many dwellings in history, feminism, and pop culture with care and play. Swaying among this coven is Pam herself, embodying the witch in a tender spiritual memoir woven through the cultural sense-making. *Waking the Witch* goes beyond edifying and enjoyable, casting a spell that might wake your own connection to magic, beauty, and meaning."

—Taisia Kitaiskaia, author of *Literary Witches: A Celebration of Magical Women Writers* and *Ask Baba Yaga: Otherworldly Advice for Everyday Troubles*

"Students and scholars will savor *Waking the Witch*'s historicism— which is brilliant—and practitioners will thrill to its understanding and inspiration. In a world of boundless choices, this is one of the singularly finest works for understanding modern witchcraft. It will never leave my bookshelf."

—Mitch Horowitz, PEN Award–winning author of *Occult America* and *The Miracle Club*

"Pam Grossman's brilliant examination of the witch in history, literature, politics, and contemporary culture provides much-needed insight into our convoluted and deeply held beliefs about feminine power. With wit and wisdom, scholarship and sass, Grossman reveals why witches both frighten and fascinate us, and why witchcraft's popularity is growing today as women reclaim their birthright after centuries of infamy. *Waking the Witch* is a must-read if you want to understand gender politics today or seek to enjoy a more fulfilling relationship with the women in your life.

Prepare to be pleasantly awakened as you meet your own inner witch, reconnect with her origins, and see how honoring her can transform your world."

—Skye Alexander, author of *The Modern Guide to Witchcraft* and *The Modern Witchcraft Spell Book*

"Conjuring a contemporary perspective on the witch in both fact and fiction, Pam Grossman lays the breadcrumbs, connecting the corners from devilish cohort to bubblegum hero and all the identities between. Sublime, witty, and often deeply personal, she draws you into her circle, that of the Divine Feminine and her Earthly practitioners."

—Nicola Scott, *Wonder Woman* comics artist and cocreator of *Black Magick*

"My heart thrills in gratitude for this book and for everything Pam Grossman contributes to the study, practice, and pleasure of witchcraft. With rare insight and a flair for nuance, *Waking the Witch* explores ambiguous territories few writers dare to tread. As only a practicing witch could do, Grossman engages the witch archetype even in the liminal spaces where she becomes most difficult. Witches are myths, are monsters, are sisters and sirens, and witches are REAL. Fearless and brilliant, this book is a must-read for anyone interested in spirituality with intelligence."

—Amanda Yates Garcia, author of *Initiated* and cohost of the *Strange Magic* podcast

WAKING

the

WITCH

REFLECTIONS ON
WOMEN, MAGIC, AND POWER

PAM GROSSMAN

G

GALLERY BOOKS

NEW YORK LONDON TORONTO SYDNEY NEW DELHI

G

Gallery Books
An Imprint of Simon & Schuster, Inc.
1230 Avenue of the Americas
New York, NY 10020

Certain names and other characteristics of those portrayed have been changed.

Excerpts of letter from Remedios Varo to Gerald Gardner from *Letters, Dreams, & Other Writings* by Remedios Varo, translated by Margaret Carson. Translation copyright © 2018 by Margaret Carson. Used by permission of Wakefield Press. All rights reserved.

Excerpts of "A Spell to Bind Donald Trump and All Those Who Abet Him" from *Magic for the Resistance: Rituals and Spells for Change* by Michael H. Hughes, copyright © 2018 by Michael H. Hughes. Used by permission of Llewellyn Publications. All rights reserved.

Some portions of this book have previously appeared in *Sabat Magazine, Ravenous Zine*, and *Huffington Post*.

First Gallery Books hardcover edition June 2019

GALLERY BOOKS and colophon are registered trademarks of Simon & Schuster, Inc.

For information about special discounts for bulk purchases, please contact Simon & Schuster Special Sales at 1-866-506-1949 or business@simonandschuster.com.

The Simon & Schuster Speakers Bureau can bring authors to your live event. For more information or to book an event, contact the Simon & Schuster Speakers Bureau at 1-866-248-3049 or visit our website at www.simonspeakers.com.

Interior design by Jaime Putorti

Manufactured in the United States of America

10 9 8 7 6 5 4 3 2 1

Library of Congress Cataloging-in-Publication Data
Names: Grossman, Pam, author.
Title: Waking the witch : reflections on women, magic, and power / Pam Grossman.
Description: New York : Gallery Books, 2019.
Identifiers: LCCN 2018054467| ISBN 9781982100704 (trade pbk.) | ISBN 9781982100711 (ebook)
Subjects: LCSH: Witches. | Women—Miscellanea.
Classification: LCC BF1571.5.W66 G76 2019 | DDC 133.4/3—dc23
LC record available at https://lccn.loc.gov/2018054467

ISBN 978-1-9821-0070-4
ISBN 978-1-9821-0071-1 (ebook)

For Matt,
the most charming man I've ever met

I fear, and I love, I love, and I fear,
The Far Away Ladies now hovering near.

—Helen Adam
"At Mortlake Manor"

Contents

WAKING
the
WITCH

Witches have always walked among us, populating societies and storyscapes across the globe for thousands of years. From Circe to Hermione, from Morgan le Fay to Marie Laveau, the witch has long existed in the tales we tell about ladies with strange powers that can harm or heal. And although people of all genders have been considered witches, it is a word that is now usually associated with women.

Throughout most of history, she has been someone to fear, an uncanny Other who threatens our safety or manipulates reality for her own mercurial purposes. She's a pariah, a persona non grata, a bogeywoman to defeat and discard. Though she has often been deemed a destructive entity, in actuality a witchy woman has historically been far more susceptible to attack than an inflictor of violence herself. As with other "terrifying" outsiders, she occupies a paradoxical role in cultural consciousness as both vicious aggressor and vulnerable prey.

Over the past 150 years or so, however, the witch has done

another magic trick, by turning from a fright into a figure of inspiration. She is now as likely to be the heroine of your favorite TV show as she is its villain. She might show up in the form of your Wiccan coworker, or the beloved musician who gives off a sorceress vibe in videos or onstage.

There is also a chance that she is *you*, and that "witch" is an identity you have taken upon yourself for any number of reasons—heartfelt or flippant, public or private.

Today, more women than ever are choosing the way of the witch, whether literally or symbolically. They're floating down catwalks and sidewalks in gauzy black clothing and adorning themselves with Pinterest-worthy pentagrams and crystals. They're filling up movie theaters to watch witchy films, and gathering in back rooms and backyards to do rituals, consult tarot cards, and set life-altering intentions. They're marching in the streets with HEX THE PATRIARCHY placards and casting spells each month to try to constrain the commander in chief. Year after year, articles keep proclaiming, "It's the Season of the Witch!" as journalists try to wrap their heads around the mushrooming witch "trend."

And all of this begs the question: *Why?*

Why do witches matter? Why are they seemingly everywhere right now? What, exactly, *are* they? (And why the hell won't they go away?)

I get asked such things over and over, and you would think that after a lifetime of studying and writing about witches, as well as hosting a witch-themed podcast and being a practitioner of witchcraft myself, my answers would be succinct.

In fact, I find that the more I work with the witch, the more complex she becomes. Hers is a slippery spirit: try to pin her down, and she'll only recede further into the deep, dark wood.

I do know this for sure though: show me your witches, and I'll show you your feelings about women. The fact that the resurgence of feminism and the popularity of the witch are ascending at the same time is no coincidence: the two are reflections of each other.

That said, this current Witch Wave is nothing new. I was a teen in the 1990s, the decade that brought us such pop-occulture as *Buffy the Vampire Slayer*, *Charmed*, and *The Craft*, not to mention riot grrrls and third-wave feminists who taught me that female power could come in a variety of colors and sexualities. I learned that women could lead a revolution while wearing lipstick *and* combat boots—and sometimes even a cloak.

But my own witchly awakening came at an even earlier age.

Morganville, New Jersey, where I was raised, was a solidly suburban town, but it retained enough natural land features back then to still feel a little bit scruffy in spots. We had a small patch of woods in our backyard that abutted a horse farm, and the two were separated by a wisp of running water that we could cross via a plank of wood. When we were little, my older sister, Emily, and I would sometimes venture to the other side, where we could feed the horses (an act that still scares me to this day) and pick fistfuls of clover. But the majority of our time was spent on our side of the stream, threading ourselves through the thicket of trees that served as our personal forest. In one corner of the yard, a giant puddle would form whenever it rained, surrounded by a border of ferns. We called this spot our Magical Place. That it would vanish and then reappear only added to its mystery. It was a portal to the unknown.

These woods are where I first remember doing magic—

entering that state of deep play where imaginative action becomes reality. I would spend hours out there, creating rituals with rocks and sticks, drawing secret symbols in the dirt, losing all track of time. It was a space that felt holy and wild, yet still strangely safe.

As we age, we're supposed to stop filling our heads with such "nonsense." Unicorns are to be traded in for Barbie dolls (though both are mythical creatures, to be sure). We lose our tooth fairies, walk away from our wizards. Dragons get slain on the altar of youth.

Most kids grow out of their "magic phase." I grew further into mine.

My grandma Trudy was a librarian at the West Long Branch Library, which meant I got to spend many an afternoon lurking between the 001.9 and 135 Dewey decimal–sections, reading about Bigfoot and dream interpretation and Nostradamus. I spent countless hours in my room, learning about witches and goddesses, and I loved anything by authors like George MacDonald, Roald Dahl, and Michael Ende—writers fluent in the language of enchantment. Books were my broomstick. They allowed me to fly to other realms where anything was possible.

My very favorite book was *Wise Child* by Monica Furlong, a story about a young girl who gets taken in by Juniper, a kind and beautiful witch who lives at the top of a hill in the Scottish countryside. Juniper is feared by the local townsfolk because she doesn't practice their religion and because she is a woman who lives on her own. She teaches Wise Child the ways of natural medicine and magic, and shows her the kind of love that a mother might. The villagers come to them in secret whenever they are in need of healing, but in public, Juniper and Wise Child are shunned. Witches, I learned from the book, are complicated creatures, sources of great comfort and great terror. And no matter how good a witch might be, she would often become the target of misunderstanding at best and persecution at worst.

The witch is always at risk. Nevertheless, she persists.

Though fictional witches were my first guides, I soon discovered that magic was something real people could do. I started frequenting new age shops and experimenting with mass-market paperback spell books from the mall. I was raised Jewish but found myself attracted to belief systems that felt more individualized and mystical and that fully honored the feminine. Eventually I found my way to modern Paganism, a self-directed spiritual path that sustains me to this day. I'm not unique in this trajectory of pivoting away from organized religion and toward something more personal: as of September 2017, more than a quarter of US adults—27 percent—now say that they think of themselves as spiritual but not religious, according to Pew Research Center.

Now, I identify both *as* a witch and *with* the archetype of the witch overall, and I use the term fluidly. At any given time, I might use the word *witch* to signify my spiritual beliefs, my supernatural interests, or my role as an unapologetically complex, dynamic female in a world that prefers its women to be smiling and still. I use it with equal parts sincerity and salt: with a bow to a rich and often painful history of worldwide witchcraft, and a wink to other members of our not-so-secret society of people who fight from the fringes for the liberty to be our weirdest and most wondrous selves. Magic is made in the margins.

To be clear: you don't have to practice witchcraft or any other alternative form of spirituality to awaken your own inner witch. You may feel attracted to her symbolism, her style, or her stories but are not about to rush out to buy a cauldron or go sing songs to the sky. Maybe you're more of a *nasty woman* than a devotee of the Goddess. That's perfectly fine: the witch belongs to you too.

I remain more convinced than ever that the concept of the witch endures *because* she transcends literalism and because she has so many dark and sparkling things to teach us. Many people get fixated on the "truth" of the witch, and numerous fine history books attempt to tackle the topic from the angle of so-called factuality. Did people actually believe in magic? They most certainly did and still do. Were the thousands of victims who were killed in the sixteenth- and seventeenth-century witch hunts actually witches themselves? Most likely not. Are witches real? Why, yes, you're reading the words of one. All of these things are true.

But whether or not there were actually women and men who practiced witchcraft in Rome or Lancashire or Salem, say, is less interesting to me than the fact that the *idea* of witches has remained so evocative and influential and so, well, bewitching in the first place.

In other words, the fact and the fiction of the witch are inextricably linked. Each informs the other and always has. And so, it's from this fuzzy, fabulist focal point that I regard her in the following chapters—and in general. I'm fascinated by how one archetype can encompass so many different facets. The witch is a notorious shape-shifter, and she comes in many guises:

A hag in a pointy hat, cackling madly as she boils a pot of bones.

A scarlet-lipped seductress slipping a potion into the drink of her unsuspecting paramour.

A cross-dressing French revolutionary who hears the voices of angels and saints.

A perfectly coiffed suburban housewife, twitching her nose to change her circumstances at will, despite her husband's protests.

A woman dancing in New York City's Central Park with her coven to mark the change of the seasons or a new lunar phase.

The witch has a green face and a fleet of flying monkeys.

She wears scarves and leather and lace.

She lives in Africa; on the island of Aeaea; in a tower; in a chicken-leg hut; in Peoria, Illinois.

She lurks in the forests of fairy tales, in the gilded frames of paintings, in the plotlines of sitcoms and YA novels, and between the bars of ghostly blues songs.

She is solitary.

She comes in threes.

She's a member of a coven.

Sometimes she's a he.

She is stunning, she is hideous, she is insidious, she is ubiquitous.

She is our downfall. She is our deliverance.

Our witches say as much about us as they do about anything else—for better and for worse.

More than anything, though, the witch is a shining and shadowy symbol of female power and a force for subverting the status quo. No matter what form she takes, she remains an electric source of magical agitation that we can all plug into whenever we need a high-voltage charge.

She is also a vessel that contains our conflicting feelings *about* female power: our fear of it, our desire for it, and our hope that it can—and will—grow stronger, despite the flames that are thrown at it.

Whether the witch is depicted as villainous or valorous, she is always a figure of freedom—both its loss and its gain. She is perhaps the only female archetype who is an independent operator. Virgins, whores, daughters, mothers, wives—each of these is defined by whom she is sleeping with or not, the care that she is giving or that is given to her, or some sort of symbiotic debt that she must eventually pay.

The witch owes nothing. That is what makes her dangerous. And that is what makes her divine.

Witches have power on their own terms. They have agency. They create. They praise. They commune with the spiritual realm, freely and free of any mediator.

They metamorphose, and they make things happen. They are change agents whose primary purpose is to transform the world as it is into the world they would like it to be.

This is also why being called a witch and calling oneself a witch are usually two vastly different experiences. In the first case, it's often an act of degradation, an attack against a perceived threat.

The second is an act of reclamation, an expression of autonomy and pride. Both of these aspects of the archetype are important to keep in mind. They may seem like contradictions, but there is much to glean from their interplay.

The witch is the ultimate feminist icon because she is a fully rounded symbol of female oppression *and* liberation. She shows us how to tap into our own might and magic, despite the many who try to strip us of our power.

We need her now more than ever.

What follows, then, is an exploration of the archetype of the witch: meditations on her various aspects and associations, questions she's conjured throughout my life, and lessons I've learned from walking the witch's path.

And it is a permission slip for you too to identify with her, should you feel yourself falling under her spell.

Look around. Look within.

The witch is waking up.

Chapter 1

THE GOOD, THE BAD,
AND THE WICKED

"You're a good witch, right?" the CEO of the company I work for asks me as we sit drinking Aperol Spritzes in a splashy West Village restaurant in Manhattan. She takes a quick sip, then peers over her glass at me with a nervous smile.

"Of course," I reply with a dismissive laugh, and then quickly change the subject. It's not that I'm lying. It's more that I've been down this road many times before, and it's one I don't particularly feel like navigating tonight. The one where I'm prompted to discuss my personal beliefs and otherworldly extracurricular activities as a matter of small talk, trying to make the inquirer feel at ease all the while. The one where I have to fit myself into one of two Oz-ian boxes: good witch or bad witch.

I don't hide my witchly self. Frankly, I don't think I could if I tried. Between my podcast and writings and other magic-oriented projects—let alone my predilection for diaphanous dark fabrics and lunar jewelry—at this point in my life, what you see is what you get. But where things can get tricky is how my identity as a witch squares with all of the other roles I hold: As a daughter-in-law to two Episcopal priests, say. As a stranger being introduced to a new person at a friend's party. As a public figure who represented a major corporation for fourteen years. No matter the positive PR of late, using the word *witch* as a personal descriptor still puts people on edge.

My instinct is to try to allay their fears: No, I'm not satanic (though the Satanists I've met are actually quite nice and not at all what you'd imagine!). No, I don't do spells to hurt anybody (not anymore, at least!). No, I'm not evil (no more than anyone else who is trying their best but is ultimately subject to the foibles of humanity!). No, no, no, I will not curse your marriage, blight your crops, sour your milk, drink your blood, or slaughter your children. Don't worry, I promise: I'm not here to do the devil's bidding!

Witch is a word I've chosen for myself. In part, it's shorthand to signify that I'm a practicing Pagan, common parlance within a large community of people who have found an approach to spirituality that is outside of (though not necessarily in opposition to) the five or so dominant world religions. I follow the holy wheel of the year and the cycles of the moon, doing rituals and seasonally appropriate celebrations. I honor nature and the divinity that is inside me and all living beings, and I strive to spread light and to be in service of something higher than myself: Spirit, the gods, the Goddess, the Mystery—that which language is too restrictive to name.

I have also done all of this while paying my rent on time, having a meaningful day job, donating time and resources to causes I believe in, and supporting my husband, friends, and family through thick and thin.

I think I'm a pretty great witch, thank you very much.

To complicate matters, in witchcraft circles there are other classifications beyond "good" and "bad." Some speak of "white witches," or witches who pledge to do no harm, and "black witches," or those who will resort to hexes—though this language is quickly falling out of favor due to its racist undertones. Some speak of "left-handed" versus "right-handed" magic, signifying whether or not one is focused mainly on individual self-development as opposed to being beholden to a group or universal deity. Some practice "chaos magic," which sounds rather alarming but simply refers to a kind of postmodern "whatever works" approach that blends images and techniques from different religions or genres, sometimes in unorthodox or even humorous ways.

As with all categorical systems, interpretations of each of these terms vary, and lines between them can be blurry. Furthermore, many people are attracted to witchcraft *because* it is highly individualized. There is no one book or single leader or unifying set of dogmata, which means you learn as you go. You research, you experiment, and you evolve as you encounter others who have also been drawn to this path.

The vast majority of practitioners I know are some of the most compassionate and curious people I've ever met. They value love and knowledge above all else, and in many cases you wouldn't necessarily know they are witches unless they told you. I know witches who are lawyers, chefs, teachers, advertising executives, artists, accountants, nurses, and everything in between. Doing witchcraft is a way for us to strive to be the best version of ourselves, to honor the sacred, and ultimately to try to make the planet a better place. It also allows for the fact that both light *and* darkness can offer great gifts. And while there is often some overlap in how we practice, everybody does things a bit differently. We may cast spells, do rituals, meditate, seek guidance from systems like astrology or tarot. We may honor our ancestors, celebrate nature's cycles, ask for help, give thanks. We may be looking to heal or to be of spiritual service. But no matter what form our magic-making takes, for many of us, the word *witch* signifies that we are people who actively embody the paradox of having a transcendent experience while feeling more deeply connected to ourselves and each other, here on earth.

I call myself *witch* for other reasons, too. It is a means of identifying how I carry myself in the world, and the kind of energetic current I wish to be a conduit for.

At any given time, it can signify that I am a feminist; someone who celebrates freedom for all and who will fight against injustice using every tool at her disposal; a person who values intuition and self-expression; a kindred spirit with other people who favor the unconventional, the underground, and the uncanny. Or it can simply refer to the fact that I am a woman who dares to speak her own mind and display the full gamut of human emotion—behavior that is still met by society with judgment or disdain. Like many others these days, I use this word with both absolute conviction and with my tongue in my cheek. And like many such epithets, it is loaded and coded. I'm thoughtful about how I use it, when and why and with whom, because it is a word that carries weight, even as it liberates.

It resists being flattened or reduced. It bristles at binary. And that's also why I love it, because, hey, so do I.

★ ★ ★

RIGHT OFF THE batwing, the problem with witches is that they have *always* been difficult to define.

Most books about the history of the witch tend to begin the same way. They start with the word itself: where it comes from, what it means, and how the writer intends to use it in the forth-coming text.

Many of them will tell you that the etymology of the word *witch* is unclear. Most sources say it's derived from the Old English *wicca* or *wicce*, meaning "male or female magic-worker," respec-tively. Some say that those in turn come from words associated with bending, or with wicks, or with willows. Or that it's a permu-tation of older words for "wisdom" or "wise." And so, they often conclude, the witch is someone who has knowledge about how to shape reality, to make changes happen at will.

Now all of this is in reference to the Western witch with its dis-tinctly European context. But nearly every culture has its version of witches, let alone many flavors of magical people including sor-cerers, soothsayers, oracles, healers, and shamans. For the purposes of this book, I'm going to focus primarily on the English-derived word *witch*, as that by itself is intricately complicated.

So, what do we mean when we use it?

Well, it turns out, that depends.

In Ronald Hutton's book *The Witch: A History of Fear, from Ancient Times to the Present*, he begins by stating that there are currently no fewer than four common meanings of the word *witch*. To paraphrase: someone who uses magic for malevolent means; any person who uses magic at all (whether good, bad, or neutral); a follower of nature-based Paganism, such as Wicca; and a figure of transgressive female power. Many historical books like his tend to focus on the first definition. After all, witches have been associated with evil since they first apparated on the scene.

But today these definitions blur together, informing and influencing each other. The witch wouldn't now be a feminist icon, for example, without that primary malevolent meaning to riff off of and rail against.

Malcolm Gaskill writes about what he calls the "murkiness" of the witch archetype. In his book *Witchcraft: A Very Short Introduction*, he states, ". . . [W]itches resist simplification, and are as diverse and complicated as the contexts to which they belong: economy, politics, religion, family, community, and mentality. . . ."

Or as Jack Zipes puts it a bit more succinctly in *The Irresistible Fairy Tale*: "We use the word 'naturally' in all Western countries as if we all know what a witch is. We don't."

But perhaps my favorite statement on the matter is from Margot Adler, who writes in her monumental book on modern Paganism, *Drawing Down the Moon*: "The lexicographical definitions of *witch* are rather confusing, and bear little relation to the definitions given by Witches themselves."

Well, you might suggest, we can at least look at the facts, and start at the beginning of human civilization, when magic was believed by most everyone to be real. The trouble is, the toil is, a clear history of the witch as such is impossible to concretize, though there have been some admirable attempts. As those books will tell you, myriad rich traditions of folk magic, witchcraft, and shamanism span the globe. Many of these beliefs have existed for thousands of years, and still do, and they have been practiced by people of all genders.

But how does all of that get us to the point where we are now, when Merriam-Webster's primary definition of *witch* is "one that is credited with usually malignant supernatural powers; *especially*: a woman practicing usually black witchcraft often with the aid of a devil or familiar"? When did that "*especially*: a woman" come to pass? After all, there have always been male and gender non-conforming practitioners of magic who have been called—or who call themselves—witches. Gerald Gardner, the founder of the religion that came to be called Wicca, was a man. And yet, the vast majority of people persecuted in the name of witchcraft have been female.

If a group of people were asked to draw pictures of a witch today, each would most likely use a similar visual shorthand: a woman with a black pointy hat and long hair, probably on the mature side, and accompanied by a broom, cauldron, and/or feline. When I asked a member of the Unicode Emoji Subcommittee why the universal emoji of a person with a pointy hat and wand was named *mage* rather than *witch*, he told me, "I requested that the names for fantasy characters try to avoid gender connotations. . . . Witch is usually assumed to be feminine (although I know better!). . . . [W]e also mentioned wizard or warlock but those are typically thought of as masculine. I suggested 'mage' because I thought it was a good shortening of the phrase 'magical person,' and the default imagery (according to Unicode's guidelines) should be 'gender neutral.' "

Putting the issue of gender aside for a moment, we must then come to the witch's intent, and here is where the "good witch / bad witch" question gets further muddied. Many of our modern ideas of the villainess witch come from faulty historical sources.

For example, the scholars who have suggested that the diabolical "confessions" of witchery during the European and colonial New England witch hunts should be taken as evidence of real witchcraft practice have largely been discredited. Furthermore, relatively few reliable records survive from those incidents. Much of our witch-related imagery comes from either witch-hunting manuals written by the obviously biased hunters themselves or from refutations of these manuals by other writers of the age.

The actual witch trial "transcripts" shouldn't be taken at face value either. First of all, it's an understatement to say that the accused were perhaps not the most reliable of narrators, fighting as they were for their lives under unfathomably cruel circumstances of physical torture and psychological desperation and/or delusion. Second, the documents that contain these so-called confessions were often kept improperly, and many of them no longer exist, if indeed they ever did in the first place. For instance, our understanding of America's most famous historical witch incident, the Salem witch trials, is piecemeal at best. As Stacy Schiff writes in her book *The Witches: Salem, 1692*: "No trace of a single session of the witchcraft court survives. We have accounts of the trials, but no records. . . . The Salem record book has been expunged. . . . Over one hundred reporters took down testimony. Few were trained to do so. They were maddeningly inconsistent." What the witch trials actually proved is that non-magical human beings are capable of the very malice and murder that they fear from so-called witches.

On the flip side, many of the nineteenth and twentieth century texts that planted the seeds for positive depictions of witches—including the modern religion of Wicca—have also been called into question. Books such as Charles Godfrey Leland's *Aradia, or the Gospel of the Witches*, Sir James George Frazer's *The Golden Bough*, Margaret Murray's *The Witch-Cult in Western Europe*, Robert Graves's *The White Goddess*, and Marija Gimbutas's *The Language of the Goddess*, to name just a few, contributed to a more sympathetic—or even romantic—notion of witches, yet they have all been subject to much subsequent scrutiny and debate regarding their validity. As meaningful as it can be to pull witches out of the hell pit and onto the pedestal, by today's academic standards these more starry-eyed spins on witchcraft are based on conjecture, flawed scholarship, or outright poetic license.

Additionally, these witch "histories" are cobwebbed with details from legends, myths, and fairy tales. Our assumptions about witches have accumulated over centuries to form a dark layer cake of associations. Stories about fictional witches and ideas about "actual" witches are forever contaminating each other and then morphing into newer versions. This is why I believe it's more effective to talk about the witch as a symbol than as a reality, real as she may sometimes be.

Nonetheless, it's fair to say that up until the past century or so, whenever a witch appeared in stories—whether fiction or alleged nonfiction, as in the case of real-world witchcraft accusations—she was almost always a danger-maker who tried to bring about the downfall of children, upstanding women, and good, clean men. And it's this reputation that means that, no matter how hard you scrub, you can never completely get the stink of sulfur off her.

SO IF THE witch has been a sort of monstress for millennia, how did we reach the point where the possibility of being a "good witch" was even on the table? We'll be looking at many iterations of this in the following chapters, but there are a few particularly important links in the chain.

Despite centuries of bad press, popular attitudes toward witches began to shift in the mid-nineteenth century, catalyzed in large part by French historian Jules Michelet's 1862 book *La Sorcière*. In it, Michelet suggests that the word *witch* was a slur that the Church used against any gifted female healer or "High-priestess of Nature." He writes that these sorceresses, as he calls them, were tragic figures, having been oppressed and nearly obliterated by such male-dominated forces as the Catholic Church, feudal governance, and science: "Where, indeed, could she have taken up her habitation, except on savage heaths, this child of calamity, so fiercely persecuted, so bitterly cursed and proscribed?" He then details how these sorceresses take matters into their own hands by starting their own satanic religion where, unlike in the Church, womanhood and nature were celebrated.

La Sorcière is one of the earliest popular works that is sympathetic to witches, as well as being an impassioned and lyrically written dissertation on the systemic subjugation of female power overall. Though it's filled with historical inaccuracies and plenty of the author's own fantasies, its effect on the popular conception of witches was substantial.

In 1863, Michelet's book was translated into English under the far more titillating title *Satanism and Witchcraft*, and its direct influence can be seen in the work of the twentieth-century poets, filmmakers, and artists, including the Surrealists, who incorporated Michelet's romanticized vision of the witch into their work. There was also a loose adaptation of the book in 1973 via

Mushi Production's psychedelic animated adult film *Kanashimi no Belladonna* (or *Belladonna of Sadness*), which was rereleased in theaters in 2016. But the impact of Michelet's sorceress expands far beyond these obvious reinterpretations. In fact, it can be directly linked to the most famous fictional witches of all time.

WHEN L. FRANK Baum's book *The Wonderful Wizard of Oz* was released in the year 1900, it forever stamped the concept—and terminology—of good witches and bad witches into popular consciousness.

In Baum's original story, there are actually two good witches. First, there is the Witch of the North, whom Dorothy meets upon her arrival in Oz after her house crushes the Wicked Witch of the East, post-tornado. The Witch of the North is an old woman dressed in glittering white, who gifts Dorothy with magical Silver Shoes (as they are in the original text—ruby was only for the film). She also gives her the "witch's kiss": a mark on Dorothy's forehead that will be a source of protection and safe passage for her and her friends throughout the tale.

Glinda, the Good Witch of the South—and the only witch deemed by Baum to be worthy of a first name—doesn't actually appear until the end of the story, though leading up to this we're told that she's the most powerful witch of all. When Dorothy and her companions finally meet Glinda, they are impressed by her red hair, blue eyes, and youthful looks (despite her significant age, we're told). They're also moved by her generosity. "You are certainly as good as you are beautiful!" Dorothy cries, after Glinda offers customized treasures for the Tin Woodman, the Cowardly Lion, and the Scarecrow. This kind and lovely witch then teaches her how to use the Silver Shoes to get back home to Aunt Em.

It's a spectacular story, not only as a parable about friendship and truth-seeking, but also due to its exceptional originality. The Emerald City, the Yellow Brick Road, magical slippers, a brave farm-girl protagonist, and, of course, the good and bad witches are all now seemingly timeless icons from what some have called "the first American fairy tale." But several of these ideas were not invented by Baum out of whole cloth. In fact, a great many of them can be traced to the influence of his mother-in-law, the suffragist and equal rights pioneer Matilda Joslyn Gage.

Gage was a follower of Theosophy, the nineteenth-century gnostic religious movement that brought Eastern mystical thought to the West. She would have been familiar with the ideas that one can go on a spiritual journey up thirteen golden stairs to find enlightenment at the Temple of Divine Wisdom, and that one can reveal the ultimate truth behind all world religions by metaphorically lifting the veil of illusion (or peering behind a curtain, perhaps). Interestingly, the Theosophical Society was started by another mighty woman, Madame Helena Petrovna Blavatsky, one of the few female spiritual leaders of the age, who was often slandered and called a fraud by the press during her life. Still, Theosophy had many adherents, and it does still today. Encouraged by Gage, Baum and his wife, Maud Gage Baum, became members of the Theosophical Society's Chicago chapter on September 4, 1892. (He also began writing his stories down on paper at his mother-in-law's behest.)

Like many suffragists, Gage was also an abolitionist, and her childhood home in Fayetteville, New York, was part of the Underground Railroad. "I think I was born with a hatred of oppression," Gage is quoted as saying at the 1888 International Council of Women, before recounting her memories of sheltering slaves and attending antislavery gatherings.

Baum's good witches of Oz are abolitionists of a sort as well, as slavery runs rampant in the wicked witches' domains. When the Wicked Witch of the East is killed at the beginning of the story, the Good Witch of the North tells Dorothy, "She has held all the Munchkins in bondage for many years, making them slave for her, night and day. Now they are all set free, and are grateful to you for the favor...." And the Wicked Witch of the West has the Winkies as her slaves. Dorothy experiences a taste of slavery herself when the Wicked Witch holds her captive: she is worked to the bone in the witch's kitchen for days on end, and the Lion is locked up as well. Dorothy's first act after the witch is killed is to free the Winkies, who declare the day a holiday to be celebrated every year.

Most significant to Baum's development of the "good witch" concept, however, was Gage's 1893 treatise *Woman, Church, and State*, published just five years before her death. In it, she writes that the subjugation of women happening in her time was comparable to the European witch hunts. She believed that the witches of Western Europe were persecuted because their wisdom was a threat to the patriarchal Church. As Gage writes: "Whatever the pretext made for witchcraft persecution we have abundant proof that the so-called 'witch' was among the most profoundly scientific persons of the age. The church having forbidden its offices and all external methods of knowledge to woman, was profoundly stirred with indignation at her having through her own wisdom, penetrated into some of the most deeply subtle secrets of nature:

and it was a subject of debate during the middle ages if learning for woman was not an additional capacity for evil, as owing to her, knowledge had first been introduced in the world."

From her perspective, calling brilliant women "witches" was a way for the Church to demonize them and rationalize bringing about their demise. (Or as Lisa Simpson would put it 115 years later, "Why is it whenever a woman is confident and powerful, they call her a witch?")

And where did Gage get this idea? At least in part from Jules Michelet's *La Sorcière*, which she cites multiple times throughout her book's footnotes.

Though Gage's writing was hugely influential upon the advent of American feminism, it must be noted that, like *La Sorcière*, it is filled with inaccuracies. We now know that a good portion of the women and men who were put to death during the witch hunts were likely from lower, uneducated classes, and thus probably not among the "profoundly scientific persons" she had envisioned. Gage is also responsible for further circulating the now disproven claim that nine million witches were put to death in Europe— scholars today estimate the figure as being somewhere between fifty- and two hundred thousand.

Regardless, her reframing of the witch hunts captured the imagination of many of her readers, including that of her son-in-law. If not for Gage, L. Frank Baum might never have conceived of good witches at all.

In sum, Gage's feminist fingerprints are all over Oz, and her legacy of good witches remains vital through this day. As Kristen J. Sollée puts it in her book *Witches, Sluts, Feminists: Conjuring the Sex Positive*: ". . . Gage embraced a reclamation of the divine feminine as her spiritual practice, and is the first known suffragist to reclaim the word 'witch.' . . . Without Gage, witches might still be viewed as solely evil in popular culture."

One might say that Matilda Joslyn Gage was the O.G.: Original Glinda.

IN 1939, NEARLY forty years after Baum's book was published, MGM released the motion picture *The Wizard of Oz*, and Glinda's question to Dorothy, "Are you a good witch or a bad witch?" has been reverberating ever since. The film became a classic for many reasons, but certainly one of them is that it injected Baum's idea of good witches into the cultural bloodstream of the masses. It also opened the door for later glamorous witch characters such as Veronica Lake's Jennifer in the 1942 film *I Married A Witch*; Kim Novak's Gillian Holroyd in the 1952 movie *Bell, Book, and Candle*; and Elizabeth Montgomery's Samantha Stephens of the 1960s ABC television show *Bewitched*. If Michelet, Gage, and Baum helped bring the witch out of the shadows, then Hollywood pulled her into the spotlight.

MGM's version of Glinda set the template for an onscreen witch who was not only good, but beautiful to boot. She was played by film and stage star Billie Burke, who was also the wife of the legendary Broadway producer Florenz Ziegfeld Jr., of *Ziegfeld Follies* fame. Notably, Burke was fifty-four years old when she shot *Oz*—nearly twenty years older than Margaret Hamilton, who played the hideous hag the Wicked Witch of the West.

In the film, Glinda and the nameless Wicked Witch are set up as the ultimate dichotomy: Glinda is a living confection, ecstatic in star-spangled pink, part fairy, part flamingo. Her preferred method of transport is flotation, and when she shows up in a shimmering soap bubble, all trills and ruffles, we know immediately that she is a benevolent being. She has a starry scepter and wears a crown evocative of Mary, Queen of Heaven. Glinda, then, is no less a saint. Celestial, airy, and a stickler for elocution, she is girlish and glistening. More than that, she is a mother figure, a guardian, a giver. She is kindness in full bloom.

The Wicked Witch of the West is her diametric opposite. Angular and shrouded in black, she greets us in a cacophony of screech and caw. She is a woman enflamed, a creature of fire and desire, with her libidinous laugh and hard-on for scarlet slippers. Her movement isn't float, it's flight—arrow-direct forward motion, broom between her legs, leaving a trail of smoke behind. She is living singe, all freedom and speed and scorch. Even at the beginning of the film in her guise as her doppel, the mean Miss Gulch, she rides a bicycle—a rather independent activity for a woman of the 1930s. Unlike her rosy-hued, hermetically sealed counterpart, this witch feels the air on her skin as she rides. But she is also a chthonic character, queen of an upside-down underworld, living in a gray castle on top of a mountain range that resembles a row of jagged teeth. The Wicked Witch's skin is a lurid green, evocative of poison and envy and plague. Her pea pallor and overall color palette tell us that she is a sickening deliverer of death.

Ironically, the character of the Wicked Witch of the West was most threatening to the actor who played her. The green makeup was copper-based and, as the Oz Wiki says, "potentially toxic," and it could only be removed with alcohol, a highly painful process thanks to its antiseptic sting. It was also difficult for Hamilton to eat anything while in costume, and she had to ingest mostly liquids or else have her food broken into little bits and fed to her by a production assistant. Several sources say that Hamilton's skin stayed tinged green for weeks after the filming was complete. Even more harrowing, her costume caught on fire while she was shooting the Munchkinland scene, leaving burns on her face and right hand. She had to miss two months of filming to recover. As it is so often with witches, the line between villain and victim was smudged with soot.

Still, Hamilton seems to have had a deep appreciation for getting to play such an iconic role. In fact, she reprised it several times later in life, including in a 1976 episode of *Sesame Street* (which only aired once due to complaints from parents), as well as for a 1980 photo shoot by Andy Warhol that he incorporated into a print for his 1981 *Myths* series. Kids who might have cowered from her in 1939 grew into adults who applauded her. One can find audio online of her and Judy Garland appearing together on *The Merv Griffin Show* in 1968, nearly thirty years after *The Wizard of Oz* was released. In the clip, Garland is quite charming, but it's Hamilton and her raucous, ornithological cackle that gets the biggest audience response. There's an Old English word, *kench*, which means "to laugh loudly." I could listen to Hamilton's kenching all day.

The Wicked Witch of the West is shrill, no question—and even more perverse, she revels in her shrillness. And it's perhaps this that makes her so beloved. She's frightening, yes—so much so that chunks of her dialogue got cut after the film previewed to an audience of terrorized children. But more than that, she seems to be having an absolute ball. Even when she's melting, she is *living* for herself, making proclamations about her own "beautiful wickedness." Her actions are condemnable, but I'll give her this: she has no shame and no remorse. And this kind of wickedness strikes me as immensely appealing. That witch is one brazen broad.

There is a clip that surfaced online recently of a seventy-two-year-old Margaret Hamilton appearing on *Mister Rogers' Neighborhood* in 1975, and I haven't been able to stop watching it. She enters his house clutching a sort of a bowling bag–shaped purse and her famous pointy black hat. She is wearing pearls and a pink striped suit. The semiotic choice of this—the Wicked Witch in Glinda pink—thrills me to my core.

Mister Rogers guides her gently to the plaid sofa, where she perches with her hands folded like a foreign dignitary, beaming.

"I'm interested to know about how you felt about playing that Wicked Witch in *The Wizard of Oz*," he says.

MARGARET HAMILTON: Well, I really was very thrilled. . . . I had done it very often . . . when I was a little girl at Halloween. . . . Lots of children would rather be a witch than almost anything else. There are lots of other things you can pick out, but that's the one I loved, and so when I had the chance to do this, I was very, very happy about it.

FRED ROGERS: Girls and boys like to play witches, don't they?

MH: Yes, they do, yes, they certainly do.

FR: And when you feel as if you'd like to play something a little bit scary, a witch is a fine thing to play.

MH: She has lots of things about her. I've always felt that . . . sometimes the children feel that she's a very mean witch, and

I expect she does seem that way. But I always think that there are two things about her: She does enjoy everything that she does, whether it's good or bad, she enjoys it. But she also is what we sometimes refer to as frustrated. She's very unhappy because she never gets what she wants, Mister Rogers. You know, most of us get something along the line. But far as we know, that witch just never got what she wanted, and mainly she wanted those ruby slippers. Because they had lots of power, and she wanted more power. And I just think that sometimes we think she's just a mean and a very bad person, but actually you have to think about her point of view. That it wasn't as happy a time as she wanted it to be, because she just never got what she wanted.

The entire exchange moves me—Rogers treating Hamilton with such reverence, Hamilton speaking about her witch of a lifetime with a deep sense of compassion and, dare I say, love.

It's her reframing of wickedness that resonates with me most of all. There's no question that the Wicked Witch of the West is the antagonist of the Oz story—she is a murderess and a tyrant, and many of her actions are nothing short of evil. But her unbridled enjoyment rubbing up against her unquenched appetite for more, more, MORE is what really makes her character spark. And both of these things—female delight and female desire—are so often demonized.

We call "witch" any woman who wants.

Margaret Hamilton and I are far from the only ones who have considered the Wicked Witch's side of things. I was fourteen when Gregory Maguire's novel *Wicked: The Life and Times of the*

Wicked Witch of the West, was released in 1995, and I immediately fell in love with it. The idea of bringing this odd, emerald-colored Oz-ian out of the cesspool and into the center of the story appealed to my own underdog sensibility. I wanted to know more about this magical footwear marauder.

Maguire's first trick in *Wicked* is that he gives our witch a name: Elphaba, an homage to L. Frank Baum's initials. After casting this seven-letter spell, he then transforms her from a generic villain into a fully fleshed-out protagonist, with nuance, motivations, and an entire backstory. We learn that she is the child of a rape, that her mother is a drug addict and her adoptive father is a zealot, and that her green skin is a source of deep shame and disgrace throughout her life. However, she is also a gifted scholar and a defender of the oppressed: she becomes a civil rights champion on behalf of talking "Animals," who are being discriminated against and treated like second-class citizens. She suffers unbearable losses: Fiyero, the love of her life, is captured and most likely murdered during a police raid, and her sister, Nessarose, is crushed to death by the house that Dorothy inevitably twists in on. Maguire's revisioning of the Wicked Witch's story becomes one about politics, persecution, and personal pain. It asks us to consider the factors that can turn a good guy into a Big Bad.

I related to this when I read it, because I too felt perpetually misunderstood, and I welcomed any story that treated social rejects with tenderness and compassion. This retelling of the witch's tale evidently hit more nerves than mine. It was adapted into a critically acclaimed Broadway musical in 2003 and went on to win three Tony Awards. And it continues to be one of the most successful shows in history, surpassing $1 billion in total revenue in March 2016 and becoming Broadway's second-highest-grossing show in July 2017, trailing only *The Lion King*. *Wicked* is also being developed into a nonmusical television show by ABC, and a musical feature film by Universal Pictures. Soon the whole world will get to sing along to the Wicked Witch's lament.

Feeling like a freak, an outsider, or misunderstood is, ironically, a pretty common experience. We watch the witch with great interest, because some part of us wants her to win. After all, we too fear being crushed, drowned, vanquished by the alpha Dorothys. Each of us harbors a secret wish to be spotlit and adored, warts and all.

THERE IS ANOTHER aspect of Hamilton's appearance on the Mister Rogers show that's significant too. It's clear that they both intend to allay the fears of the many children who found the Wicked Witch of the West to be the stuff of nightmares, to render her relatable and more human.

Mister Rogers asks her if it was hard work to make *The Wizard of Oz*. She says yes, then goes on to describe the difficulty of wearing the green makeup all day, and how she went to great lengths to make sure it wouldn't come off, even when she was eating her lunch. She also expresses her dismay that she frightened so many kids:

> MH: . . . Sometimes, Mister Rogers, I'm a little unhappy because lots of children are quite scared by her and that always makes me feel a little sad, because I don't think any of us thought, you know, that it would be as scary as sometimes it seems to be. But when you understand her—when you realize it's just pretend and that everybody can do it—

you can do it, little boys as you say do it, little girls do it, and sometimes when you get older you play at Halloween time that you're dressed up as something else. . . .

FR: And all witches don't have to be bad, either.

A bit later, Mister Rogers asks if she'd like to try on her costume again. Hamilton agrees, saying she'd love to and that it would be fun. He opens a trunk and begins taking out pieces of her infamous black outfit. When she sees the garments, her face lights up. "Oh my! How nice, yes!" she exclaims, and begins to dress.

She puts her skirt on and ties it, then pats her hips.

MH: Look at here. Something to put things in! Even witches have to have pockets.

FR: It's helping me just to see you get into these things.

MH: Oh, I'm glad.

FR: . . . to know that you're a real lady who got dressed up to play this part.

He helps her put on a black blouse with billowing sleeves, then asks her to turn around so he can show the back to the viewers. "This is a real zipper back here, just like the zipper on my sweaters," he explains.

She spins back around, now dressed. "There!" they say in unison. She giggles. "Isn't that fun?" she asks. "You look great!" he says. They are obviously both a bit giddy.

She puts on the cape and gives it a swirl. Then she fixes the iconic veiled hat on her head and smiles to the camera.

"Now, there's your old friend, the Wicked Witch of the West!" she says with a chortle.

At Mister Rogers's request, she does the voice and the famous cackle. He says it would be fun to talk like that, and he tries to imitate her, cackling back.

"You can!" she exclaims. "They all can. You can do it too!"

It's clear they're getting a kick out of each other.

Mister Rogers then asks if she has grandchildren. She says she has three, and recounts their names and ages, and remarks that she's very lucky to have them. The segment ends with her still in costume, leaving to visit one of Mister Rogers's friends.

MH: . . . I'll go just as I am.

FR: Oh, you will?

MH: Is that all right?

FR: Oh, that'd be fine for the neighborhood.

MH: I think that would be fun.

And they say their good-byes. She ducks under the doorframe to accommodate her towering headgear.

"There I am!" she remarks, and exits the set.

The first few times that I watched this clip, I was overcome with emotion. So much of it touches me: the admiration they show each other, these legendary rulers of their respective imaginary neighborhoods. The unapologetic joy they take in the Wicked Witch's scariness. The mix of pride and vulnerability of Hamilton, now nearing the end of her life, and returning to a part she played four decades earlier with respect and pleasure and grace.

But what moves me most of all is the delicate dance that she and Mister Rogers do of trying to diffuse people's fears while still not robbing the witch of her magic. Yes, they tell us, it's just pretend. But it's also real and accessible to YOU. And isn't that the most wonderful wizardry of all?

It's a similar position that I've found myself in repeatedly throughout my life, this posture of simultaneous revelation and preservation of mystery; of letting myself be scary while still having the urge to reassure others that I'm no threat. This resistance to fixing myself to any one pole.

So often we try to classify. To put one another into distinct, labeled envelopes, and then seal them shut with the flick of a tongue. We resist nuance at every turn, and that goes tenfold for women. They are prudes or sluts, passive or pushy, babes or bitches, harlots or hags. If you show interest in fashion and beauty and sparkly dresses, you're considered vapid, a lightweight, and dismissed or discredited. If you voice your opinions or ambition, or talk too often or laugh too loud, you are domineering, thirsty, a harpy, a nag.

Perhaps the greatest gift that L. Frank Baum has given us is the vision of a full Technicolor spectrum of female power.

Yes, I'm a good witch and a good person. But I also embrace complexity. I intend to wear a black cape over my proverbial pink gown. To laugh too loud and get real mad and defend myself and the people I care about. I want more out of life than to float gently along in a bubble. I want to wear the pointy hat *and* the crown. To live as vividly as I can, as I am. To be wicked and winsome and wild and whole. I want to be more than either/or.

But my heart's true desire is to live in a magical land that values all of it: the goodness of Glinda, the glee of the Gulch witch, the artistry of Margaret Hamilton, and the promise of Matilda Joslyn Gage. To call that place home.

TEEN WITCH:
SPELL CASTS FOR OUTCASTS

Sabrina Spellman didn't have a last name for the first thirty-four years of her existence as a pop-culture character. Blond, mod, and mischievous, Sabrina the Teen-Age Witch, as she was originally called, first appeared in *Archie's Mad House* #22 in October 1962. "I hope you didn't expect to find me living on some dreary mountaintop . . . wearing some grubby old rags and making some nasty old brew," she says, lounging on the floor with records and magazines surrounding her. "No . . . we modern witches believe life should be a ball! . . . Besides soft, gracious living doesn't reduce our powers one iota!" She goes on to tell us that witches can't cry, they can't sink in water, and they mustn't fall in love, else they risk pissing off Della, the glamorous head witch. Inevitably, this third detail proves especially problematic for boy-crazy Sabrina.

To complicate matters, per witch tradition, she's supposed to do hexes and mean magical pranks, but she just can't resist using her powers for good. Sabrina helps her friends with their romantic entanglements, decorates her room in cheery colors, gets local townspeople out of scrapes. Sometimes her spells work, but more often than not, they backfire: she'll accidentally target the wrong person, and even her jinxes end up having unintended happy consequences. "I've got to try and be a good wi . . . I mean a *bad* witch, and not disgrace the family!" she says to herself in a June 1970 appearance. A new hitch is introduced as the series progresses: no one can know her true identity—not even her boyfriend, Harvey Kinkle, a sweet klutz whom her Aunt Hilda can't stand.

Throughout the series, whether in the comics or subsequent television shows, Sabrina finds herself torn between obeying authority and following her heart. She often longs to be a regular teen, at times wishing her powers would leave her entirely. Sentiments like these hint at the pathos shared by so many teen girls, as they are caught between the desire to conform to one's social group and the need to establish oneself as an independent young adult.

These conflicts proved to be far more resonant with readers than Sabrina creators George Gladir and Dan DeCarlo originally imagined: "I think we both envisioned it as a one-shot and were surprised when fans asked for more," Gladir is quoted as saying in 2007. Due to popular demand, Sabrina became a recurring character in the *Archie's Mad House* and *Archie's T.V. Laugh-Out* comic book series, as well as appearing in several animated TV shows. Eventually she became the star of her own spin-off comic book series in 1971, setting the template for generations of teen witches to come.

The tone of the early Sabrina comics is light and low-stakes, a projected fantasy by male creators about what a teenage girl would do, could she do anything. She makes magic pizza, saves a music festival from being shut down by grumpy old townsfolk, finishes her homework in record time, and, of course, tries to make boys fall in love with her. But she's also a product of her age, evolving with the styles and mores of the times. In April 1971, she's enlisted by her groovy older cousin, Sylvester, to help him spread the word about the "New Witch Movement." He turns up to the house on leave from Salem U wearing a fringed leather jacket and bell-bottoms. "All I'm trying to say is that us magic cats of today don't go around scaring people in those crazy Halloween suits, flying on brooms, that's from the Old Establishment!" he proclaims, echoing the sentiments of the flower-power generation, and zapping Sabrina's go-go style into hippie chic.

The Sabrina character has reincarnated several times over since then, with each iteration becoming more complex and showing more nuanced understanding of the teen-girl psyche. While her love life remains a concern across generations, as time goes on her most pressing issues become about reconciling her identities as a witch and a high school student, and learning how she can exercise her powers more effectively.

I first became familiar with her when I was fifteen, via the 1996 sitcom *Sabrina the Teenage Witch* that was created by Nell Scovell. It starred Melissa Joan Hart from the Nickelodeon show *Clarissa Explains It All*, and it ran until 2003. The show is upbeat and goofy in tone, with a laugh track and plotlines about magical mix-ups and spells gone wrong. But unlike in the early comics, nineties-sitcom Sabrina is given a backstory: her father is a witch but her mother is mortal, making her a sort of hybrid between the magical and the mundane. She's also given the Spellman surname (Scovell named her after a real-life family friend, Irving Spellman), making her a more fleshed-out, relatable character.

This series starts off on the night of her sixteenth birthday, when aunts Hilda and Zelda discover Sabrina asleep and levitating above her bed. Her powers have just activated, they tell us, and it's time for them to tell her who she truly is.

Being a witch isn't easy. We watch Sabrina try to learn how to cast spells and use magical ingredients, and at first she's not so hot at it. She accidentally turns a mean cheerleader into a pineapple, and causes school mayhem when she uses "truth sprinkles" in her home-ec Bundt cake, causing a candor epidemic. Throughout the series she navigates mishaps of love, friendship, and family, and she struggles to learn when it is appropriate to use her powers, and how. The nineties Sabrina show is a female coming-of-age story with dimension, if a doggedly cheery one. No matter how challenging her problems are, supernatural or otherwise, she and her aunts always come up with a solution in the end.

In the 2010s, all of the Archie gang went through an edgy revamp, with the additions of social media scandals and plenty of sex. They've also been given a much more sinister vibe, thanks in large part to writer Roberto Aguirre-Sacasa, who introduced the undead and other occult elements into Archie's world with his *Afterlife with Archie* series. *Riverdale*, the hit CW TV show that Aguirre-Sacasa developed, has reimagined the Archie story as a sort of *Twin Peaks* for teens, heavy on the drugs, mist, and murder. He and artist Robert Hack have also given Sabrina a far more mature tone in 2014's *The Chilling Adventures of Sabrina* comic series, which was adapted into the hit 2018 Netflix television show of the same name.

This latest Sabrina has some elements from prior versions. We find her again with a 1960s aesthetic, in homage to her midcentury roots. As in the 1990s sitcom, *Chilling Adventures* also hinges upon her sixteenth birthday, when she must choose whether or not to have a "dark baptism" and become a full witch in the Church of Night coven, like her father was. In this more adult spin, however, we also learn that she can't be defiled before the ritual, despite her devotion to her sweet and hapless boyfriend, Harvey.

Sabrina's aunts are flesh-eating witches, and her initiation into their coven consists of her having to sign the Book of the Beast and commit herself to serving Satan whenever he calls upon her. She will also have to renounce her relationships with Harvey and her friends. When it comes time to make her choice, she waffles, realizing that the Church of Night is just another hypocritical institution that peddles "freedom" while keeping its members subservient to a male overlord.

This new rendition of Sabrina is conscious of equal rights issues, with concerns about feminism and social justice worn proudly on its sleeve: When their gender non-conforming friend Susie is bullied by a bunch of jocks, Sabrina and her pals start the Women's Intersectional Cultural and Creative Association (or WICCA), a club at school with a mission to fight gender discrimination, racism, and censorship.

It is also by far the darkest version of Sabrina we've seen yet, with a watercolor wash of horror, and intentional nods to such occult thrillers as *Rosemary's Baby* and *The Exorcist*. The depiction of the cannibalistic Church of Night coven is satirical to be sure, skewering early modern Christian beliefs about satanic witches—but there's enough blood and impending doom to make the series feel genuinely unsettling. This Sabrina isn't bothered with decorating her room or getting straight As. She's too busy drowning her sexist principal in a flood of spiders, raising zombies, and exorcising demons both real and metaphorical.

ADOLESCENCE IS ITS own special horror show, and so it makes sense that the witch turns up in so many allegories about youth. Seemingly overnight, our social groups stratify, our identities are taxonomized, and we find ourselves in a tyrannical dominion of in-crowds and losers. Popularity becomes a new standard to be measured by. Some of us are wanted, some of us are worthless, and most of us are worried about our place in the pecking order.

It's also a time when we begin to feel divided inside, wishing to be singled out as special and longing for belonging at the same time. We try to establish ourselves as individuals and begin to bear the weight of other people's opinions of us. We're consumed by crushes and lust, and we ache for reciprocity. The demands of our familial responsibilities begin to chafe against our platonic or romantic allegiances. And on top of all of that, there's added pressure to get good grades and be good-looking. For many of us, to be a teenager is to be a literal misfit. You don't fit into the right community or clothing. You don't feel comfortable in your own skin.

Puberty is arguably one of the most ghastly physical changes we go through. We fall subject to the body's awkwardness, its seething wants, its sudden betrayals. The teen body is a body on display during a time when so many of us would rather remain out of view. It inconveniences us, embarrasses us. It turns us into objects of judgment and desire. It is a liminal entity, stuck between childhood and adulthood, suddenly wanting to be adorned and adored. It shifts in size and shape and functionality, and there is nothing we can do to stop it—a transmogrification in real time.

Though there is no question that teenage years are difficult for most people of all genders, the cis female pubescent body has its own specific markers of new breasts and new blood. We're warned that these things will appear, and that it will be sudden. That we'll have to acquire special items to accommodate our new forms. We're taught to mold our chests appropriately in preparation to be seen, but that menstruation must always remain hidden and that it will hurt. And if we engage in sexual activity, there's a good chance we might do it too soon or not soon enough, and that sex is going to *really* fucking hurt, quite possibly with tearing and yet more blood. We're told about other girls, older girls, who were humiliated or harmed. We lean in close and listen: Ghost stories around a cafeteria table. Whispers three times in a bathroom mirror.

The teen girl becomes aware of eyes on her. She is an oddity, a spectacle. And so she trains in the art of allure, the art of defense, the art of transformation. Fairy glamour in the form of eyeshadow and "contouring" can disguise her infinite insecurities and roiling wishes. She learns that the attention her body receives will be weaponized. That she has power, and that power can be wielded.

The combination of physical changes, swelling hormones, and a newly emerging labyrinth of social taboos often causes feelings of helplessness, hauntedness, or being halfway human. No surprise, then, that young women flock to stories about witches. These tales enact this tension, rendered more romantic thanks to the added luster of magic. These shape-shifting characters provide a potent metaphor for teen girls' own rapid fluctuations, as well as their fantasies about gaining control at a time when they have anything but.

★ ★ ★

MY FAMILY MOVED to a nice town called Morganville "for the schools." From kindergarten through tenth grade, I got a solid education there, and I know what a rare and lucky thing it is to grow up somewhere that is well-resourced and relatively safe. But one of the rotten by-products of a commuter town with good schools is the classism that permeates the social scene. There were kids in my grade who lived in McMansions and who would be offered a choice between a BMW or a nose job on their seventeenth birthdays. These were kids who wore the "right" clothes, the definition of which would change year to year: from Umbro shorts to Samba sneakers to Hypercolor T-shirts to Z. Cavaricci pants, which you knew were real because of the white label on the fly. For girls, hairstyles evolved from huge Jersey bangs (which I sported for years in a tumescent, sticky crown) to locks straightened with a hot iron into strips of gleaming fettuccine.

I was well-liked enough at the start of seventh grade, even briefly accepted by the popular kids. But my interests in making art and having "deep" conversations made us quickly part ways. My braces, frizzy hair, and flat chest certainly were no help. I drifted through different circles, not quite fitting in anywhere, too sensitive for the stoners and too strange for the straight-A-ers. I felt rootless and lonely.

As I moved further from the in-crowd, my clothes got darker, looser. I raccooned my eyes with black eyeliner and wore talismans around my neck: a key, a crescent moon, a brass bullet shell with the Nicole Blackman poem "Daughter" rolled up inside, mezuzah-style. My wardrobe was a way to stand out and swathe myself in shadows at the same time.

I was turning into something else.

I floated away from middle school's social nucleus and with-drew deeper into a world of my own crafting.

Unlike Sabrina, I didn't join a coven or go through some elab-orate initiation. My earliest experiments in doing my own teen magic were based on whatever I could get my hands on in the sub-urbs. *Mall witch* is a phrase that's bandied about these days with derision, but that's what I started out as. In Monmouth County, New Jersey, the closest suppliers of any sort of witchcraft material were the occult sections of mall bookstore chains like B. Dalton and Waldenbooks. If I was lucky, I would get my parents to drive a bit farther out, to shops like Red Bank's Magical Rocks or Mount Holly's Ram III Metaphysical Books (which is where I got the idea that I wanted to be a "metaphysician" when I grew up, as evidenced by games of MASH I recently found scrawled in an old notebook). If the occasion was super special, I got to go to the witchcraft mecca that was New Hope, Pennsylvania, where I would buy books like Raymond Buckland's *Advanced Candle Magick* and my first set of tarot cards, the Sacred Rose deck by Johanna Gargiulo-Sherman, which were drawn to look like medieval stained glass.

My parents were cautiously supportive. Artists themselves, they encouraged my individuality and were happy to see me pursue my interests, as long as I kept communication open with them. But at school, my interest in magic remained a largely private and soli-tary pursuit. I wasn't ashamed of it, exactly—my discretion arose from an urge to protect one of the few precious things that was mine alone. When you're a weird kid, you learn to put guardrails around the things you love. You keep them hidden heart-deep, lest someone try to take them, mock them, or co-opt them out of cruelty or just plain clumsiness.

I spent a lot of my spare time writing poetry, reading, and painting pictures onto which I'd glue craft-store oddities and scraps from vintage science books. We had two VCRs at our house, and I rigged them up so I could make VHS mix tapes of music videos I loved or super-cuts of every moment in a movie where the moon makes a memorable appearance.

But when I wasn't making art, I was making magic.

Most of my early spells were focused on the boys I had crushes on, desperately hoping to make them love me back. I also started doing occasional castings for a few trusted friends who were pining for people who might or might not be pining back.

There was the spell I did for Rebecca, my sister's friend, who was hiding in my room during a house party, after she told me she was lusting after some "hot guy" who was downstairs. I lit some candles, did some incantations, sprinkled her with some "love powder" that I'd bought at a new age shop, and sent her on her way. They made out that night.

There was the spell I did after spending hours picking out the perfect crystal at East Meets West, a mystical goods shop in Monmouth Mall. I came home and charged it with love magic, and then gave it to Keith, a ruddy-faced boy who was playing the role of the king in our school's production of *Once Upon a Mattress*. This attempt was not so successful, as he largely ignored me throughout the run.

Not every spell was benign, though.

During eighth grade, there was a girl I loathed. She was a rich little twit named Tiffany who represented everything I stood against. It was bad enough that she was vapid and snotty, but to make matters worse, she was dating Marc Fleishman, a boy I was

in love with. Something had to be done. I had a book of medieval magic that contained some darker workings than what I was
used to. Its spells listed ingredients like toad's feet, black eggs, and
freshly tanned leather. I was going to have to improvise.

I found a spell entitled "To Seek Vengeance Against One's
Enemy." I didn't have the bladder of a chicken, but I did have a zip-
lock bag. I didn't have raw sugar, but I did have packets of Sweet'n
Low. I followed the steps as best I could in the kitchen one night
when my parents were out. I mixed the ingredients together on
the stove, adding cinnamon, garlic powder, black pepper, and a
yearbook photo of Tiffany to the boiling water. I dropped in a
piece of pleather that I'd cut from an old purse and pricked nine
times with a pin, per the book's instructions. I spat in the pot. I
pictured misfortune befalling her. I said her name.

The next morning, Tiffany showed up to school covered with
boils. She had laid out in the sun the day before and fallen asleep
"oiled and foiled." Her skin was an outbreak of sun blisters, on
which she had smeared some sort of greasy ointment, making
her even more grotesque. She looked like a scabbed sea creature,
some sort of mottled rockfish. She was hideous and she knew it.
And she was visibly upset, walking around all day with her face
shielded by her hair. The spell had worked.

At first, I felt exhilarated and dangerous—a righteous sense
of justice. But as the day went on, a thick, mute fear crept in.
What have I done? My guilt and remorse compounded the more I
thought about it. As much as I was thrilled by the spell's efficacy,
I hated knowing that I was the one who'd made her suffer, and I
fretted about what dark forces I might have unleashed.

Lying in bed that night, I was kept awake by visions of her sad, swollen face. I decided that I would never do this to another person again. Curses to curses. Hexes no more.

INVARIABLY. TALK OF teen witches circles back to *The Craft*, the 1996 film that launched a thousand covens. I was fifteen when it was released, and couldn't have guessed then what a cult classic it would turn into. Today it's held up as one of the most influential films about witches ever made, and there's a lot to love about it. Fans often cite its deliciously nineties costumes (chokers! dressy vests! peasant skirts with boots!) and its thrilling, no-holds-barred depiction of vengeful teen girls. Many women of color have also remarked about how meaningful it was for them that one of the film's four witches is a black woman, something that was—and still is—all too rare, as archetypal witch iterations so often default to white. Lastly, the film has an air of authenticity about it that most witch flicks lack. Wiccan priestess Pat Devin worked as its consultant to ensure that many of the rituals and props resembled those of her own practice. And two of the film's stars, Fairuza Balk and Rachel True, had actual interest in the occult when they got the roles—and still do. Balk went on to own an LA occult shop called Panpipes for several years, and she currently sells her own magically charged artwork online. True now has a thriving tarot-reading business called True Heart Tarot. (In a bit of further witch trivia, there are stories about how during the shoot of the film's pinnacle seaside ritual, actual bats landed on the "magic" circle, waves crashed with shocking force, and the entire crew lost power during Balk's final chant. But I digress.) Many practicing witches around my age often talk about this film as being a big inspiration for their own exploration of witchcraft, and its attempt at realism is one of the reasons why it struck a chord.

But there's also a lot about *The Craft* that's problematic.

At the start of the movie, we're introduced to our protagonist, Sarah, a transfer student with a suicidal past who is plagued by uncanny goings-on. On her first day at her new school, she meets Nancy, Bonnie, and Rochelle, a group of gothed-out girls who are looking for a fourth member to complete their coven. After Rochelle sees Sarah make a pencil magically stand on its point during French class, she is convinced that Sarah is the one they've been waiting for.

At first it seems that Sarah has finally found safe harbor with her sister outcasts. Together, they can now call in the four directions (something that practicing witches do in real life, albeit with variation). With their powers now supercharged, they each set about to make their personal wishes come true. Sarah casts a love spell on Chris, the boy she likes, despite the fact that he'd spread nasty rumors about her when she refused to sleep with him after one date. ("I know it's pathetic," she says, in one of the film's clumsy attempts to rationalize her ongoing crush on a cruel skeezebag.) Bonnie uses witchcraft to heal disfiguring scars on her back and make herself more beautiful. Rochelle, the film's only black character, casts a vengeance spell that causes a racist bully's hair to fall out. And ringleader Nancy uses magic to invoke the (fictitious) god Manon, which results in her abusive stepfather dying from a sudden heart attack. This leaves her and her mother with a hefty sum from his insurance policy that allows them to move out of their leaky trailer and into a fancy LA high-rise.

Understandably, the girls are intoxicated by their newfound

capabilities. They use magic to change the color of their hair and traffic lights and to forge a deeper connection with the spirit of Manon. They also exude more sexuality as their magic grows, both in their deportment and in their personal style. As Rachel True, the actor who played Rochelle, told me, "Our skirts get shorter as our powers get stronger." Sexing and hexing become entwined, as they so often do when it comes to depictions of witches. For a time, these teens are on a joyride, emancipated from the bounds of adolescent victimhood and attracting whatever outcomes they desire.

But soon their original spells get out of hand, and Sarah becomes trepidatious about continuing to use magic in this way. Chris, the boy who now "loves" her, becomes a stalker; the now more beautiful Bonnie turns narcissistic; Rochelle's racist bully is seen crying in the gym shower as so much of her hair falls out that she's rendered a high school Gollum. Nancy desires ever more power, and after doing a dark invocation spell, her own magic turns deadly. Tensions reach a climax when Chris's witchcraft-induced obsession with Sarah culminates in his attempt to rape her (a highly fraught message by today's standards—are we supposed to think that Sarah brought this on herself?). She escapes his grip and runs to the haven of her coven, shaken and disheveled and covered in dirt. When Nancy hears what happened, she is livid. She goes to a party that Chris is attending and tries to seduce him. When he resists, she changes her face into Sarah's, succeeds, and then berates him for treating women like whores. "*You're* the whore!" she screams, then uses her magic to send Chris tumbling out the window to his death.

Sarah, now fully convinced that Nancy is evil, tries to stop her with a binding spell that doesn't work. A violent showdown between Sarah and Nancy ensues. Sarah, tapping into the goodness and power from her deceased mother (also a witch, natch), finally defeats Nancy by crashing her into a mirror in a shower of glass shards. At the end of the movie, the other two witches attempt to make peace with Sarah. Their magic is gone, they tell her, and they're wondering if hers is still there. Sarah responds by conjuring a lightning bolt to snap a tree branch that falls at their feet: a warning that they should never approach her again. In the film's final scene, we see Nancy strapped down to a bed in an insane asylum as she babbles hysterically about Manon, presumably writhing until the end of her days.

When I first saw this film as a teen, I had mixed feelings. I was put off by the fact these teenagers' rituals resembled so many of my own. Was this the path I was walking? Was I also going to be punished by sinister fates? At the same time, there is a cool factor that the film sells, which I found hard to resist: the witches are rebels adorned in leather jackets, black lipstick, and strands of fashionable talismans. They spell-cast against a soundtrack of nineties alternative rock songs and Graeme Revell's moody synth-meets-Middle East score. "Watch out for those weirdos," a bus driver warns them, in one of the film's most iconic scenes. "We are the weirdos, mister," Nancy replies over her dark sunglasses, before flashing a Cheshire smile. These girls have supernatural swagger. I wanted that too.

Ultimately, though, the tone of the film struck me as patronizing and a bit mean-spirited. The lesson seemed to be: Don't dabble in the dark arts, ladies, or you'll get what's coming. Don't be too powerful, too strong, too much. *The Craft* reinforces the idea that teen girls are utterly devoid of self-control or self-reflection. That unleashing their fullest potential is to invite mayhem and destruction. At one point, the proprietress of an occult bookshop the girls frequent says that magic is neither black nor white. That the only good or bad is in the heart of the witch. I suppose Sarah is supposed to be a good witch, in the end—but doesn't she use magic to hurt Nancy and the others? We're invited to admire the way these girls refuse to be victimized, but they also get carried away—*just as girls always do.* Better, perhaps, to just grin and bear it than to meddle in things that are beyond one's "limited" understanding. Check yourself before you wreck yourself.

It's not that I couldn't relate on some level. My own early experiments with magic were driven by a lot of the same impulses: wanting love, revenge, control. I too was driven by the desire to live a life of my own devising, and like Sarah, I had learned firsthand how awful it felt to voluntarily inflict harm on another person (albeit with far fewer casualties). But I bristled at the film's implications that for most young women, their interest in magic would inevitably dwarf their sense of right and wrong.

Watching the film again as an adult, I'm still not totally comfortable with it. We're given very little backstory on any of the witches, and we're not asked to sympathize with their personal traumas until well into the movie, so their characters are flattened into caricatures. I wish we were made to care more about them, but instead the film turns into a cautionary tale about what happens when girls are left unmonitored. *The Craft* is like an occult version of *Heathers*, another film about high school vengeance taken much too far. We're supposed to identify with these underdogs and to feel vicarious satisfaction when their revenge plots work. But then we get castigated when their targets suffer and the girls get swept up in power trips. The film slaps us five, then slaps our wrists.

But even this is not my least favorite aspect of *The Craft*. What truly leaves a sour taste in my mouth is the film's depiction of female friendship. The girls are not terribly nice to one another, even before things go south. They join forces out of necessity, not true kinship, and in the end, Sarah finds herself alone. I would have loved to see the witches form a true alliance based on mutual caring and concern. Instead, the movie reinforces the tired stereotype of girls stabbing each other in the back. Even if they had to learn harsh lessons or fight dark forces, their bond could have helped them be even more ferocious and fantastic.

This movie is a horror fantasy in which snakes appear out of nowhere and witches hover above the floor. But perhaps, for the filmmakers, the idea of a united group of young women was just too implausible.

MY SAVING GRACE during my teen years was my best friend, Molly. She was even shorter than I was, a fact emphasized by hair that reached nearly to her knees. We shared a similar taste in music and a love of bizarre films. We passed notes in school and gifted each other with old cigar boxes filled with charms, old toys, rocks and seashells, and torn-out pictures from *Sassy* magazine. We decorated my basement as if it was our own art installation, with doll heads hanging from the ceiling with purple ribbon, Kate Moss ads, vintage children's book illustrations, photocopied *Sandman* comics pages, and stills from Disney cartoons. We spent hours dressing up in costumes and having "arty" photo shoots, doing our best to emulate images that we came across from photographers like David LaChapelle and Floria Sigismondi and makeup artist Kevyn Aucoin. We made collaged shrines of our heroes and

mocked "poseurs" and assholes we saw on TV and at our high
school. We watched tons of *Liquid Television* and argued over
which of us was Daria and which was Jane.

We dreamed of directing movies, or working for MTV, or
maybe being in a band. We wanted to make things, anything.
Mostly, we wanted to make something of ourselves, even if we
didn't know what exactly, or how. But the thing we knew for sure
was that we wanted out. We couldn't wait to escape our snob-
filled, cookie-cutter, boring-ass town.

When we were freshmen in high school, Molly and I fell quite
happily into a group of kids, mostly guys, who loved Marilyn
Manson and monster movies. We were inseparable, gathering
each weekend at the home of two brothers whose parents were
famously permissive—all the more ironic since their dad was a
cop. Though they lived in a suburban development, they kept a
pet pig named Hammy. He was an ugly dirigible of a creature who
gloomed around the house, always seeming on the brink of attack.

The eight or so of us spent countless hours together, drinking
beer and listening to music and sneaking into creepy R-rated movies like *Seven* and *The Crow: City of Angels*. We'd make videos of
one another and play rounds of "Would You Rather?" *Would you
rather have wings or fins? Would you rather be invisible or have the
power of teleportation?* We'd have relatively chaste sleepovers, doz-
ing in piles on the couch in front of episodes of *Mystery Science
Theater 3000*, slogged out on Chex Mix and Budweiser. Molly
and I had found our tribe. They were our band of Lost Boys, and
we were the Wendys.

Eventually, we started dating a couple of them, Ryan and Tom,
who were best friends as well. I made out with Ryan for the first

time at his house while *Children of the Corn* played on his VCR. It was love.

Molly went to Tom's one night—their first time alone together. She was pretty nervous, and I was nervous for her. She and Tom were both on the shy side, so it was anyone's guess who would make the first move, if it happened at all.

I did a spell.

I started by trying to telepathically send Molly a message of bravery and held an image in my mind of them kissing. I remember pacing the upstairs hallway of my house in front of the mirrored closet doors, back and forth, back and forth, chanting, gathering energy, feeling a sort of furry electricity running up and down my arms. Back and forth back and forth gathering gathering gathering until—astonishingly—a shudder of lightning and a loud crack of thunder.

I couldn't believe it. Was it a coincidence? Or had I somehow summoned it? I still don't know.

A phone call from Molly later that night confirmed what I thought must be true: yes, they had kissed. We compared notes on the times: they lined up. The spell had worked.

The following year things changed. We found ourselves replaced by younger, faster models, two girls named Nicki and Angie who smoked incessantly and whose primary party trick was masturbating under their jeans while everyone watched. Our relationships with Ryan and Tom were long over. The clan got way druggier, and we watched our friends downshift into full-on burnouts, now more interested in swapping stories about getting their dogs high than discussing weird cartoons. Marijuana didn't agree with me. The first time I smoked it, my throat closed up and my heart sped so fast I was convinced I was going to die. After that, I was too scared to try anything harder.

And so we were now outside our group of outsiders, and Molly and I found ourselves at sea. Still, we stayed connected to each other, holding a golden cord between us that kept us from drowning entirely. We made each other mix tapes, had candy-mad sleepovers, and continued dressing up in our best New Jersey avant-garde. We starting going to live shows, eventually making pilgrimages into Manhattan to see our favorite musicians play. Björk at the Hammerstein. Tori Amos at the Beacon Theatre. Rasputina at the Bowery Ballroom. PJ Harvey, Prince, Bowie, Portishead. Artists who lifted us out of our misery, and into a world of the fantastical, the cinematic, the Anywhere-but-Here.

One night, Molly and I did a ritual in the woods behind my house. We decided to dress ourselves in "ceremonial garb," and the best we could pull together was a couple of white clearance rack Victoria's Secret nightgowns that we wore beneath a few things we found in my mom's closet: a wine-colored bathrobe and one of her old graduation gowns. Our plan was to dance beneath the moon as a gesture of some sort of offering, but our goals beyond that were admittedly vague.

We dug a pit and filled it with sticks but couldn't get the fire to light. One of us got the idea to take balled-up newspaper and coat it with hairspray. That did the trick. We smoked clove cigarettes and tranced out staring into the flames. We fluttered our hands in the air and started to sway, until we felt a wave of energy wash over us. We didn't know what it was, but it felt as if something divine had been dropped over our shoulders. The wind picked up and the flames grew higher and higher, until they threatened to spread.

We panicked and extinguished the fire shortly thereafter, but the thrill lasted far beyond those thirty or so minutes. We didn't care if those kicked-up forces were chemistry or a chimera. What we had conjured was connection: to each other, and to something that felt bigger than ourselves.

WHEN WE FIRST meet Louise Miller in the 1989 film *Teen Witch*, she's a boxy-sweatered nerd with only one friend. She spends her free time in her school drama department, and she has no suspicion that she is destined for anything other than languishing on the bottom rung of the social ladder. One day she happens upon a strange amulet in the prop closet. At first she thinks nothing of it. But then she meets Madame Serena, the neighborhood psychic, who informs her that she is, in fact, a reincarnated witch. Serena explains that the amulet Louise found is a sort of battery that contains her magic, and that she will be able to access these powers when she turns—you guessed it—sixteen.

When Louise's birthday comes and her abilities awaken, she revels in her powers, and uses them to her advantage. She casts a spell to make herself popular, transforming from an ugly duckling into a denim-and-tulle-wearing swan. With this sudden confidence, she seduces the cutest boy in school away from his cheerleader girlfriend—though she resists the urge to charm him with a love spell. She's not quite so restrained with her magic in other circumstances: she turns her annoying little brother into a dog and retaliates against a nasty teacher by causing him to disrobe in front of the entire class.

It's all fun and games, until things inevitably go awry. The demands on her social life become overwhelming, and she ends up alienating her best friend—the only one who ever truly liked her before she became a witch (and who also happens to be one of the most appalling rappers in cinematic history—best if you just see it for yourself). Louise also can't tell if the school hunk truly cares about her, or if it's just her magically induced popularity that has caught his attention. Once again, our teen witch has a crisis of identity: Where do her loyalties lie?

The film ends with Louise smashing the amulet on the ground at the school dance, having decided to renounce magic in favor of true love. (She does keep her bitchin' wardrobe, though.) The takeaway? Witchcraft is a shortcut, a cheat code in the game of life. Best not to use it, because if you do, you'll never feel as if you've earned anything on your own. But it can also be read as an analogy for other forms of illusion: if you rely too much on keeping up false appearances, you'll never know if people like you for who you really are.

As with Louise's and Sabrina's catalyzing sixteenth birthdays, it is common for teen witch stories to have the protagonist's powers activate when she "comes of age," a clear metaphor for puberty and the double-edged sword of sexuality. Sometimes her witchcraft is a threat, and sometimes it's an asset. In some instances she inherits her magic, but in others it's self-taught or bestowed upon her by another person. But often her new abilities are something that she must learn to hone with practice and restraint, or else relinquish entirely. She must make decisions about the kind of witch she wants to be.

In the YA book series *Beautiful Creatures* (for the record, also a highly underrated 2013 film), Lena Duchannes comes from a line of "Casters." As family lore tells it, on her sixteenth birthday she will be "claimed" as either a Light Caster or a Dark Caster—and she is terrified of the latter. Is her destiny to be good or evil? Who is she, really? Her impending metamorphosis fills her with dread.

In *The Girl Who Drank the Moon*, Xan the witch accidentally feeds moonlight to an orphaned baby named Luna, imbuing her with magic that she is too young to control. Xan then casts a spell on Luna in order to contain her powers. When Luna turns thirteen, the dormant magic begins to burst out of her and wreak all sorts of havoc. She must learn how to put these new skills to use, lest they cause more damage.

Sunny, the Nigerian-American protagonist of Nnedi Okorafor's *Akata Witch*, is twelve when she has her first vision. She begins her story staring into a candle after all of the electricity in her village has gone out. Suddenly she sees an image of "[r]aging fires, boiling oceans, toppled skyscrapers, dead and dying people." She leans in so close to the flame that her long hair catches fire, and her mother has to cut off 70 percent of it. She feels overwhelmed by her gifts, until she gets guidance from friends and magical teachers.

And in Greg Rucka and Nicola Scott's comic series *Black Magick,* we are shown in a flashback how witch and homicide detective Rowan Black has come into her powers. After her thirteenth birthday party, we see her in a car being driven somewhere by her mother and grandmother. "It's hard not being able to tell anyone," Rowan says. Her mother replies, "They wouldn't understand, Ro." Next we see the three of them arrive in the woods, where they are greeted by some witches. The group then guides Rowan through a ritual that involves submerging her in a magical pool where she sees all of her previous lives flash before her in water bubble mirages. She has been initiated, or "awakened," as the witches say. For the next three months, Rowan enters a deep

depression. She starts acting out in school, crying uncontrolla-
bly at home, and experimenting with dark magic. We learn that
watching herself be tortured and persecuted, lifetime after lifetime, has become too much to bear, and she can't stand the pain
that comes with learning about who she really is. This montage
ends with her mother dying in a car crash, and an evil entity seems
to be responsible. While it's not implied that Rowan caused the
death exactly, it's clear that she is now suddenly caught up in some
sort of occult battle. Like it or not, she must pull herself together
in order to grow up and become a fighter on the side of good, both
as a witch and as an agent of the law.

Adolescent witches have to learn control and discernment, just
as teen girls must with their burgeoning sexuality and protean
senses of self. These stories portray magic as a mixed blessing: a
source of vast potential, and a mechanism of possible destruction.
The teen witch is a key ready for ignition, a match with a promise
to inflame.

WHEN I WAS fifteen, I became subject to invisible forces of a different kind.

In November of 1996, I was called to the principal's office.
Grandma Trudy was there waiting for me, and I was to leave early
with her. When we got to her car, she told me that my sister was
undergoing some sort of breakdown at college, and that my mom
was flying to Savannah to be with her. Then she drove me to the
mall and bought me a burgundy velour top from The Limited,
which is how I knew that things were dire, because Trudy never
paid full price for anything. It was my sophomore year of high

school, and my sister's first semester at Emory University. And it was the start of the worst years of both of our lives.

Emily was brought home, and she was different. The sweet and loving sibling I had known was not this person who stood before me. To my young eyes, she seemed possessed, and each day she waged a war inside herself to either cast the demon out or give over to it entirely. She lashed out and lambasted everyone around her, transfigured with fury. Her fits were ferocious, verbally and sometimes physically. She would career from racing highs to abysmal lows, devoid of logic, resistant to reason. When she wasn't paralyzed and screaming on the floor, she was hard to keep up with. She crashed cars. Took too many pills. Heard voices. Became frenzied with laughter or obsessed with the same repeated thought. One day she ran away barefoot, holding a cordless phone.

Mostly, though, there was crying. Unceasing torrents of tears. Emily's sorrow was bottomless, her need unmeetable. My sister, the ocean. The human typhoon.

Anyone who tried to comfort her came under attack. She hated everyone who loved her. She hated how she felt. She hated what she was doing to us, and hated us for trying to make it stop. She was convinced that everyone was against her, and that medical treatment was some sort of punishment. The psych ward was a prison, and she saw us as her jailers. Still, she had to be admitted. Over the ensuing months, I watched her go in and out of mental health facilities, as doctors tried to adjust her meds, teach her coping strategies, keep her safe. She'd eventually be diagnosed with manic depression. It's a term that has since gone out of vogue—now they call it bipolar disorder—but it is an apt descriptor of her breakneck swings in mood, and the unpredictable extremes of her behavior.

When she was in the hospital, it was heartbreaking, but when she was home, it was cataclysmic. Each day she was our natural disaster, an erratic weather pattern whose gales threatened to blow us all away. My parents and I became our own crisis unit, coming up with strategies for how to help her and to help each other. We knew it wasn't her fault, and that nobody suffered more than she did. But the three of us also had to figure out ways to survive. Like any triage team, we began working in shifts. When my parents were just too tired, or couldn't get through, I took my turn at her side.

I wish I'd been one of those teen witches with psychic abilities that suddenly switched on. If they had, I could have seen the future, in which my adult sister would not only stabilize but thrive, thanks to a combination of finding the right medicines, getting good therapy, and becoming a committed practitioner of Buddhist meditation. But back then, I had no way of knowing that she'd eventually be herself again, let alone go on to inspire thousands of people—myself included—with the story of her own recovery.

Instead, my newfound power was both a blessing and a burden. For some reason, in the throes of her maelstroms, I was the only one Emily seemed to hear.

She would shout and wail in repeating loops of lamentation, and I would listen and comfort her for hours. When she was drifting into delusion, I held her feet on the ground. I could talk her down from whatever ledge she clambered onto. It was me who convinced her to check herself in for treatment, time and time again. It was me who seemed to be able to soothe the beast, to keep the demon at bay. I was her guardian angel. Her keeper. Her magical sage. She needed constant attention, and I felt I had no choice but to give it to her. I thought I was her savior, staving off death. At times she seemed to think so too.

It was a gift I never asked for. And it was one I soon came to resent, because it had a very short shelf life. After each transformative conversation, each completed rescue mission or successful exorcism, I'd still find her hours later crumpled in a shrieking ball, and I'd be her adversary once again. I wrote poems about her, comparing us to Orpheus and Eurydice, me descending into the dark to fetch her from the Hades of her own head, trying desperately not to look back lest I lose her forever.

Our household was an emotional battle zone, a lattice of tripwires. Loud was scary, but quiet was worse. At any given moment, something, someone, could go off.

My room became my refuge. It was a suburban shrine, plastered with holy icons. I covered the walls with mythical images and pictures of my favorite musicians, artists, writers, and actors— matron saints who offered me hope that the adult world was a place webbed with shimmering filaments of imagination. I singlehandedly kept Fun-Tak in business, rolling ball after ball of the oily blue gum between my fingertips and sticking it to the four corners of every postcard and poster and cutout and printout, scraps of paper and poems, each promising to keep watch until my eventual escape. I put glow-in-the-dark stars on the ceiling, celestial-patterned throws on the chair and floor. I stuffed it with so many candles I'm surprised I didn't burn the whole house down. This was my cocoon, my cauldron. A magic hut I constructed in the heart of the wilderness, safe and lit from within.

★   ★   ★

ONE OF THE most beloved teen witches of all time is Willow from *Buffy the Vampire Slayer*. When we first meet her, she is Buffy's best friend and a member of what they dub the Scooby Gang—a group of friends (plus a rather dashing school librarian named Giles) who fight vampires and solve metaphysical mysteries. Studious, reliable, and computer-savvy, Willow spends copious amounts of time in the school library to research ways that Buffy can combat the various ghouls that have overtaken their fair town of Sunnydale. Willow discovers that she can do magic, and her spells become one of the primary weapons in the arsenal of Buffy and the crew.

As the series progresses and the girls go off to college (conveniently at the same university near the town they grew up in), Willow becomes more deeply devoted to witchcraft, poring over dusty old books and ultimately joining a Wiccan student club. Here she meets a witch named Tara, and their relationship becomes the subject of one of pop culture's most groundbreaking LGBTQ+ arcs—the first fully developed lesbian love story on US television. They find that being together enhances their powers: a beautiful metaphor for coming out of the closet, broom or otherwise. Their first kiss causes them to literally levitate off the ground.

Their euphoria is short-lived. Soon Willow becomes addicted to witchcraft, seeking bigger and bigger highs, and endangering herself and her friends in the process. When Tara is killed by a stray bullet, Willow's grief is so deep that her powers turn evil. Her eyes and hair turn black, and veins are visible through her skin. She wants vengeance, she wants justice, she wants Tara back. And in seeking these things, she goes on a rampage that nearly destroys the world.

She's in the midst of conjuring a literal apocalypse when her best friend, Xander, intervenes with love and a forgiving heart. Giles then takes her to the English countryside to train in a new form of magic that is based on nature and light.

Willow's magic is a proxy for emotional extremes. It externalizes the colossal feelings of youth that threaten to take us over. Looking back at it now, I also see Willow's story line as a metaphor for addiction or mental illness. It shows how when a person is in pain, they can demolish not only themselves but everyone around them. But it also offers hope that with the right treatment and support, recovery is possible for all involved.

BY THE SPRING of 1997, I was struggling badly. At home, I was a walking Richter scale, hypersensitized to my sister's seismic shifts.

I hated most of the kids in my school, and I was dating a goth boy named Anthony who was arty and broody, true to form. We'd drive around in his car, listening to Tricky and Nine Inch Nails, then preen around the mall in lavish makeup, frilly outfits, and the requisite Doc Martens. He was a couple years older than me, and we both knew he'd be off to college soon, an umbra that hung over me for months. My only friends were him and Molly, and none of us were happy. My grades were slipping, and my moods were black. I made miserable artwork, images of bleeding girls and splintered faces. When I wasn't consoling my sister, I spent most of my free time at home alone, door closed, music blasting. I'd stay up late scribbling poems and casting spells until I fell asleep, then wake up late the next morning, drained and glassy-eyed.

As Emily's episodes got worse and my powers of consolation seemed to decrease, I tried to put as much distance as I could between her and me. I discovered that I could access the roof through the window in our upstairs bathroom, and I'd sneak out there whenever she went on one of her tirades. I'd put on headphones, turning the volume all the way up on my Walkman to muffle the sounds from below. Then I'd lift my arms up to the sky and pray for protection. *Help me, Artemis. Help me, Nuit. Please, Great Goddesses of Night, hear my call in the dark.*

To my parents' immense credit, though they had their hands full with my spinning sister, they recognized that I also needed a lifeline, and they scrambled to keep me from hurtling into space. They checked in with me as often as they could. They sent me to therapy. And they researched other ways to get me extra support.

There was a place they had heard about that had helped one of their friends' kids. It was a tiny private school, but an unconventional one. There were no uniforms, and it was run by a poet named Lois Hirshkowitz who commuted from Manhattan every day. She had long gray hair, which she wore in a bushy ponytail, and her bony, freckled fingers were covered in rings that looked like watch gears. At my admissions interview, she regarded me with seriousness, asking me lots of questions and listening intently with a flinty, glittering gaze. I liked her classroom, with its single long table, fireplace, and floor-to-ceiling wall of books. And I liked the way she made me feel, as though my words were worthy of consideration. It would be a big change, especially considering I only had two years left of high school. But I decided I would give it a try. It couldn't be worse than the school I was at, I reasoned, even though it would mean an hour-long bus ride back and forth. I liked the idea of having this woman as my teacher. I liked the stillness I felt when I was with her. She was quiet, and her classroom was quiet, but both seemed to be teeming with words beneath the surface. I was living in a haunted house. For now, quiet didn't sound so bad.

Lakewood Prep was a mix of Professor X's school for mutants and the Island of Misfit Toys. I went from having five hundred kids in my grade to being one of twelve. We were all very different from one another, but when you're in a class that small, you turn into a sort of family, with all that word implies. Each of us was there for a different reason, but we all shared a need for a little extra help that the public schools weren't equipped to provide.

There was the writer with trichotillomania, who wore a wig to cover up the bald spots she had from pulling out her hair. One girl was a former heroin addict, who had pet ferrets and drew pictures of giant-eyed superheroes. There was a hilarious boy whose father was an upstanding law enforcement officer by day and a child beater by night. My eventual boyfriend, Eddie, was a sweet and gifted musician with a tumultuous family life and a propensity for trying any drug he could get his hands on.

And there was me. A purple-lidded poetry chick with a super-sick sister and an obsession with the occult.

Mrs. Hirshkowitz taught two classes: poetry and contemporary fiction. She took us seriously as writers and readers, assigning us books by Nadine Gordimer, Toni Morrison, Geoff Ryman, and Patrick McCabe. We read poetry by Sharon Olds and Molly Peacock and plays by Tom Stoppard and we wrote every single day. As a teacher, Mrs. H.—as we called her—was encouraging but had high standards. She was kind, but she didn't mince words if there was something she thought could be improved upon, whether in our writing or our general conduct. I also learned that despite her understated composure, she had a sly sense of humor, and when she laughed, her whole face cracked like crème brûlée and her eyes flashed with wicked pleasure. I loved how she used words, not just in her own poetry but when she spoke. She had a way of undercutting a grandiose statement with dry informality: "I think that's sort of astonishing," she would say when she liked something I had written. I thought she was sort of astonishing too.

When I was in her class, I knew I could write about absolutely anything, and that it would be okay. Welcome, even. Reams of poems about my sister unspooled out of me. Emily was my monster and my muse. If I couldn't control things at home, at least I could contain her on paper. I learned how to bring internal chaos into crisp creative focus. With each poem, I wrote myself a little bit stronger: magic words to heal a stricken heart.

HERMIONE GRANGER IS only eleven when we first meet her, but she's a teenager for most of the Harry Potter series. She is brilliant, righteous, and deeply devoted to her studies. She is also a bit of an outcast. Because she has two nonmagical, Muggle parents, she is subject to ridicule by some of the crueler students at school who call her a Mudblood—a slur that implies that she is less pure than those who are born into wizarding families. Hogwarts School of Witchcraft and Wizardry offers her dear friendships and caring teachers who help her develop her craft. But it is also where she grows up and learns that the world can be a punishing, dangerous place.

This could turn her bitter or cause her to experiment with evil, as so many teen witches do. But J. K. Rowling makes choices with her character that reveal a far more optimistic opinion about powerful young women. As the books go on, Hermione gets involved with activism and becomes a champion of the downtrodden. When she learns that house elves are unpaid and given no time off, she starts the Society for the Promotion of Elfish Welfare (SPEW) to raise awareness about their working conditions. She knits the elves socks and hats that have the power to set them free—all of this decades before the pink pussy hats of the 2017 Women's March. And she develops into a community organizer, encouraging Harry to form Dumbledore's Army, a secret student group focused on self-defense spells, so that they might ready themselves for possible attack from the villain Voldemort. Throughout the series, Hermione is a crusader for goodness, using both her brains and her compassion to fight for equality and save the day several times over.

Like the other teen witches who came before her, she makes mistakes and missteps on her journey to becoming a better witch. But she never becomes corrupted by power and she is never overtly sexualized. Nor does she have to give up her magic in the end. Instead, she learns how to hone her natural talent and apply it to causes that she cares about. If Hermione is the teen witch of the generation that came after mine, I'd say things are boding rather well for the future.

IT'S EASY TO trivialize the teen witch trope, just as it is tempting to roll one's eyes at teenage girls in general. This young witch is not above the heartbreaks and mind-quakes that occur every day at home and at school. She wants to kiss the cutest boy, she wants to ace the math test, she wants to be invited to the party at the most popular kid's house. She wants to feel pretty, sure. But she also wants to feel powerful. As if life is not something happening to her, but rather something that she can impact herself.

For better or worse, teen witches crave a sense of justice. They turn mean girls into mice, teachers into toads. They want to see the worthy get rewarded and the cruel get what's coming. And so they start covert groups and have clandestine meetings. They plot and scheme ways to set things right.

If they're lucky, they'll receive guidance from others further along the path, mentors or friends who will circle around them and help give their spells shape. These allies will keep them from incinerating the entire cheerleading squad and hand them the antidote to any poison they may unwittingly ingest.

It is dangerous to be different, and it is especially hazardous to be a female in flux. At any moment, one might be ridiculed, locked away, cast out. The teen witch is an avatar of the miseries, insecurities, and strange proclivities that so many of us keep knotted within as we navigate our young lives.

But she also offers a way to combat adversity. The most satisfying of her stories teach us that we don't need to fear or diminish our innate power—we just need to choose how to best direct it. The teen witch helps us grow more fully into ourselves.

Chapter 3

SYMPATHY FOR
THE SHE-DEVIL

L est one think that fear of female sexuality evaporates once teen girls reach adulthood, I offer the satanic witch for consideration. Here is a woman so depraved that she'd rather dance with the devil in the pale moonlight than spend time with a respectable, churchgoing husband. *Quelle horreur!*

In films from *Häxan* to *The Devils* to *The Witches of Eastwick*, we see this dynamic play out. Devilish witches are Girls Gone Wild. They're unruly, unholy. They will ruin your life.

Witches and demons have long been brimstone bedfellows, as evidenced by witchcraft stories that involve diabolical relations of every flavor. In most tellings, the witch becomes Lucifer's lover, eager servant, or gleeful emissary, and she joins a cabal of other witches and ghouls who are tied to him for all eternity. Usually the devil first presents himself as a ticket out of her dull life, an emancipator who will provide her with endless pleasure and omnipotence. Though he may initiate their interactions and show up expressly to tempt her, becoming his consort is often depicted as voluntary on her part. She makes a pact with him or signs his book in an act of conflagrant consensuality, thus agreeing to do his bidding in exchange for power, riches, and/or nefarious nooky on the regular. In many of these narratives, her chosen identity as a witch is chalked up to her own shortcomings. She is lacking in willpower or faith. She is horny. She is bored. She's a satanic sex bomb just waiting to go off.

And go off she does. She fornicates with demons. She kills babies and makes a magical flying ointment out of their flesh. Her airborne travels take her to unwitting villages that she curses with misfortune and death. When she returns to the devil's side, she joins his other followers in acts of perverse worship involving orgies and gorging and goats, oh my.

But where did this infernal image of the witch come from?

In the Western world, belief in demons and witches can be traced back to ancient Mesopotamia, and both archetypes were later adopted by the Persians, Hittites, and Hebrews. Early Greek and Roman literature is rife with seductive sorceresses like Circe, Medea, Canidia, and Pamphile, women who used charms and potions for love or revenge, and often to the detriment of the men who encountered them.

Characters such as these were inspired in part by real life. The Greeks began a systemic classification of different types of magicians by the fifth century BCE, including the *goēs* who specialized in ghosts, *pharmakeis* (m) or *pharmakides* (f) who specialized in potions, and the *magos* who were generalized service magicians that practiced *mageia*, which eventually turned into the English word *magic*. Warnings about evil magic and the people who used it were seen throughout the ancient world, and there are records of the punishments that would be meted out were one to get mixed up in such dangerous activity. But it was the Romans who began persecuting magic-workers in earnest. By the third century CE, the use of *veneficium*—a combination of magic and poisoning—was outlawed in Rome, and it was usually women who were prosecuted for it.

But our fly-by-night, lusty devil-witch resulted from the crossing of several mythological streams.

One of the most famous tales we have of a woman being a magical, evil sex monster is that of Lilith, Eve's predecessor, and the supposed original apple of Adam's eye. Lilith's story as Adam's first wife got popularized in the eighth century CE thanks to a text called *The Alphabet of Ben Sira*. It stated that God created both Lilith and Adam from the earth, but that she refused to lie beneath him during sex, believing that they were equals since they were made from the same material. Adam declared that he was superior to her and declined her request to be on top. Furious, she uttered God's true name—an enormous sin in Jewish tradition—and then flew away from Eden. In some versions of the story, Lilith then copulates with Samael, the angel of death, and bears thousands of children, thus earning the moniker Mother of Demons. God sends three angels after Lilith, and they tell her that if she doesn't return to Eden, they will kill a hundred of her children each day. She refuses and begins murdering human babies in retaliation for the death of her own offspring. Per Jewish folk tradition, it was believed that only a magical amulet with the names of the three angels could ward her off and protect human newborns from being killed by her.

In feminist reframings of the 1960s and onward, Lilith became a symbol of female independence, and she continues to be a favorite among modern witches today. Her refusal to submit to a man and her choice of living on her own terms resonates with unconventional women, many of whom believe that Lilith was written out of the Bible due to misogyny. *The Alphabet of Ben Sira*, where she's first said to have been Adam's wife, was actually written at least five hundred years *after* the book of Genesis, but whether this story was passed down orally before then is anybody's guess.

While the character of Lilith may not appear in the Bible, her origins long predate it. Her name is most likely derived from *lilītu*, a class of female storm demons from Mesopotamian mythology. The first written record of Lilith or Lilitu as a singular deity is from ancient Sumer around 2000 BCE. According to myth, she is the "dark maid" who makes her home inside a *huluppu* tree in the garden of the goddess Inanna. Lilith's other companions in the tree are a bird and, yes, a serpent. In this story, Lilith, the bird, and the serpent all refuse to leave the tree, and Inanna is beside herself. She calls upon the god Gilgamesh, who arrives in fully armed regalia ready to throw down, and the three interlopers flee. According to Diane Wolkstein and Samuel Noah Kramer's translation: ". . . Lilith smashed her home and fled to the wild, uninhabited places."

The book of Genesis was written approximately 1,500 years after that of Inanna and the *huluppu* tree, and its Edenic tale echoes this one. And while the story of Lilith the demoness ex-wife wasn't to be written down for another five centuries after the Old Testament was, there is a mention of the word *lilith* in Isaiah 34:14. Various translations have interpreted this word to mean "night monster," "creature of the night," or "screech owl."

There is also a theory that the *lilith* creature eventually permutated into the Latin *strix* of Roman lore, which is a supernatural night owl who would prey upon young children while they slept. The word *strix* eventually came to refer to a woman who could transform herself into this deadly winged creature. In Germanic areas, it was also believed that she was a cannibal who ate people of all ages, and not just the young. *Strix* eventually evolved into *stria* or *striga*, words that, throughout Roman and Germanic regions, came to mean any maleficent, magical woman. Ultimately *strega* became the Italian word for "witch," and the association of witches with owls remains to this day.

Belief in these terrifying she-beings circulated throughout much of Europe, and the shape-shifting lady with the insatiable appetite took on many other forms. Eventually she morphed into the hellacious sex-crazed witch of the early modern era.

But before we get to her, let's meet her piquant paramour.

THE DEVIL HAS gone through multiple rebrands over the years (pardon the pun). Until the Middle Ages, he had been a relatively minor player in Christian theology. Satan is mentioned very seldom in the Bible, and there is no clear description of his appearance either. The character as we now picture him—the tempter of souls with his signature hooves, horns, and pitchfork—is in fact a conflation of many different elements, and a full survey of them would merit an entire book in itself. But briefly, some of his predecessors include: "the satan" or *satanas* of the Old and New Testaments, described as a "heavenly prosecutor" sent to test and harass humanity, most famously Job; the serpent in the Garden of Eden; the red dragon in the book of Revelation; Lucifer, the fallen angel, whose image has been largely influenced by Milton's *Paradise Lost* of the mid-seventeenth century; and a hearty dusting of Pagan deities (especially the horny-in-all-senses-of-the-word fertility god Pan) sprinkled on top for a randy kick.

Some have suggested that the Church's rekindled interest in Old Scratch was a strategic response to the sudden influx of Greek and Arabic texts about ceremonial magic that were being translated during the twelfth and thirteenth centuries. The leaders of the Church began to worry that these foreign occult influences were putting down roots in their own godly garden. Unlike the folk traditions or "low magic" that some of the poorer or "simpler" local citizens might still have been practicing, this literary magic was a threat to the Church because it appealed to a more intellectual class—including the clergy themselves. Churchmen behaving like sorcerers? Something had to be done. And so, Catholic leaders began to frame this foreign magic as "demonic," and any practicing magicians of this new, bookish type were smeared as devil worshippers.

In the thirteenth and fourteenth centuries, the Church began actively focusing on the dangers of demonic possession, and it was during this period that the employment of magic was declared an act of heresy. This was made official via Pope John XXII's 1326 bull, *Super illius specula*, which states:

> *With grief we discover, and the very thought of it wrings our soul with anguish, that there are many Christians only in name; many who turn away from the light which once was theirs, and allow their minds to be so clouded with the darkness of error as to enter into a league with death and a compact*

with hell. They sacrifice to demons and adore them, they make or cause to be made images, rings, mirrors, phials or some such things in which by the art of magic evil spirits are to be enclosed. From them they seek and receive replies, and ask aid in satis- fying their evil desires. Alas! this deadly malady is increasing more than usual in the world and inflicting greater and greater ravages on the flock of Christ.

The bull then goes on to say that anyone who teaches, stud- ies, or practices these evil deeds or who is in possession of books that contain such information will be excommunicated and tried "before competent judges for the infliction of all and every pen- alty which heretics are subject to according to law. . . ."

And so the seeds of Satan were planted by the Church itself, which began an active campaign to inform people about this new threat. Dominican and Franciscan friars started traveling to cit- ies and far-flung mountain towns throughout Western Europe to inform the public that to practice magic was to be a heretic, and that those who did so were in league with the devil.

Cue the original Satanic Panic.

And enter the demonic witch, stage left.

Records show that in the 1420s, a series of satanic witchcraft accusations and subsequent deaths took place in Western Europe, including in the Valais region of the Alps, the Languedoc area of France, and the city of Rome, with the earliest being an incident in the Pyrenees Mountains in 1424. These incidents can be traced directly to places where friars visited to preach. While the locals may already have had their own beliefs in owl monstresses, noctur- nal cannibal women, and meddlesome village witches, the visiting friars were responsible for contributing the concept of devil-worshipping magic-makers who had to be stopped at all costs.

Two men in particular are credited with identifying witches specifically as old women: a French theologian named Jean Gerson, and an Italian friar named Bernardino of Siena. As time went on, however, people of all ages and genders were accused. Suffice it to say, rumors began to escalate and spread, sending stories of satanic witches crashing throughout Europe in waves for the next three hundred years, peaking between 1580 and 1630 and declining by 1750 or so. The colonial American Salem witch trials of 1692 came rather late in the order of events and its fatalities were relatively small in number compared to the tens of thousands in Europe. The specific details about allegedly witnessed witchcraft acts varied from region to region and person to person. However, some similar motifs emerged.

The concept of a satanic witches' gathering—the Witches' Sabbath or *sabbat*, as it was sometimes called—came in large part from a few key mid-fifteenth-century texts including Johannes Nider's *Formicarius*, the anonymously written *Errores gazoriorum*, and Claude Tholosan's *Ut magorum et maleficioreum errores* (the titles just trip off the tongue). Witchcraft treatises such as these were shockingly graphic. They described the Witches' Sabbath as a demonic orgy, replete with feasting, dancing, and sordid coital acts between witches, demons, and the devil himself. They would sometimes make mention of the *osculum infame,* or Kiss of Shame: a gesture of greeting that involved the witch kissing the devil's anus. Other such Sabbath horrors were cataloged and spanned a wide range of deviance from cannibalism to bestiality to participation in the Black Mass, a perverse inversion of the

Catholic Mass sometimes said to involve semen, menstrual blood, or urine. There's also frequent mention of the witches' usage of dead baby parts to create the flying ointments that they would use to travel to their gatherings. (They had to murder the babies first, naturally.) The participants in the Sabbaths were rumored to be naked, maniacal, and totally out of control. They were unrepentant sinners, quite literally hell-bent on satisfying their dark urges and intent on pleasing their Dark Lord.

Once possessed by him or one of his demon lackeys, the witches would return to their villages or cities to wreak further havoc. They were often accompanied by familiars—magical animals or imps who would assist their misconduct. Sometimes it was believed they could also turn themselves into animals so that they might enter into innocent people's homes and farms unrecognized. Crucially, they would get to and from locations by flying, though their method of transport varied from poles to brooms to cooking forks to simply taking the shape of a winged creature themselves.

And so by the turn of the sixteenth century, our baby-killing, devil-fucking, creep-all-day, party-all-night witch was born.

ONE BOOK TOWERS above the rest as having had a great deal of influence on the shaping of the witch as a diabolical figure—and a female one at that: the *Malleus Maleficarum* or *The Hammer of Witches*. It's often stated that this infamous witch-hunting manual was first published in Germany around 1486 by "Kramer and Sprenger," (a good name for an infernal law firm if I ever heard one). Recent scholarship suggests, though, that Jakob Sprenger's name wasn't added to the book until 1519—more than thirty years after it was published—presumably to give it more credibility, since he was a respected Dominican friar.

Regardless, we do know that the primary, if not sole, author was Heinrich Kramer, a Dominican inquisitor with a major vendetta against women. Though it's true that his writings were informed by centuries of societal beliefs about female inferiority, he was a master of misogyny and paranoia in his own right.

As Malcolm Gaskill states: "It's not very historical to call Heinrich Kramer a superstitious psychopath, but he was up that end of the medieval spectrum."

Or in digital age lingo, one might say that he was ". . . one of witch hunting's most notorious trolls," per Kristen Sollée.

I might add that he was a vile person whose pathological fear of women caused him to create one of the most idiotic and despicable documents of toxic masculinity the world has ever seen.

Kramer wrote *The Hammer of Witches* to educate the reader about how to identify witches and their behavior, counteract their magic, and then go about trying and sentencing them, often to their death. He warns that witches are the most dangerous people there are, because they "give homage to the very devils by offering them their bodies and souls." In a section entitled "That Witches Deserve the heaviest Punishment above All the Criminals of the World," he writes, "The crimes of witches, then, exceed the sins of all others. . . . [H]owever much they are penitent and return to the Faith, they must not be punished like other Heretics with lifelong imprisonment, but must suffer the extreme penalty."

He writes of their penchant for infanticide, bovinicide, cannibalism, mind control, causing miscarriages, and raising hailstorms. Another favorite witch pastime, according to Kramer,

was to render men impotent by tricking them into thinking that
their penises had been removed entirely: "There is no doubt that
witches can do marvelous things with regard to male organs. . . .
But when [dismemberment] is caused by witches, it is only a matter of glamour; although it is no illusion in the opinion of the suf-
ferer." So let's get this straight: witches could copulate with devils,
commit murder, and change the weather itself—but causing the
actual loss of such an important extremity was too much for
Kramer to fathom: *Don't worry, boys, it's just a trick of the eye!* Even
all-powerful witches could not breach the sanctity of the boner.

He describes the pact that each witch makes with the devil,
sometimes in a solemn group ceremony, sometimes in private: She
swears to devote herself to him, renounces the Christian faith, and
promises to bring him more followers. She is also to make certain
"unguents" from the bones and limbs of dead babies, especially
baptized ones. In exchange, she will receive prosperity, a long life,
and, presumably, a steady supply of red-hot devil dick.

Kramer frames all of this by stating that, of the two sexes, it
is usually women who are witches for a host of reasons that he
details at length: they are more gullible, more impressionable, and
more indiscreet than men, and "feebler in both mind and body."
He expounds on all of this for several paragraphs, citing historical and biblical examples, and quoting from other male writers to
prove his points.

Most importantly though, Kramer emphasizes that women are
more susceptible to the lure of witchcraft because of their inexora-
ble libidos: ". . . [S]he is more carnal than a man, as it is clear from
her many carnal abominations." He explains that this is because
women were born defective, since they come from Adam's bent

rib: "And since through this defect she is an imperfect animal, she always deceives."

Yes, according to Kramer, all women are lying whores. It's not our *fault*, mind you: baby, we were born this way.

The most frequently quoted line from the *Malleus*—and arguably the book's thesis statement—is: "All witchcraft comes from carnal lust, which is, in women, insatiable." He goes on to say, "Wherefore for the sake of fulfilling their lusts they consort even with devils." No wonder we fly off to fuck incubi. The men just can't keep up.

Kramer's ideas about emasculating witch-women were given a big boost: Johannes Gutenberg's printing press had been operational by 1450, and his innovation in movable type technology was instrumental in replicating and disseminating witch texts and imagery throughout Europe. The *Malleus Maleficarum* was republished an estimated thirty times over the next two hundred years, during which it allegedly became second only to the Bible in terms of sales. Per Montague Summers's introduction to the 1948 English edition: "The *Malleus* lay on the bench of every judge, on the desk of every magistrate. It was the ultimate, irrefutable, unarguable authority." As such, it set the standard for who witches were (i.e., women), and how they should be punished (with brutality). So, though ideas about sexually promiscuous female devil-worshippers certainly existed before this, it's fair to say that the *Malleus Maleficarum* sealed the deal. It wasn't just a *femme fatale* that Kramer helped create. It was a *femme infernale*.

Image is everything, and a second text was also instrumental in codifying the visuals of the witch. In 1489, a German legal scholar named Ulrich Molitor wrote *De lamiis et pythonicis mulieribus* (often translated in English to *On Female Witches and Seers*) as a response to *The Hammer of Witches* and in several instances refuting some of its statements. But what is perhaps most significant about Molitor's work is that it was accompanied by six woodcuts by an anonymous artist—arguably the first illustrations of witches to be widely replicated. With captions such as "Two Witches Cooking Up a Storm," "Transformed Witches Ride a Forked Stick Through the Sky," and "Witch and Devil Embracing," these six pictures cemented the image of the witch as a lascivious shape-shifter, with loose hair and looser legs. This book was reprinted in more than twenty illustrated editions and was seen by many of Germany's most prominent artists, who would go on to render their own interpretations of these sexed-up, hexed-up temptresses.

Artists of the age, such as Albrecht Dürer and his student Hans Baldung Grien, were influenced by witchcraft writings such as these and the pictures that accompanied them, and they began including the licentious witch as a figure in their own "cabinet art." These were works that were bought by wealthy men for their private—*very* private—collections of what Yvonne Owens calls "classically inspired religious pornography." Drawings by Dürer, Baldung, and their students showed naked women of all ages engaging in witchcraft and thereby summoning demons and other destructive forces. Images like theirs had a sneaky duality to them. On the one hand, they served as illustrated morality allegories that warned the viewer to, as Linda C. Hults puts it, "Control your women, or the devil will usurp your authority." At the same time, they were blatantly titillating pictures, intentionally giving the collectors a risqué rush. As happens so often when it comes to arousal, shame and judgment were part of the equation: *take a good long look at this very bad thing.*

ALARMING IMAGES AND salacious anecdotes about these witchly devil-doers went viral. They showed up in printed witch-hunting texts and artists' renderings, sermons of preachers, leading questions by witchcraft prosecutors, and rumors among citizens themselves. The power of suggestion cannot be overstated in regard to why so many of the same elements showed up repeatedly in the so-called confessions of the tens of thousands of people who were accused of practicing witchcraft in Germany, France, Switzerland, Italy, Spain, Denmark, Scotland, Ireland, England, Iceland, Hungary, Poland, Russia, Luxembourg, and the Netherlands.

Many have written about the hardships of daily life in these regions at the time, such as a high infant mortality rate, challenging weather conditions, illness, and economic strife. These struggles left people vulnerable and looking for a scapegoat—or a goat-footed demon lord and his witch mistresses in this case. They began accusing their own neighbors of witchcraft, and blaming one another for any misfortune that befell their families.

And the results were horrific. Though it's impossible to determine an exact number, contemporary historians estimate that up to two hundred thousand people throughout Western Europe were accused of practicing witchcraft, and approximately half of them lost their lives because of it. Trials took place throughout the continent. Practices for identifying witches were excruciatingly painful, humiliating, and sometimes fatal. Witch hunters would examine the bodies of the accused to see if they had a "devil's mark," which signified the sealing of an infernal pact and was believed to be made by Satan himself either with a flaming-hot iron brand or by raking his claws over the witch's flesh. They also searched for a "witch's teat," which was an extra nipple that a witch was thought to have in order to suckle her familiar or imp. Any moles, protuberances, discolorations, or birthmarks on the skin of the accused were deemed suspicious and would be stabbed with a pin. If the flesh did not bleed, that meant the person was a witch. There was also the "swimming test." The suspect would have a rope tied around their middle, and then be flung into a body of water. If they floated, it meant they were guilty, for the water "rejected" the witch's evilness. If they sank: Oops! Guess they were innocent after all! Often the accused were tortured until they confessed or died, whichever came first. At other times, they were jailed without hope of release. "Proven" witches were executed outright, usually by burning or hanging.

Though it's true that people of all genders were accused of being witches, it's estimated that between 75 and 85 percent of those killed were women. There have been many theories as to why that is, touching upon everything from socioeconomics to biblical beliefs. But when we remember the vehemence of the *Malleus Maleficarum*, I think it's safe to chalk it up to good old-fashioned generalized misogyny.

Regardless, it's clear that from the end of the fifteenth century onward, one of the prime images of the witch that was being fed to civilians was that of the satanic, sexually deviant female. Clear, too, is that virtually all of those narratives were driven by men—popes, preachers, demonologists, magistrates, artists, writers. Certainly, witchcraft *accusers* came in all genders. But even the most infamous story of female finger-pointing ended up being distorted by a fella.

★ ★ ★

I **WAS A** freshman in high school the year we read Arthur Miller's *The Crucible*, the 1953 play that is largely responsible for bringing the history of the Salem witch trials into popular twentieth-century consciousness. And the story of one of its lead characters, the witchly pot-stirrer Abigail Williams, is a rather fine example of the way in which a male author's sexual hang-ups can reshape reality.

When Miller's play begins, Reverend Samuel Parris is fretting over his ten-year-old daughter, Betty, who is lying motionless on a bed. He had observed her dancing in the woods with his seventeen-year-old niece, Abigail Williams, alongside his slave, Tituba, and ten or twelve other girls. The audience soon learns that Abigail and co. were in fact doing some sort of unseemly magic ritual involving blood and nudity, and that Abigail was trying to put a deadly curse on Elizabeth Proctor, the wife of her thirtysomething former employer and former lover, John Proctor. Though Reverend Parris doesn't actually know the ritual's intent, he is afraid the villagers will think it is witchcraft, a conclusion that will threaten his livelihood and smear his good Christian name.

John Proctor arrives, and he and Abigail have a scene alone. We learn that she was fired as his housemaid because his wife, Elizabeth, discovered their affair. Abigail approaches him with lust in her eyes, and insists that he is there because he still has feelings for her. He denies it:

PROCTOR: Abby, that's a wild thing to say—

ABIGAIL: A wild thing may say wild things.

Proctor tells Abigail to put their affair out of her mind—it's in the past. This sets her off in a tearful fury: "You loved me, John Proctor, and whatever sin it is, you love me yet!" Salem hath no fury like a horndog scorned.

Shortly after this, Abigail finds herself being questioned by another reverend about her activities in the woods. Not wanting her curse on Elizabeth Proctor to be found out, she accuses Tituba of forcing them to do the ritual. The slave denies it at first: "I don't compact with no Devil!" But when she is threatened with hanging, Tituba says that she told the devil she would not work for him. Desperately looking to deflect blame, she then says, "Mister Reverend, I do believe somebody else be witchin' these children. . . . [T]he Devil got him numerous witches."

These witches could be anyone, or anywhere. And we all know what happens next.

As if possessed, Abigail and Betty suddenly start crying out the names of various villagers in town and accusing them of being seen with the devil.

The Salem witch trials commence. We're told that the girls of the village are behaving as if they have been attacked by witchcraft, screaming and convulsing on the floor. The accusations escalate, and several villagers are put in jail.

Later in the play, we learn that Abigail has accused Elizabeth Proctor of using a magic poppet to remotely stab her in the stomach with a needle. John Proctor goes to court to defend his wife, but soon finds his own allegiance called into question. When his servant, Mary Warren, begins to testify that the girls' antics are a hoax, Abigail accuses Mary of bewitching her with a freezing cold wind. Abigail cries, "Oh heavenly Father, take away this shadow!"

Proctor, convinced she is lying, shouts, "How do you call Heaven? Whore! Whore!"

He finally confesses their prior affair to the court, to prove that Abigail has a motive for trying to have his wife hanged.

PROCTOR: . . . She thinks to dance with me on my wife's grave! And well she might, for I thought of her softly. God help me, I lusted, and there *is* a promise in such sweat. But it is a whore's vengeance, and you must see it. . . .

Elizabeth, unaware of her husband's admission, then takes the stand. When she is asked about the affair, she denies it to save her husband's reputation, but ends up getting him convicted instead. The trial comes to a close, and John Proctor's final line in the scene is: "You are pulling Heaven down and raising up a whore!"

In the final act, we learn that Abigail has disappeared, having stolen Reverend Parris's life savings and boarded a ship with one of the other girls. John Proctor is about to be put to death, and the only way to save himself is if he "confesses" to being in league with Satan and names other people as being "with the Devil" as well. He starts to do it, but then can't bring himself to go through with it. He decides he'd rather be hung, and is led offstage to die. The reverend begs Elizabeth to plead with her husband: "Go to him! Take his shame away!"

But she responds, "He have his goodness now. God forbid I take it from him!"

It's a damn(ed) dramatic story. Who could resist the tale of a sexy, spell-casting Jezebel bringing about the downfall of her ex-lover and inciting a town massacre along the way? *The Crucible*'s

Abigail Williams is a whorish home-wrecker—and a teen witch as well—whose anger and trickery send an innocent man to his death. Even more, she gets away with it, and we're left feeling sorry for the doomed Proctor and his poor, pure wife.

As an allegory, too, it's highly effective. After all, Miller's primary intent in writing it was to draw a parallel between Salem hysteria and the McCarthyism of his own age in the 1950s, during which hundreds of innocent people were investigated for being alleged Communists under the direction of Senator Joseph McCarthy, and subjected to hearings by the House Un-American Activities Committee. The accused were encouraged to name others who might have Communist sympathies, else they risked losing their livelihoods or being imprisoned.

Miller wanted to show how even though these events were 250 years apart, both were predicated on the paranoia and blame-laying that can corrode society from the inside out. His play is one of the primary reasons we use the term *witch hunt* today to describe any circumstance where a community aggressively tries to root out its own transgressors, usually under false pretenses (more on that later). There's no question that *The Crucible* has gone down in history as one of America's great theatrical masterworks. It won the Tony for Best Play when it debuted on Broadway in 1953, has been produced globally countless times, and has remained a constant presence in high school curricula in the decades since its first performances. *The Crucible* is how many of us are taught about the Salem witch trials, its legacy forever entwined with American history.

I was a sophomore when the 1996 film adaptation came out, and one could see how Daniel Day-Lewis's John Proctor might have fallen for Winona Ryder's Abigail Williams, smoldering beauty that she is. Per the film's screenplay (which Miller wrote as well), their initial lust for each other, and the onslaught of Williams's "hysterical" accusations when he rejects her, is Proctor's eventual undoing.

Here's the thing though:

The real Abigail Williams was actually eleven years old during the Salem trials, not seventeen (and certainly not twenty-four, Ryder's age when she appeared in the film). And John Proctor? He was sixty, not in his "middle thirties," as Miller writes, and as Daniel Day-Lewis was when he played the role. There is no proof that there was any sort of romantic relationship between Abigail and John whatsoever, nor did she ever work in the Proctor household.

Similarly, there is no evidence that any gathering in any woods actually took place, and certainly not a nude one involving sanguineous slurping.

Of course, as a playwright, Miller is given creative license, and he made many other theatrical choices that openly contradict public record. As he states himself in a disclaimer at the beginning of the script, "This play is not history in the sense in which the word is used by the academic historian." Some key characters in the play are actually conflations of several real people, and both Cotton Mather and Tituba's husband, John Indian, are left out entirely. Tituba, the voodoo-practicing "Negro" slave, was in fact most likely a South American Indian (some have theorized that she was from an Arawak village in present-day Guyana or Venezuela) who was sold to the Parris family's sugar plantation in Barbados.

Some of these decisions were intentional, and some were perhaps based on erroneous history books that Miller was reading at the time. But it is clear that the primary plot driver for the play—a lusty teenage witch out for vengeance—was a complete fabrication on his part.

What Williams and her convulsing compatriots did was awful—some might say unforgivable. Her accusations and testimonies are largely responsible for the actual executions of nineteen human beings and the deaths of several others. And who knows the truth of why she did it? Perhaps she was hallucinating on ergot-tainted rye, as some scholars have surmised. Perhaps she was really bewitched, or suffering from conversion disorder, the current term for "hysteria." Perhaps she was just a tween girl living in a highly oppressive society who desperately needed to blow off steam—a child caught doing something naughty with the help, who lied to cover herself, and whose lies then carried her away on a fatal flight of fancy. I could be like Arthur Miller and make up a story of my own: that a young girl was sexually abused by a senior citizen and then spun out of control because it was too much for her to process. But that would be a fabrication, based on nothing but my own biased, wild imaginings, and influenced by the conversations and events of my own time and place.

We don't know much about what happened to the real Abigail Williams after the trials of Salem. According to court documents, she gave her last testimony on June 3, 1692, and then disappeared from public record entirely. Her activities and whereabouts have remained a mystery to historians, and her grave site is unknown.

Still, in Miller's epilogue of the play, he writes, "The legend has it that Abigail turned up later as a prostitute in Boston."

The Crucible makes John Proctor into a kind of a martyr, a proud man who would rather face death than have diabolical lies ruin his good name. It seems Miller saw himself in Proctor. After all, he was distraught when director Elia Kazan, his friend and frequent collaborator, gave testimony to the House Un-American Activities Committee in 1952, betraying several of their left-leaning actor and playwright colleagues. When Miller himself was called before the committee in 1956, he refused to name names of suspected Communists, and was subsequently blacklisted from Hollywood.

Yet in the writing of this play, Miller gave young Abigail's name a sexual tarnish for generations to come.

MILLER WAS IN fine-standing tradition, as throughout the twentieth century witches became a frequent subject of erotica. In the 1920s, Hollywood photographer William Mortensen began making a series of pictures called *A Pictorial Compendium of Witchcraft and Demonology*. It contained images of nude women posing with ghouls, nude witches in states of ecstasy flying on brooms, and nude heretics being tied up in chains or lashed to wooden stakes, adding some S&M to the T&A. Though considered by some to be in poor taste at the time—Mortensen was famously called "the Anti-Christ" by Ansel Adams—these pictures have since resurfaced in galleries and museum shows, remarkable not only for their sensational subject matter and arresting compositions, but for Mortensen's inventive photo manipulation techniques.

The 1960s and 1970s saw the development of an entire genre of hot 'n' heavy witches. Witchsploitation films and pulp publications arrived on the scene, with titles like *Virgin Witch* and *Bitchcraft*, featuring images of vixens engaged in any number of naked and depraved occult activities. Some of these, such as the documentary *Witchcraft '70,* purported to educate the public about modern witchcraft, while including plenty of images of witch kink throughout. Others were more up-front with their salaciousness. The 1970 German film *Mark of the Devil* was about a witch hunter in eighteenth-century Austria and was notorious for its graphic scenes of beautiful women being tortured. "Rated V for Violence," the film's poster read, and vomit bags with the words "Guaranteed to upset your stomach" were given out as promotional materials.

The 1970s also brought on new scholarly thinking that heightened the racy reputation of witches. It was already well-documented by this point that the "flying ointment" that witches supposedly used to fly to the Sabbath was most likely not actually made of baby parts. Writings as far back as Giambattista della Porta's *Magia Naturalis* of 1558 posited that it was probably an unguent of hallucinogenic plants, such as belladonna, that induced phantasmagoric visions and flying sensations in its applicant. Thus, the stories of witches flying, dancing, and demon-boning weren't true, but they weren't entirely false either—it was just a long, strange trip. But it was anthropologist Michael Harner's 1973 book *Hallucinogens and Shamanism* that put forth an idea about just how that ointment might have been applied. According to Harner, witches were associated with broomsticks, because women did in fact use broom handles as "an applicator for the atropine-containing plant to the sensitive vaginal membranes. . . ." In other words, the witches' brooms may have been psychotropic dildos, giving their women one hell of a ride.

GROWING UP JEWISH. I wasn't raised with much talk of the devil or hell or even sin. Still, I learned firsthand how tempting the dark side could be. Before puberty, I tended to get crushes on baby-faced boys: Davy Jones from the Monkees. Joey McIntyre from New Kids on the Block. Macaulay Culkin from *Home Alone*, even though I knew our love was doomed because he was much too old for me (I was nine, he was ten). These guys were cherubic and nonthreatening, and they made my heart flutter. But as I got older, it was two devilish characters who set off sparks in a spot a bit lower than my cardiac region: Jareth the Goblin King in *Labyrinth*, played with rakish aplomb by David Bowie and his codpiece, and Frank N. Furter in *The Rocky Horror Picture Show*, performed with corseted relish by Tim Curry.

It strikes me now that both of these characters were sexually ambiguous (or omnivorous, in Frank's case) dudes in makeup, which some might consider in itself outside the boundaries of propriety. But gender-bending aside, Jareth and Frank are similar in another way: they are supernatural sin-peddlers to innocent ingénues—and both look damn good while doing it. I knew they were supposed to be dastardly, but I found them rather dashing instead.

Labyrinth's heroine, Sarah, played by a young Jennifer Connelly, is a fifteen-year-old brunette in the suburbs who is obsessed with magic and make-believe. Miserable about being forced to babysit her infant half brother one night, she chants a spell for Jareth the Goblin King to come and take baby Toby away. Much to her regret, her wish comes true, and Toby is abducted. And so she must undo her mistake and go rescue her brother from Jareth's labyrinthine kingdom. Jareth sets many traps and tricks to thwart her, but he has another motivation: he wants to seduce Sarah and have her worship him for eternity.

In a scene reminiscent of Snow White and the poisoned apple, Sarah is given a peach that Jareth has drugged, and she falls into a hallucinogenic trance. She dreams that she is transported to a masquerade ball, where Jareth appears wearing a horned mask. They dance to a love song called "As the World Falls Down," and Sarah is entranced by him, her mouth agape for the entire three minutes of screen time. Suddenly a clock strikes, and she is shaken out of her stupor. She awakens to find herself in a trash heap with no recollection of what has just occurred.

Looking back on all of this now with my adult brain, I see how troubling their age difference is (Connelly was fifteen when she played the role, and Bowie was nearly forty), not to mention how disturbing it is to watch a woman be roofied with fresh produce. But as a kid, I wasn't thinking about gender dynamics or sexual authorization. Watching *Labyrinth* was the first time I remember finding a villain attractive. Right or wrong, all I knew was that he turned me on.

And he was designed to. Jim Henson, the film's director, wanted to cast a rock star who exuded charisma and sex appeal, and David Bowie certainly ticked those boxes (apparently Michael Jackson was on Henson's short list as well). Brian Froud, *Labyrinth*'s conceptual artist—and a legendary illustrator in his own right— explained that they wanted Jareth to be a mash-up of Sarah's desires. As he told *Empire* magazine in 2016: "We're not looking at reality, we're inside this girl's head. . . . There are references to all sorts of things in his costume. There's the danger of a leather boy in his leather jacket, which also has a reference to the armor of a certain type of German knight in it; there are references to Heathcliff from *Wuthering Heights*; and the tight trousers are a reference to ballet dancers. He's an amalgam of the inner fantasies of this girl."

Of course, this is all a projection of a man's fantasies about what a teenage girl might desire—a fantasy of a fantasy, if you will. But in my case, at least, they were right on the money, so I'm cutting them some slack.

At the end of the film, Jareth and Sarah have a final confrontation. She fumbles with the magical incantation that will defeat the Goblin King and set her and her baby brother free, but she can't quite recall the ending. Suddenly it dawns on her. Looking directly into his eyes, she says: "You have no power over me."

The words break the original pact she made with Jareth (not to mention, they echo nicely with Glinda's pronouncement to the Wicked Witch of the West in *The Wizard of Oz*: "You have no power here. Begone!"). Next thing we know, Sarah is back at home, with her baby brother safely in his crib.

I adore *Labyrinth*'s opulent costumes, the magic of Henson and Froud's puppets, the irresistible soundtrack (I still consider "Underground" to be one of Bowie's greatest songs, and I will fight you on that). I believe its feminist message about a young woman who uses her wits to rescue a boy, and to reject an abusive man, makes up for its flaws. Sarah's quest is one of the earliest examples of the Campbellian hero's journey that I can recall being exposed to that had a female at its center.

Objectively speaking, the Goblin King is a manipulative man who preys on an underage girl, while framing himself as the victim. Sarah's final words to him are a mantra of victory, which still give me chills when I hear them. They are the ultimate utterance for a woman, or for anyone, really, who finally acknowledges their own strength and sets themselves free. My head knows this. My heart knows this.

And yet. All I'm saying is Bowie's pants might be worth giving up a baby brother for.

Tim Curry's Frank N. Furter is even more goth-looking and transgressive than Bowie's Goblin King. *The Rocky Horror Picture Show* was released in 1975, eleven years before *Labyrinth*, but it came into my consciousness afterward. I was a teenager when I rented it from our local Blockbuster. The VHS cover's blood-red lips and gory typeface intimidated me, and I told myself I could stop the movie at any time if it got too scary. That it is a comedy was the first of several surprises.

Frank N. Furter was like nothing I'd ever seen before: a six-foot-tall man with thigh-high stockings, patent-leather platform heels, a spangled bustier, and bulging biceps. He's sinister, but seductively so, and driven by boundless lust. Part Dr. Frankenstein, part Dracula, he creates a male sex slave named Rocky in his laboratory. He also beds wide-eyed betrothed visitors Janet and Brad (played by Susan Sarandon and Barry Bostwick, respectively), in one of cinema's early examples of bisexuality. Janet in particular transforms from a prim and proper lady into a full-on sex fiend, romping around the castle in her bra and undies and sleeping with Rocky, breaching her pending marital bond and vexing her host in one fell swoop. Throughout the film, Frank is accompanied by a retinue of debauched weirdos, and the spirit of their shared home is downright bacchanalian. In a climactic musical number, he croons:

Give yourself over to absolute pleasure
Swim the warm waters of sins of the flesh

Eventually it becomes clear that Frank is also a tyrant and a murderer, and his followers finally stage a coup that leads to his death. Our devils must be vanquished, after all, especially the ones who on the surface seem the most alluring. But oh, how I mourned his passing. The world seemed far less interesting without Frank's raving immoderation.

Jareth and Frank are rightly and justly defeated, as they are each truly evil, despite their glittering groins.

But I confess these films left me with a bit of a sulfur tooth for stories where the devil never gets his due, and our girl gets her rocks off instead.

HISTORIAN JULES MICHELET understood the attraction of the Prince of Darkness when he wrote the aforementioned sympathetic witch book, *La Sorcière,* in 1862. He felt that you couldn't blame women of the Middle Ages for turning to Satanism. According to him, they were constantly being abused, neglected, and told they were unclean, so why not seek out an empowering alternative? In his words: "The Devil only, women's ally of old and her confidant in the Garden, and the Witch, the perverse creature who does everything *backwards* and *upside down*, in direct contradiction to the world of religion, ever thought of unhappy womanhood, ever dared to tread custom underfoot and care for her health in spite of her own prejudices."

Sylvia Townsend Warner's 1926 marvel of a novel *Lolly Willowes* is an extension of this line of thinking. It begins with us meeting Laura Willowes right after her beloved father dies, leaving her domestically untethered. The year is 1902, and Laura, a spinster at the ripe old age of twenty-eight, is pressured to move into her brother's London home with his wife and their two daughters, who call her Aunt Lolly (a name she despises). She resents giving up her days full of botany, brewing, and outdoor frolicking which she so enjoyed. She finds London life excruciatingly dull with its routine, niceties, and endless obligations, especially as she has fallen into the role of a nanny for her two dull nieces. She never gets time to meander on her own, for ". . . she was too useful to be allowed to stray." After twenty or so years of doing her familial duties, and the coming and going of the war, Laura finds herself desperate for a change.

Each fall, she starts to feel a dark pull to escape: "Her mind was groping for something that eluded her experience, a something that was shadowy and menacing, and yet in some way congenial." In time she grows used to this "recurrent autumnal fever," and treats it with long twilight walks and bouquets of rare flowers until the season subsides.

One day she stumbles upon a greengrocer full of country provisions. There, she finds herself lost in a reverie of plums and turnips and homemade jam, imagining their idyllic origin point. She buys an armload of chrysanthemums, and the florist adds a few sprays of beech leaves to the bouquet. These leaves cause Laura's heart to flood with longing: "They smelt of woods, of dark rustling woods like the wood to whose edge she came so often in the country of her autumn imagination."

Then and there, this now forty-seven-year-old Laura decides she will move to the country and live on her own. She will answer this tenebrous call at long last.

Despite her brother's protests, she moves into a house in the hamlet of Great Mop, renting a few rooms from a landlady named

Mrs. Leak. Laura soon begins to fall in love with her new home, and finds herself enamored of the wildness of her surroundings, and of her burgeoning independence.

Things are disrupted, though, when her nephew, Titus, comes to live with her. The gregarious young man's presence overwhelms her, and she falls back into the role of a submissive auntie. She becomes desperate to have her private woodland life back. One day, on a too-rare walk by herself, she cries out in a desolate field: "Oh is there *no* help?" She feels the atmosphere shift, and realizes that something—or someone—has heard her. When she returns to her cottage, she finds that a white kitten has mysteriously appeared. When she goes to pet him, he scratches her, drawing blood, then curls up to sleep. It immediately dawns on her: "She, Laura Willowes, in England, in the year 1922, had entered into a compact with the Devil." This kitten is her familiar, and she is now a witch.

The last third of the book has her attending a Witches' Sabbath, where she learns that Mrs. Leak and most of the villagers in Great Mop in fact are all witches. In the days to come, her nephew mysteriously becomes beset by such miseries as curdled milk and a wasp attack, and he eventually falls in love and leaves town with his new fiancée. Laura is finally alone and revels in her new identity as a witch. She realizes that she had been targeted by Satan way back in London, and that it was he who lured her to this new life of liberty. She calls him "the loving huntsman" (also the subtitle of the book), for though he has preyed upon her, he did so gently, and in doing so ultimately led her to true happiness.

At the end of the book, she and the devil meet at last, and she tells him that he has saved her:

I think you are a kind of black night, wandering about and succoring decayed gentlewomen. . . . That's why we become witches: to show our scorn of pretending life's a safe business, to satisfy our passion for adventure. . . . One doesn't become a witch to run round being harmful, or to run round being helpful either, a district visitor on a broomstick. It's to escape all that—to have a life of one's own.

Lolly Willowes was a best seller upon publication but then fell into relative obscurity until the *New York Review of Books* republished it seventy-three years later in 1999. I didn't encounter it myself until 2011. I was thirty years old, and it quickly took a place in my personal literary pantheon. I was touched by this story of a woman who rejected the expectations that society imposed upon her and who dared to heed a bigger call. Her loving huntsman wasn't a villain. Rather, he delivered her from the evil of patriarchal conventions. She was stifled, and he gave her a wide field to fill with her fullest potential.

It reminds me of another woman who was writing at the same time as Warner. In Virigina Woolf's 1929 book of lectures *A Room of One's Own,* she wrote: "When, however, one reads of a witch being ducked, of a woman possessed by devils, of a wise woman selling herbs, or even of a very remarkable man who had a mother, then I think we are on the track of a lost novelist, a suppressed poet, of some mute and inglorious Jane Austen, some

Emily Brontë who dashed her brains out on the moor or mopped and mowed about the highways crazed with the torture that her gift had put her to. Indeed, I would venture to guess that Anon, who wrote so many poems without signing them, was often a woman."

I don't know what Lolly Willowes goes on to do after her encounter with her devilish redeemer. Maybe she writes poems or books, or simply spends her days wandering aimlessly in the woods. But I'm glad that she gets to decide.

ONE FINAL STORY of bedeviled liberation: an art house horror film that came out in 2015. Robert Eggers's *The Witch* occupies a space that's part folkloric, part historical (its subtitle is *A New England Folktale*), which makes it the ideal vehicle for examining this dark archetype. The movie takes place in colonial New England around the year 1630, and it centers on Thomasin, an adolescent Puritan girl with Noxzema-fresh skin and flaxen hair that she keeps tucked under layers of plain clothing like the good Christian lamb that she is. The film begins when her father is cast out of their village due to a religious disagreement. He takes his wife and five children to set up their own family homestead, determined to live a humble life of the Lord. Their new farm is small and isolated, nothing around save a barren field, a creek, and some very menacing woods. Their only company besides one another is a dog, a horse, two white goats, and one black goat that the children name Black Phillip. And their days are grueling, filled with fervent prayer and Bible readings, endless wood to chop, and rotten corn to harvest. No one seems to work harder than Thomasin, who is assigned every task imaginable by her parents, from milking the animals to washing clothes to looking after her four precocious siblings, including newborn baby Samuel. One day Thomasin is playing peekaboo with Samuel out by the water on the edge of the woods. After a few rounds of making him gurgle happily, she opens her eyes one final time and is horrified at what she sees: the baby has disappeared. Cut to a scene with an old witch in a red cloak carrying the baby through the woods and into her hut. We then see a montage of terrors: first the baby alive by firelight, then the witch making some sort of bloody potion that she proceeds to rub all over her naked body and broom. Finally we see her flying in the night sky toward the full moon. Clearly, the witch has used the infant as the primary ingredient for her flying ointment. Samuel is now purée de bébé.

Meanwhile, Thomasin's family begins to fray at the seams. The distress of the missing child, the punishing circumstances of rural living, and the parents' extreme religious fervor all form an oppressive cloud that threatens to smother them all. Thomasin's sexual development is a threatening force of nature as well: her brother Caleb keeps staring at her cleavage, and her mother begins blaming her for every mishap, eventually conspiring to send Thomasin away to work as a house servant for another family. Before this comes to pass, Thomasin and Caleb go off into the wood on horseback determined to find an alternate solution. They discover a dead hare in a trap their father set, and are overjoyed, knowing the extra food will be a boon to the family. On their way home, another hare crosses their path—presumably the witch's familiar or the witch herself in animal disguise—startling the horse and dog. The siblings are separated: Thomasin falls from the horse and is knocked unconscious, while Caleb gives chase and gets waylaid in another manner entirely. He stumbles upon the woodland hut, and a beautiful, buxom brunette opens the door. She kisses him passionately, and then we see her now wizened arm grab him from behind. She's the witch, this time wearing a glamour, and we know Caleb is in dire straits, and that his sin of lust has led him down a dark road indeed. When he returns to the farm, he is naked and in some sort of trance. His jaws seem to be sealed shut, and his parents pull an entire apple from his mouth. After hours of prayer, bloodletting, and frenzied religious babbling on Caleb's part, he eventually dies, leaving the mother bereft and furious. She is convinced it is witchcraft, and soon the family accuses Thomasin of being the witch in question. Thomasin denies it and accuses her younger twin brother and sister in turn, saying that they talk to Black Phillip, the goat. Their father, at the end of his rope, locks all three of them—Thomasin and her twin siblings—in the goat pen, and buries Caleb's body. Things escalate from here: The witch shows up in the locked pen, where we see her mouth covered in goat's blood. The next morning the father finds the pen split open with Thomasin lying shell-shocked on the ground. The two white goats are dead, the twins are missing, and Black Phillip is on the loose. In a violent crescendo of horrors, both parents meet their demise: The father is rammed in the stomach by Black Phillip, and a pile of firewood collapses on him. The mother attempts to choke Thomasin to death, so Thomasin axes her in the head in self-defense.

With her family all now either dead or missing, Thomasin is totally alone. She looks to the wood, then goes back into the goat pen, removes some of her bloody clothing, and falls asleep in her shift. When she awakens, it is nightfall. She walks over to Black Phillip with a lit torch, hair loose.

THOMASIN: Black Phillip, I conjure thee to speak to me.

BLACK PHILLIP (*seductively*): What dost thou want?

THOMASIN: What canst thou give?

BLACK PHILLIP: Wouldst thou like the taste of butter? A pretty dress?

And then, in the film's most quoted line:

BLACK PHILLIP: Wouldst thou like to live deliciously?

He asks if she sees a book before her, then asks her to remove her clothes. We see him—now in human form—put his hands around her naked shoulders. She says she doesn't know how to sign her name. He says he will guide her hand.

After their exchange, Thomasin walks into the woods. She sees a ring of naked women dancing in a frenzy around a fire. The witches begin to levitate. The camera closes in on Thomasin's face. She is laughing and shuddering in ecstasy, as the firelight illuminates her bare, blood-spattered flesh. She rises into the air, high among the treetops, her arms spread wide like wings.

The end of this film has been read in many ways. Some viewers have interpreted it as a tragedy: Thomasin's entire family has turned against her before becoming victims of a supernatural villain themselves. And she herself ultimately succumbs to evil, proving her family's suspicions right all along. She's left an orphan with no one to turn to save Satan himself, so turn to him she does. On its surface, *The Witch* chronicles an innocent young woman's downfall, after her church and her entire community have failed her. Once left to her own devices, into the devil's arms she flies. Perhaps it's a morality tale, or at least a perverse fantasy about what happens when female power goes unchecked.

But I think that analysis does a great disservice to the character of Thomasin and to Eggers's script. Her life up to this point has been one of abuse and entrapment. Throughout the film, she is brutalized and blamed by her parents for their every hardship. Her safety is jeopardized, and she's treated like a workhorse to be traded to another household when her own deems her too dangerous. Her entire family's sexuality is repressed by a severe religious practice, and they are starved in all senses of the word: for food, for pleasure, for any sort of catharsis. Her father's pride and stringent beliefs are what got them banished from their community in the first place. He is the one who put the shackles of biblical literalism and fanaticism on this family, and it's because of him that they are forced to live under merciless circumstances. That Thomasin becomes his fall woman is a shrewd allegory for how patriarchal and religious oppression has so often punished females for male misdeeds. Thomasin is living in hell already. After all that she's been through, Black Phillip's offer of lipids and luxury seems a solid trade for one's eternal soul. Add in some delicious living, and you'd sign too.

The witch of the wood is Eggers's brilliant composite of so many witch beliefs: she is by turns a horrid hag, a temptress, a night-rider, a murderess, a servant of evil, and, ultimately, an independent and sexually awakened young woman. She might be the film's antagonist, but, by gods, she seems to be having far and away the most fun of any of them. When Thomasin becomes a witch herself, perhaps it is a downfall. But at least she's falling upward.

In the film's final image, she's cruciform, perhaps being sacrificed to an unholy goat god. But the other side of crucifixion is resurrection. She's smiling and flying and freer than she's ever been. And in watching her, I too felt a sense of release.

WHEN ALL IS said and done, these Mephistophelian fictions beg the question: How much agency do these witch women actually have? Haven't they just traded one patriarchal prison for another? After all, the devil is, by all accounts, a dude, and now he is their master and keeper. Must phallocentrism exist even in the inferno? But for me, that oversimplifies the point. I think these tales about devils and witches represent something more, for they are commentaries upon the fallacy of female deficiency. They offer a different kind of fantasy: a vision of a world where women can live unrestrained and unashamed. In these stories, the witch is lit up at last: not from being burned at the stake, but rather from the blaze of her own inner fire.

Chapter 4

BODY MONSTERS

At the opening of her 2012 exhibition of scratchy, nude self-portraits, the globally acclaimed artist Tracey Emin said, "My work is about not wanting to have a child. In society, if you don't want to have children, people think that you're a bit of a witch." And she's right. Women who don't have children are treated as worrisome. *Is there something wrong with her body? Is there something wrong with her mind? Does she envy my family? Is she wishing us ill?* At best, a woman of childbearing age or older who doesn't have kids sparks curiosity. At worst, she's seen as a violation of the natural order.

I know a little something about the taboo of childlessness myself, as a married woman in my thirties who has elected not to become a parent. After years of discussions with my husband, my friends, my therapist, my deities, and myself, I've figured out that my reason for not having kids is both very complicated and the simplest thing in the world. What it boils down to is this: my desire to have them is outweighed by my desire not to. Non-moms like me are growing in number. According to a 2017 Pew Research study, nearly 1 in 5 American women of childbearing age don't have children, whereas in the 1970s it was 1 in 10. Nonetheless, those of us who are childless are still seen as abnormal. We occupy a particular and peculiar promontory of womanhood that can be splendid in its solitude, but also prone to sudden windy gusts of confrontation. Over the years, I've been subjected to involuntary heart-to-hearts with concerned relatives, nosy half-jokes from colleagues, and cringe-worthy conversations with strangers who suddenly blanche and scramble to turn what they thought was innocuous small talk—"How old are your kids?"—into a skein of assurances or panicked "let's change the subject quick" non sequiturs. Or there are the acquaintances who get adamantly defensive about their own choices, telling me how much they love being parents and how it's the most meaningful and worthwhile thing they've ever done. They are the ones who wistfully suggest that maybe I'll change my mind, as if "meaningful and worthwhile experience" hadn't ever occurred to me when I was making my Progeny: Pros/Cons list. In these moments I'm treated like a glitch in the software. Or worse: a pity.

I think of the witches I grew up with, the forest dwellers and fortune-tellers who populated the fairy tales I loved so much when I was young. There's Dame Gothel, the witch who locks Rapunzel up in a tower after the girl's father steals vegetables from Gothel's garden. There's the witch in "Hansel and Gretel," who lures children into her candy-coated hut, so that she might roast them in her oven and eat them—I suppose preferring savory to sweet. There's the witch (an evil fairy, if we're getting technical) in the "Sleeping Beauty" tale—later named Maleficent in Disney's 1959 animated feature—who, after being snubbed when invitations to a royal christening are handed out, curses the infant princess to one day prick her finger on a spinning wheel and die. There is the Grand High Witch in Roald Dahl's 1983 book *The Witches*—played by Anjelica Huston in Nicolas Roeg's 1990 film adaptation—who unveils a master plan to turn England's children into mice so that their unsuspecting teachers will exterminate them.

All of these witch figures have something in common: they are not part of any family unit to speak of, and they have no children of their own. That they lash out and seek to abduct, murder, or nosh upon other people's offspring is a remnant of the broom-riding kiddie-killer witch of the Middle Ages, to be sure. Back then, this paranoia stemmed in part from high infant mortality rates and a lack of understanding about what was causing it. Childless women with devilish powers were as likely culprits as anything. Salem scholar Marilynne K. Roach has written that being married but having an insufficient number of children was a common reason for a woman to have been accused of witchcraft in 1692. And in John Demos's book *The Enemy Within: A Short History of Witch-Hunting*, he writes that for an accused witch, "Her family experience might also include childbearing that fell significantly below expectation. Accused witches often had fewer children than the typical woman; sometimes they had none at all." It was believed that the witch's jealousy of larger families might prompt her to curse them, to punish them for having what she is supposed to want. But even though natal care and medical knowledge on the whole have advanced significantly since then, the image of the monstrous antimother is still with us. Even today, in this age of "you do you" self-actualization, the choice to not even *try* to have children is met with suspicion. *Selfish*, *damaged*, *stunted*, *too career-focused*—whatever the descriptors, the implication is that a woman who doesn't want children is somehow deficient and therefore destructive.

In America especially, the pressure for a woman to procreate comes from every corner of her life. She gets it from a government that restricts her access to birth control and that consistently debates whether she should be able to make decisions about her own body. (Not that they're so great at supporting mothers either, mind you. The US is the only country in the developed world that does not have mandatory maternity leave, and within that same cohort, it also has the highest rate of maternal deaths.) Christianity, the dominant American religion, holds up a mother—and a virgin one at that—as the highest ideal for a woman. And then there's the relentless message from the media—not to mention one's social and familial circles—that all healthy female adults eventually have kids.

As I age, I'm reminded constantly of the children I don't have: when I spend time with my friends and their families; when I'm walking in our stroller-studded neighborhood; when I watch virtually any film or TV show about a thirtysomething woman who is struggling to balance family and career, or scrambling to have a baby before her ovaries deflate, or overcoming adversity to model for her kids that "Mommy is a hero." All of these narratives can be full of nobility and intrigue, to be sure, and I enjoy getting swept up in each of them at times. But I also appreciate alternative models of womanhood, and the witch offers that too. The witch's plotlines rarely focus on the desire to be a mother. She's busy making other things.

★ ★ ★

I'M NOT COMPLETELY lacking in maternal instincts, mind you. The love I have for my friends' children takes my breath away, and their parents happen to be especially magnificent and open-minded humans themselves. They value what I can offer their kids: a promise that in some pockets of the world, even the grown-up ones, enchantment can be found. Their daughters in particular seem to gravitate toward my witchly ways, and when they come to our apartment, they enjoy playing with my crystals and spell books (not to mention my husband's hoard of *Star Wars* toys). A few weeks ago, my eight-year-old buddy Emma told her dad, "When I'm around Pam, I believe in magic." She helps me believe in magic too.

Some of my favorite fictional witches of the past century are childless, but they still play a nurturing role to young ones. Like Juniper in my beloved Wise Child series, they become mother figures in a "found family" context—aunties or guardians who discover a new sort of magic in taking other people's children under their own weird wings. *Maleficent*, Disney's 2014 retelling of "Sleeping Beauty" starring an irresistibly campy Angelina, is one such example. She starts off as a vengeful villain, but then ends up becoming the protectress of the very princess she has cursed. It is *her* true love's kiss—not a prince's—that breaks the sleep spell and sets Princess Aurora free.

Magical nanny Mary Poppins is another such demi-mom, and she has a far witchier backstory than some realize. Her creator, the author P. L. Travers—by all accounts an unconventional woman herself—was a follower of mystical teachers like G. I. Gurdjieff, and friends with myth-making poets William Butler Yeats and George William Russell (better known as A.E.). According to Travers's biographer Valerie Lawson, "[Travers] wrote to A.E.

that her mind had become full of fantastic tales, of a witch whose broomstick would fly just as well by white magic as by black magic." A.E. encouraged her, telling her she should write a book that encompassed her many spiritual interests, and suggesting that it be called *The Adventures of a Witch*. Travers had already written a few fantastical children's stories, including one in 1926 called "Mary Poppins and the Match-Man" about a nanny who goes on a magical date with Bert, a match seller and sidewalk artist. In the story, they are transported inside one of his pictures. When she returns home to the children who are in her charge, they ask where she's been. "In Faeryland," she replies. When they grill her on the details, they tell her it doesn't sound like the Faeryland they know from stories. " 'I expect,' said Mary Poppins, 'that everybody's got a Faeryland of their own!' "

Several years later, in 1934, Travers decided to revisit Mary Poppins, this time looking at the character through A.E.'s more witchly lens. At his behest, she incorporated more mythology and magical objects. And unlike both the charming protagonist of her 1926 short story and the chirping Julie Andrews of the Disney film that Travers came to loathe, her long-form Mary Poppins is stern, temperamental, and vain despite her severe looks. In the original book, she blows into 17 Cherry Tree Lane on a gust of east wind (east being the direction of new beginnings, as any magic nerd knows). She takes her young charges, Jane and Michael, on all sorts of miraculous adventures featuring a levitating tea party, enchanted cows, and a shimmering star-girl—one of the Pleiades who's come to earth for some Christmas shopping.

In my favorite chapter, Mary Poppins's birthday has fallen on a full moon, so she escorts the children to the zoo for a special nighttime celebration. There they encounter several talking animals who all treat Mary as an honored guest. The Hamadryad—a king cobra—refers to her as Cousin and gifts her with a snakeskin. The animals form a circle around Mary and sway, as the Hamadryad hisses: "Bird and beast and stone and star—we are all one, all one. . . . Child and serpent, star and stone—all one." The children begin swaying with the snake too, caught up in the ritual until they fall asleep entranced. When they wake up the next day, Jane and Michael ask Mary about the evening's strange events. Ever the gaslighter, she replies that she has no idea what they're talking about, and that they should eat their porridge at once. The children think it must have been a dream, until they spot a golden snakeskin belt around Mary's waist. It's a section with blatantly Pagan undertones, from the significance of the full moon, to the circular dancing and chanting of the animals, to Mary's serpentine roots. When she leaves the children at the book's end shortly thereafter, the umbrella she flies away on might as well be a broom.

It's this 1934 version of Mary Poppins who appeals to me far more than the 1964 film. She's complicated and bewitching, and she cares about the children while still having enough sense of self to know when it is time for her to leave them. They love her and are changed by her, and they know they will see her again one day (and with seven Mary Poppins books and two feature films to follow, it's clear they are right). I aspire to be such a woman to the children I know. To swirl into their lives with great magic and devotion but to have the liberty to leave when the winds change. I'm lucky I have that choice.

★ ★ ★

WOULD THAT IT were all so simple. My body is mine, so I should be able to decide what to do with it and how to use it. But the issue of whether a woman becomes a mother, when, and how, is still shockingly controversial. This is in part because women's bodies have been traditionally viewed as mysterious and "other," a land of dim caverns and inexplicable lagoons. To be seen as female is to be an immediate aberration from dominant male norms.

And those who specialize in women's health care are suspect by association, especially if they are women themselves. Helping another woman with the caretaking of her own disorderly body is reason enough to be considered witchly as well.

In Barbara Ehrenreich and Deirdre English's influential 1973 treatise *Witches, Midwives, and Nurses*, they trace the historical shift from female-led, natural health care to an institutionalized medical system run by men. In it they write: "The witch hunts left a lasting effect: an aspect of the female has ever since been associated with the witch, and an aura of contamination has remained—especially around the midwife and other women healers." As the argument goes, midwives knew the proper herbs to administer to soothe pregnancy complications, to quicken and ease labor, and to stimulate the production of mother's milk. They were also learned in the ways of using plants to treat gynecological issues, as well as to prevent pregnancy or induce abortion. Because "women's stuff" happened behind closed doors, and because midwives and female healers were possessors of "secret" knowledge, this made them powerful and untrustworthy.

Near the beginning of the *Malleus Maleficarum*, our favorite Satan-obsessed sexist, Heinrich Kramer, states that he will share information in the book ". . . specifically with regard to midwives, who surpass all others in wickedness." He keeps his promise, slandering the vocation throughout the text, which includes a section entitled "That Witches who are Midwives in Various Ways Kill the Child Conceived in the Womb, and Procure an Abortion; or if they do not do this, Offer New-born Children to Devils." Unlike Kramer's other witches, midwives were considered threatening not due to their carnality per se—however directly lust may have been involved for their pregnant patients to begin with—but because they were masters of female physiology. They could seemingly control its ebbs and tides and help create life itself, or, yes, snuff it out completely through preventative or abortive measures.

One can see why midwives might have been prime suspects for witchcraft. If a child died during labor or shortly thereafter due to illness, who better to blame than the woman who was tasked with ushering that child into this world in the first place? If a person lost their life because of a disease, couldn't it be because the healer they went to put a curse on them instead? Common knowledge about physical maladies and sickness was limited, and belief in witches was real. It would be feasible to assume that supernatural forces—and the midwife-turned-witch who knew how to summon them—were responsible for these tragic losses.

All of this said, recent scholarship has revealed that there is very little evidence that many midwives were actually persecuted during the witch hunts. Yes, they were eventually eclipsed by licensed male doctors, but that likely has far more to do with the rise of patriarchally run academic and governmental institutions. And it makes sense: the knowledge of midwifery had been passed from woman to woman. Once men took charge of universities and hospitals, women were largely left out of the industry (which is probably why the clitoris wasn't fully mapped until 1998—thank you, Dr. Helen O'Connell!). The number of midwives didn't dwindle because they were burned at the stake; it diminished simply because they were women, left out and left behind.

What is true, however, is that the *idea* that midwives were witches has persisted to this day. This thinking may be based in misinformation or romanticized notions, but the sentiments are still relevant. Today, women who seek control over their own bodies or who help other women do so still send chills up conservative spines.

As I write, birth control and family planning have been under relentless attack by the Trump administration in various ways, prompting the sexagenarian Cecile Richards, then president of Planned Parenthood, to tell CNN in May 2018 that "this administration is the worst for women that I've seen in my lifetime." Not only does Trump seem to support the vice president's promise that "[w]e'll see Roe vs. Wade consigned to the ash heap of history where it belongs," he is also the first sitting president to be the keynote speaker at the annual Campaign for Life Gala held by the antiabortion group Susan B. Anthony List. His Supreme Court picks are alleged pro-life proponents as well.

For all of their railing against abortions, members of the conservative party are not big fans of reliable pregnancy prevention either. Access to female contraception in general has been under threat in the US, thanks to pressure from the religious right. In November 2018, the Trump administration issued two final rules that could allow any employer, university, or health insurance provider to drop birth control coverage based on moral or religious objections.

And earlier in the year, the US Department of Health and Human Services issued an announcement that programs promoting abstinence as the best method of teen pregnancy prevention would be strongly favored for receiving funds, despite multiple studies showing that this tactic is ineffective—especially compared with the use of contraceptives.

Legislation aside, it's jarring that several political figures have made statements revealing a true lack of understanding about how female physiology actually works, or else voiced objections to women's sexuality overall. When Missouri Representative Todd Akin was asked by a St. Louis TV station in 2012 if he felt abortion was justified in the case of rape, he infamously replied, "If it's a legitimate rape, the female body has ways to try to shut the whole thing down." Foster Friess, a major Republican political donor, was quoted as saying, "You know, back in my days, they used Bayer aspirin for contraception. The gals put it between their knees, and it wasn't that costly." And in that same year, Sandra Fluke, a law student at Georgetown University, made headlines when she gave a speech to the House Democratic Steering and Policy Committee about why female students should not be denied contraception coverage by the Catholic college. Talk-show host Rush Limbaugh responded with this spluttering pile of misogynistic illogic:

"What does it say about the college co-ed Susan Fluke [sic], who goes before a congressional committee and essentially says that she must be paid to have sex, what does that make her? It makes her a slut, right? It makes her a prostitute. She wants to be paid to have sex. She's having so much sex she can't afford the contraception. She wants you and me and the taxpayers to pay her to have sex. What does that make us? We're the pimps."

We've already covered female sex drive as a satanic force in the last chapter, so I won't open that Beelzebub's box again. But there's another insidious implication to the anti–birth control argument, which brings us back to where we started: that a woman only has value when she is breeding; ergo fornicating for pleasure and without the intent of producing offspring is unnatural or shameful behavior. As many feminist writers have pointed out, some of this thinking is not only rationalized from a standpoint of religious morality, but of economic "pragmatism." In Silvia Federici's 2004 book, *Caliban and the Witch: Women, the Body, and Primitive Accumulation*, she theorizes that the hunting of witches was in part a means of punishing any woman who was not contributing to the burgeoning capitalist workforce through reproduction. She writes that this was a particularly urgent issue in seventeenth century Europe when the population began to decline: "Against this background, it seems plausible that the witch-hunt was, at least in part, an attempt to criminalize birth control and place the female body, the uterus, at the service of population increase and the production and accumulation of labor-power."

Call it sinful or just plain selfish, but the fact remains that women have sex for plenty of reasons other than baby-making, and having the ability to do so and not get pregnant is important to them. In July 2018, the Guttmacher Institute released a statistic that "more than 99 percent of women aged fifteen to forty-four who have ever had sexual intercourse have used at least one contraceptive method"—and for the record, this certainly includes women who may have children already, or who will someday want to. Denying women birth control is to prevent them from choosing if and when they become mothers, and this decision impacts every aspect of their lives from their economic mobility to their mental and physical well-being. Women have come a long way from having to consult with midwives about their reproductive systems in hushed tones. Yet today, more than five hundred years after Heinrich Kramer declared midwives to be the worst witches of all, both the consumers and the providers of female health care are still disparaged and attacked. There are those who continue to believe that women should not be able to decide what to do with their own bodies and their own lives. And that is its own kind of evil.

WHEN TALKING OF the witch and feminine body taboos, one must bring up the topic of ickiness. Many of the ingredients she's said to use in her spells are toxic or at least terribly unsettling, from the aforementioned baby bits, to animal parts, to poisonous plants, to the biological substances of adult humans including fingernails, hair, urine, tears, and blood. Bodily fluids have historically been thought to be highly magical and therefore highly threatening elements. As anthropologist Mary Douglas wrote in her 1966 book *Purity and Danger: An Analysis of Concepts of Pollution and Taboo*: "All margins are dangerous. . . . We should expect the orifices of the body to symbolize its specially vulnerable points. Matter issuing from them is marginal stuff of the most obvious kind."

Of all of the liquids and leavings that bodies emit, there is perhaps none more feared or despised than menstrual blood. Whether because it signals that a woman is not pregnant (tragic!) or it is simply misunderstood as being an unsafe substance, menstrual taboos have been prevalent across cultures for centuries—and the belief that a woman having her period makes her impure or unstable is still with us. In the Bible, Leviticus 15:19–30 specifically details how, when a woman has her period, any person or thing that she touches is considered unclean; and in the Quran, Surah Al-Baqarah 2:222 tells men not to touch a woman during her time of the month until she is "cleansed."

But it was Roman naturalist and writer, Pliny the Elder who popularized the idea that menstruating women were possessors of dark magic. At the end of the first century CE, he wrote the following in his thirty-seven-volume *Naturalis Historia* or *Natural History*:

> *Contact with the monthly flux of women turns new wine sour, makes crops wither, kills grafts, dries seeds in gardens, causes the fruit of trees to fall off, dims the bright surface of mirrors, dulls the edge of steel and the gleam of ivory, kills bees, rusts iron and bronze, and causes a horrible smell to fill the air. Dogs who taste the blood become mad, and their bite becomes poisonous as in rabies. The Dead Sea, thick with salt, cannot be drawn asunder except by a thread soaked in the poisonous fluid of the menstruous blood. A thread from an infected dress is sufficient. Linen, touched by the woman while boiling and washing it in water, turns black. So magical is the power of women during their monthly periods that they say that hailstorms and whirlwinds are driven away if menstrual fluid is exposed to the flashes of lightning.*

It should come as no surprise then that modern depictions of witchcraft still often revolve around menstrual blood. Stephen King's 1974 novel *Carrie* was the first book he ever got published, and it set his career aloft. The story revolves around a young woman whose telekinetic powers are awakened after she is tormented by high school mean girls when she gets her first period in the locker room. "Plug it up! Plug it up!" they cry, pelting her with tampons and sanitary napkins. Carrie begins to develop her supernatural skills in secret. Her ultrareligious, abusive mother berates her, believing that Carrie is doing a form of witchcraft, which shows up in their family every three generations: "First had come the flow of blood and the filthy fantasies the Devil sent with it. Then this hellish Power the Devil had given to her." Between stress at school and stress at home, tension builds. Carrie finally snaps when she's crowned prom queen via a rigged election, and then doused with a bucket of pig's blood—another allusion to her shameful menarche. As those familiar with the novel, the subsequent films, and the eventual Broadway show know, this turns her into a vehicle of vengeance who ultimately uses her powers to bring destruction upon the entire town.

Anna Biller's 2016 film *The Love Witch*, on the other hand, turns the menses-as-malfeasance trope on its head. The story centers on a witch named Elaine who wants to find love but ends up leaving a trail of dead lovers in her wake instead. In a pivotal scene, the titular character has killed her latest conquest, and so she makes a "witch bottle" to put inside his grave, so that a part of her will always be with him. We watch her fill the bottle with her own urine and bloody tampon. "Most men have never even seen a used tampon," she tells us, a statement that's both factual and a political gesture on the part of the filmmaker. After all, most movies don't have used tampons in them either, even though millions of menstruating people see several of their own for two to seven days each month. Biller's inclusion of menstrual blood in the film is meaningful for several reasons. It is both a narrative ingredient to show her protagonist's power, and a bit of real-life silver-screen spellcraft: with this scene, a used tampon is transformed from a shameful feminine secret into a visible and powerful cultural symbol.

A BLEEDING LADY is a fright, but a postmenopausal woman just might take home the trophy for World's Most Horrifying.

The aging body is a site of terror—and the no-longer-fertile female body most of all. We see its wrinkles and sagging flesh, and we recoil. It reminds us of death. We're taught to think of it as decrepit and thoroughly asexual. Time and again, the old female physique is either cast aside or held up as a thing of evil. Though she can come in all ages and life stages, as we've seen, the witch is perhaps most often depicted as this old and putrid version. You know the stereotype: hideous, gray-haired, nose like the beak of a corvid. She's the witch who's most likely to show up in fairy tales, such as the elderly Baba Yaga in Slavic folklore, said to live in a hut that walks on chicken-leg stilts. She's the villain in horror films like *Drag Me To Hell*'s Sylvia Ganush with her crooked yellow teeth and one cloudy eye. The mere idea of "an old woman whose feet don't touch the ground" in the film *Blair Witch Project* is upsetting—we don't even have to see her to know that she is the stuff of nightmares.

In the girl/woman/hag or maiden/mother/crone triple goddess archetype popularized by writers like Robert Graves and Starhawk, the crone is the aspect that is often overlooked and undervalued in a culture obsessed with youth. Maidens and mothers are celebrated for their beauty, their unconditional love, the fruits of their bodies. Their potential. But the woman past her prime is generally something to be abhored. Where maidens and mothers are ripe, the crone is rotten. Often fictional witches are themselves afraid of mortality, from the Wicked Queen in "Snow White" to the Sanderson sisters in *Hocus Pocus* to Lamia in Neil Gaiman's *Stardust*. As such, they're double bound: punished by society for aging, then vilified for going to extremes to maintain their beauty and youth. And heaven forfend an older body that still feels lust or acts on desire. Such alleged incongruity has been feared for centuries. In *Game of Thrones*, Melisandre, the Red Woman, is a beautiful witch who practices dark sex magic. When it is revealed that she's actually an ugly old crone in disguise, it's shocking not only because she isn't who we thought she was, but because we recall that her prior table-shaking sexual sorcery was actually done by an elderly bag of bones.

One of the most famous depictions of a witch is an engraving done by Albrecht Dürer circa 1500, commonly referred to as *Witch Riding Backwards on a Goat*. It shows a naked hag with sagging breasts and skin folds, sitting astride a goat—a creature frequently used as a stand-in for carnality and diabolism, as we saw with *The Witch*'s bleating butter pusher, Black Phillip. The witch has a broom wedged between her legs—phallic and, we're meant to believe, foul. The combination of her reversed riding position, the putto standing on its head in the foreground, and Dürer's inverted monogram caused scholars to interpret this piece as a warning against sin and perversion and an allegory about going against the natural order of things. To the modern, feminist eye, it looks as though this woman is having a grand old time. But it was intended to be an image of deep discomfort, if not genuine danger. An old female body that is naked and exposed without shame is something that should never be visible, according to Dürer and his viewers. The lustful crone, after all, is the consort of the devil himself.

Still, the old witch has positive associations too. One of the most beloved crones in mythology is Hecate, the Greek goddess of witchcraft and necromancy. She is a highly powerful deity who today is often associated with the waning or dark moon. We should note that she didn't start out as an elder and was traditionally shown wearing a knee-length maiden's skirt. She later mutated into a threefold goddess, depicted sometimes with the heads of a dog, a serpent, and a horse. This triplicate form morphed into the Roman goddess Trivia, who oversaw the places where three roads crossed. Whatever her configuration, she is said to watch over boundaries, portals, and gateways. The in-between places. The land of liminality.

With the rise of the modern Wiccan movement, Hecate eventually became conflated with the crone in the triple goddess paradigm, so she is now often seen in her guise as an old woman. These days, you'll find copious images of her cloaked with long white hair twisting from beneath her hood. Hounds usually accompany her, and she holds the keys of divine mystery. She's taken on the mantle of the wise one, steeped in ancient secrets that she will reveal only to the worthy.

One thing that remains consistent about Hecate is that she is frequently shown as a torchbearer. It was she who led Demeter through the underworld each year to bring Persephone back to the surface of the earth. It is also said that the words EN EREBOS PHOS were inscribed above the main entrance to the interior of her temple in ancient Greece. These words translate to "In darkness, light," a worthy mantra for today's times if there ever was one.

Like Hecate, crones are often great helpers in stories. They are usually the ones who appear during a hero's quest to dispense advice, charms, and training. In *The Hero with a Thousand Faces*, Joseph Campbell wrote, "For those who have not refused the call, the first encounter of the hero-journey is with a protective figure (often a little old crone or old man) who provides the adventurer with amulets against the dragon forces he is about to pass." Some of my favorite fictional crone guides include: Mrs. Whatsit, Mrs. Who, and Mrs. Which in *A Wrinkle in Time*; Aughra the astrologer in *The Dark Crystal*; and Joan Clayton, a.k.a. the Cut-Wife, in the television series *Penny Dreadful*, who is both an elder witch and an administrant of abortions. Each of them offers assistance or mentorship to the hero on his or her quest, and most often during moments of crisis and self-doubt.

Rarer, though, are instances when the protagonist of a story is the crone herself.

As I get older, I find myself soaking up positive depictions of aging with the thirst of a Jericho rose. One of my not-so-guilty pleasures is watching films that feature an older female protagonist who gets a second chance at life: *Harold and Maude, Under the Tuscan Sun, The Best Exotic Marigold Hotel, Museum Hours*. I want to know that there is an alternative road for me to walk. That I won't just shrivel up and disappear, as so much of visual culture would have me believe. I want to know that vitality and self-empowerment are possible at any stage of life.

Perhaps my favorite crone heroine of all time is Marian Leatherby, the deaf, toothless, ninety-two-year-old protagonist of *The*

Hearing Trumpet, a novel written by Surrealist luminary Leonora Carrington. Marian sports a short gray beard that she finds "rather gallant," and she has a dear geriatric friend named Carmella who states, "People under seventy and over seven are very unreliable if they are not cats." Thanks to a combination of witchcraft and lavish imagination, Marian embarks on an incredible mission to escape the old folks' institution her family sent her to. Throughout the tale, she is a magical, resourceful, and ultimately powerful individual (not unlike what Carrington turned into herself, as we'll see).

These contemporary crones remind me that it's always a good idea to turn inward and connect with who I want to be rather than how I wish I looked. They also encourage me to embrace the aging process as having its own stately magic, as one becomes more adorned in experience, lessons learned, and wisdom to impart to future generations.

WITCHES ARE WRITTEN upon women's bodies, and so we must consider how the witch is worn.

According to the National Retail Federation, the witch has been the number-one Halloween costume for adults over the fourteen years that they've conducted their research, and I would wager it's been in the top spot for far longer. Though costume designer Adrian solidified our idea of witch wear via his designs for the Wicked Witch of the West in MGM's *The Wizard of Oz*, he was drawing upon much older iconography. Vintage photographs show women dressing up as witches in the decades leading up to the film, and a witch has been a go-to costume for parties, Halloween or otherwise, since at least the Victorian era.

Ardern Holt's book *Fancy Dresses Described; or, What To Wear at Fancy Balls* was so popular in the 1880s that it was published six times. It was an alphabetized compendium of costumes for well-heeled Victorian ladies, and it included this entry:

WITCH. HUBBARD, MOTHER, Mother Bunch, Mother Shipton, Nance Redfern, Dame Trot, Enchantress, Witch, and Fairy Godmother are all dressed much alike. . . . Dame Trot wears pointed hat not so high. Nance Redfern, Mother Shipton, and the Old Woman who Swept the Sky, being witches, carry a broom, and on the skirt are toads, cats, serpents, curlews, frogs, bats, and lizards in black velvet; a serpent twisted round the crown of hat, an owl in front, a black cat on shoulder. Sometimes a scarlet cloak is attached to the shoulders, and the velvet bodice is high with pendant sleeves.

Children's book illustrations no doubt had great influence upon the popular Victorian and Edwardian imagination, particularly those of fictional fairy tale and nursery rhyme author Mother Goose. Artists' renderings often feature her wearing a pointy hat—and interestingly, many have written about how her avian familiar signals that she may in fact be a lite version of the Germanic winter witch goddess Holda.

The first Mother Goose stories were published in 1697 by French fairy-tale author Charles Perrault under the title *Histoires ou contes du temps passé, avec des moralités,* or *Stories or Tales from Past Times, with Morals,* and the subtitle *Contes de ma mère l'Oye* or *Tales of My Mother Goose.* And, of course, these tales and subsequent nursery rhymes have been in circulation ever since, with

Mother Goose's image being reinterpreted as many times as the stories themselves. By the end of the nineteenth century, English editions of Mother Goose tales from publishers such as McLoughlin Brothers and Henry Altemus Company showed her wearing a black pointy hat and often holding a staff or a broom, and Arthur Rackham's illustrations for the 1913 book *Mother Goose: The Old Nursery Rhymes* crystallized her image as an old crone in a black witch's hat, riding a goose, cape flapping in the wind.

But this still begs the question: What is the origin of this pointy chapeau?

I've read several theories on this. Some believe it to be a later iteration of the Judenhut or Jew's hat, which Jewish people were forced to wear in medieval times. Others have written that during this time, many beer brewers were women, and they would wear tall, conical hats to stand out in the market. (Incidentally, there are theories that the witch's cauldron and cat come from beer brewing as well, the former to brew the beer in and the latter to scare away kitchen mice.) I've also read that this pointy headwear was simply typical fashion of the medieval elite. Wiccan priestess Doreen Valiente wrote that it came from the *copataine*, or French riding hat. Erica Jong wrote that it was the hat associated with heretics in the Middle Ages, and that between the 1440s and the 1480s, the pointed hennin hat of fashionable French women was considered devilish by clergy.

The answer may be much simpler—and rather more recent—than all of this: according to historians Ronald Hutton and John Callow, the witch's costume, hat and all, comes from the traveling gear worn primarily by working-class British women in the seventeenth and eighteenth centuries. Hutton has pointed out that the Welsh national costume adopted in the 1820s includes a tall black hat as well. (There is evidence that some upper-class British women wore this headwear too, per the unintentionally yet irresistibly witchy *Portrait of Mrs. Salesbury with Her Grandchildren Edward and Elizabeth Bagot*, painted by John Michael Wright in 1675.) This style of outfit was used later by artists to signify an outmoded woman, who was a symbol of homespun traditions and archaic ways of thinking (and, in the later case of Mother Goose—and related characters Mother Punch and Mother Hubbard—old yarns).

This illustrated witch was a parody of an old biddy or a country bumpkin, then. A clown crone who fell anywhere along the spectrum between foolish and frightening, depending on context. And her outfit was further codified by popular drawings of the eighteenth century, after the witch hunts had fully wound down. One of the most iconic depictions of a witch appears in a 1762 engraving by William Hogarth entitled *Credulity, Superstition, and Fanaticism*. It's a piece that satirizes the blind faith of religion, specifically the Methodist movement. The piece shows a preacher lecturing his congregation about evil as he holds a marionette of a devil in one hand and in the other a pointy-hatted witch riding a broomstick and suckling a feline incubus. This image made a huge impact on visual culture at the time, even though this witch herself is relatively miniature. She may well have set the standard for how we still see witches depicted in cartoons, books, and costumes today.

This witch has also gone on to influence fashion, especially in recent years. Dozens of designers have borrowed liberally from her broom closet. Hedi Slimane's spring 2013 collection for Yves

Saint Laurent featured wide-brimmed black hats, filmy black chiffon dresses, studded black leather accessories, and a dark bohemian vibe that felt very Wicked Witch of the West Coast. Gareth Pugh's spring 2015 ready-to-wear collection incorporated sequined pentagrams, Pagan poppets, and horned animal skull masks. Alexander McQueen's line has consistently nodded to witchcraft and fairy tales since its inception, and current head designer Sarah Burton has carried on that spirit. Her fall/winter 2017 collection was inspired by the traditions of Cornwall and included thick stitched ribbons reminiscent of a cloutie tree (or wishing tree) and long black folkloric dresses, as well as jumpsuits filigreed with silver tarot card imagery. Valentino, Rodarte, Elie Saab, Rick Owens, Marc Jacobs, Yohji Yamamoto, Iris van Herpen, and Ann Demeulemeester are but a few more of the many clothing designers whose lines have riffed on witchly frocks, headwear, and practices over the past decade.

And it's been heartening to see older women in recent fashion campaigns, often styled as glamorous, mystical beings, from Joni Mitchell's groovy YSL wisewoman in 2015 to Tippi Hedren's ultrachic Gucci fortune-teller in 2018. Now the crone is couture.

The witch is a muse for contemporary iconoclasts because she breaks the rules of propriety. She has little interest in satisfying the male gaze, and often revels in rebelling against it. As Hayley Phelan, the senior editor of Fashionista.com, told the *New York Times* about witch fashion: "Maxidresses and capes are not really revealing a lot of skin. . . . [These designers are] celebrating a kind of beauty that maybe appeals more to other women than to men." The fashion witch is powerful because she upends the expectations of female display in general. While she may be alluring, she's not *inviting.* Witch wear is wonderfully unwelcoming. It says, "Don't cross me," or as Carmen Maria Machado put it in a November 2018 *Harper's Bazaar* article, witch fashion is "Luxe meets feeling yourself meets fuck off." In wearing clothes that challenge the social contract of dressing to impress, one filters out any onlookers who may find her less-than-sunny exterior off-putting. She is the antithesis of the smiling blonde in the bikini. The witch fashions herself as strong and complex, not easy and pleasing. Her aesthetic evokes mystery, and even mayhem, as she subverts many of the things we're taught an attractive woman is supposed to be: passive, agreeable, a magnet for scrutiny.

While a witchy wardrobe can certainly be sexy at times, it doesn't tend to prioritize body consciousness. More often than not witchy fashion is about loose layers that veil the form or fabrics that cloak and cover. It conceals more than it reveals. It creates a shroud, albeit one emblazoned with spangles and talismanic symbols. And so the wearer is self-modulating and self-protected, a walking woven spell. If she's shocking, it's because she wants to be. This witch is a voluntary disturbance.

Women have been told over many lifetimes that their bodies are wrong and unbecoming—that they belong to other people. The fashion witch is self-possessed, first and foremost. She controls how much of herself she shows and shares.

Whether others consider her anatomy a monstrosity, or a thing of majesty, is of little concern. She knows her body is her own.

And that is true power.

Chapter 5

GIFTED SISTERS
AND SHADY LADIES

My hairstylist is also my tarot reader, and the efficiency of this pleases the pragmatic witch in me to no end. Every three months or so, I arrive at Amber King's art nouveau–decorated apartment and sit at her wooden table, where we catch up on life and sip some warm herbal concoction she has brewed. We discuss how I've been, what I'm struggling with, and what I'm hoping to accomplish. And then the real ritual begins: She reads my cards with the gilded Klimt deck that she always uses, and delivers messages to me about the state of my spiritual life with suggested next steps to take or things to be aware of. Then she washes my hair in the sort of kitchen bathtub that comes standard in so many old Manhattan apartments, before sitting me in front of her mirrored vanity. Here, she gives me my cut and, as she first explained it to me, "puts blessings into it" that pertain to my reading. The whole thing takes around two hours and costs in total what either service would cost alone. More importantly, I always leave feeling better than when I arrived.

Less weighed down by overgrown locks, sure—but also more subtly recalibrated.

The reading and the haircut are two halves of a holistic magical working. Together, they align my interior and my exterior, ensuring that I feel balanced at every level. Going to Amber is an act of self-care and a metaphysical encounter. She reorients my inner compass, then clips off all that is no longer serving me, clearing the way forward. The cut is always lovely, but what I value most of all are the insights she offers me as she literally disentangles my head. I've come to think of her as my follicle oracle.

IF FEARS AND fantasies about women's bodies have been linked to witchery, then the same is true of the female mind.

Women have long been associated with supernatural abilities, from uncanny powers of knowing, to extrasensory perception, to a strong connection with the spirit world. Even outside of mystical contexts, a persistent idea of "female intuition" implies that women have some innate sense of awareness that men do not. Personally, I'm not convinced that this is true. Even if women seem more sensitized to invisible forces or subtle emotional cues, this most likely has as much to do with socialization as biology. Perhaps people of all genders have the potential to be equally intuitive, but many men have been taught to suppress this, because sensitivity has historically been linked to femininity and weakness.

Regardless, the sentiment that women are more hardwired for otherworldy activities endures, and the current esoteric sphere seems to reinforce this generalization. The vast majority of "spiritual consultants" I've known over the years—the psychics, astrologers, energy-workers, and fortune-tellers of various flavors—have been women. At Lily Dale, the community in upstate New York where people have been going to get messages from the dead since 1879, 40 of the 51 "registered mediums" you can currently visit with are female (about 80 percent). Of the 31 featured psychics on bestamericanpsychics.com, 23 of them (or 74 percent) are women, and of the 123 California-based psychics, tarot readers, and mediums I counted on bestpsychicdirectory.com, 99 are women (80 percent). A more extensive study of gender and professional intuitives is outside the scope of this book, but I am willing to bet that the stats would remain fairly consistent.

Though certainly not all of these people would identify as witches, there is overlap between what they do and what witches have been said to do throughout time. They are all supposed to have access to the great unknown, and to provide stage directions from the spiritual world. Whether it's called a second sight, a third eye, or a sixth sense, it's usually women who are said to possess special abilities of knowing that can forewarn, inform, or illuminate.

And no matter whether they're called witches, sibyls, oracles, or seers, women like these have sometimes been revered, but are frequently reviled. The idea that their strange gifts might give them an advantage over others or enable them to hold sway over the future has often been found unnerving, to say the least.

"What do witches do?" ballet student Suzy Bannion asks a professor in Dario Argento's 1977 horror film *Suspiria*. He explains: "They can change the course of events, and people's lives, but only to do harm. . . . They can cause suffering, sickness, and even the death of those who for whatever reason have offended them."

The witches of Tanz Dance Academy live up to advance billing, and our Suzy must destroy their leader, Helena Markos, lest she be murdered herself. In the 2018 remake of *Suspiria*, the witches who run the ballet school have eerie mental capabilities. They can sense when their students are "ready" to perform occultic dance rituals, and they besiege the girls with nightmares. Their coven is devoted to a malignant deity called Suspiriorium or the Mother of Sighs, and they sacrifice dancers' lives to keep her alive. Though these witches are charismatic and alluring in some ways (having Tilda Swinton playing one of their leaders, Madame Blanc, certainly upped their glamour quotient), they are wrapped up in dark magic, and their psychic powers are a key component in their evil plans.

The fear of women with paranormal abilities has been with us for centuries. The Bible certainly doesn't mince words when it comes to witchery. Its most notorious remark on the matter is when God tells Moses during their law-of-the-land debriefing, "Thou shalt not suffer a witch to live" (Exodus 22:18, King James Version).

Or as Leviticus 20:27 puts it, "A man also or woman that hath a familiar spirit, or that is a wizard, shall surely be put to death: they shall stone them with stones: their blood shall be upon them."

Or Deutoronomy 18:10: "There shall not be found among you any one that maketh his son or his daughter to pass through the fire, or that useth divination, or an observer of times, or an enchanter, or a witch."

Here is where things get linguistically squishy, though, because other English translations of the Bible use the term *sorceress* or *woman who does magic* rather than *witch*. Likewise a person who "hath a familiar spirit" is also translated as *medium* or *necromancer*, as familiars were believed to assist them in communicating with the dead.

All of this is to say that, according to the Old Testament at least, being a person with special powers was a deal-breaker for the Big Guy in the Sky (unless he bestowed the powers himself, which he usually did to men such as Moses). This meant that if you were an occult practitioner, the Lord's adherents would make sure you paid for it with your life.

And yet in the book of Samuel, one ghost-whispering gal is shone in a far gentler light. The story of the character who has come be known as the Witch of Endor begins with Saul, the Israelite king. At a loss for what to do when his troops are surrounded by the Philistines, he implores God for guidance. God does not answer him, so King Saul decides to take matters into his own hands: he goes off with two of his men to consult a medium, hoping he'll have better luck contacting the spirit world. Only trouble is that Saul has forbidden mediumship and witchcraft in his kingdom. Talk about bad optics. So he dons a disguise and visits a woman who is still practicing necromancy on the down-low.

At first she refuses him, thinking this is all a setup. She cites the king's eradication of spirit workers, telling her visitors: "Behold, thou knowest what Saul hath done, how he hath cut off those that have familiar spirits, and the wizards, out of the land: wherefore then layest thou a snare for my life, to cause me to die?"

Saul swears to God that no harm will come to her. Whom would he like her to summon? she asks. The prophet Samuel, he tells her, and she complies. She then realizes that her visitor is, in fact, King Saul. She tells him that she sees a ghost come up from the ground like a god, and that he is old and wears a mantle. Recognizing her description, Saul realizes that the summoning has worked.

Unfortunately, Spirit-Sam is the bearer of bad news. First he admonishes Saul for calling upon him, saying that if God won't help, then what the heck is *he* supposed to do about it? He then tells his brother that the Philistines are going to take over Israel, and that Saul and his sons are going to die the very next day. See you tomorrow!

Saul falls to the ground, shocked from the news and weak with hunger. The medium insists on feeding him, butchering a fatted calf and whipping up some minute-matzo, which she serves to him and his men.

We don't hear more about her, so one can only assume that she goes on her merry, necromantic way. She also keeps her reputation intact: not only does she conduct a top-notch secret séance, but her hostess skills are aces too. Saul doesn't fare so well, as the ghost's vision plays out just as predicted. The next day, Saul's three sons are killed in battle, and after being wounded by arrows, he falls on his own sword. The Philistines overtake Israel.

It's a morally curious story, to be sure, and one that mirrors our ongoing ambivalence about consulting with those who are plugged into the ethereal plane. I also can't help but feel royally pissed off at Saul's hypocrisy. Like so many lawmakers (e.g., congressmen who purport to be against *Roe v. Wade* yet who have paid for their mistresses' abortions), he is a secret consumer of the very services he has legislated against. Not to mention that he puts our witch in a chokehold of power dynamics. She has no choice but to comply with his request that she summon Samuel's spirit, even though she knows she is putting her life at risk. I used to read this story as an act of mercy on Saul's part and kindness on the witch's. Now it strikes me as yet another tale of male privilege. It's about a man who has the power to change his own rules when it suits him, regardless of the vulnerable people he affects in the process. I like to think that when our Endorian heard the news of his death, she had a dinner of celebratory calf meat herself.

Further examination of the Witch of Endor is interesting on another front, for she is never actually referred to as a witch in the Bible. Her original Hebrew description is *ba'alat ob*, which translates roughly to "mistress of the ob." What is an ob, you ask? Interpretations vary, but it was most likely some sort of vessel or pit that would house a familiar or other ghostly entities. Sounds useful.

It seems our lady of the shades didn't come to be referred to as the Witch of Endor until many hundreds of years after her story was first written. In the Latin Vulgate Bible, which was translated by Jerome in the fourth century CE, this character is referred to as a "*mulierem habentem pythonem.*" This term is derived from the Pythia, a high priestess in ancient Greece most famously known as the Oracle of Delphi. A woman held this role from the eighth through fourth centuries BCE in the city of Pytho (itself named for the mythic serpent Python, who was slain by the god Apollo). One of the Pythia's primary functions was to enter a trance and channel words and prophecies from Apollo to those who sought her counsel. Due to twists of translation, the English terms *pythoness* and *witch* eventually came to be conflated to mean any woman with uncanny powers, though in sixteenth-century England there still seemed to be a bit of a differential. The earliest occurrence of the phrase "Witch of Endor" is found in witchcraft skeptic Reginald Scot's 1584 book *The Discoverie of Witchcraft*. He also refers to her as a "Pythonissa" in the text, though his main point is that she was most likely a fraud who used some kind of elaborate ventriloquism to trick Saul, thus neither a witch nor an oracle at all. In 1597, King James I refutes this theory in his own witchcraft treatise, *Daemonologie*, in which he claims that witches are *very* real, and very threatening indeed, but that our friend in Endor was rather more of a *pythoness* than a witch. Even Salvator Rosa's famed painting known in English as *Saul and the Witch of Endor*, has been given the title *L'ombre de Samuel apparaissant à Saül chez la pythonisse d'Endor* by the Louvre, where it now hangs. Rosa most likely wouldn't have given it any title in his native Italian, as titling art was not a common practice during his time. But in a letter dated September 15, 1668, he describes the figure in the painting as the "Pitonessa"; it seems that a picture of a pythoness, and not a *strega* or witch, was his original intent.

Suffice it to say, though *pythoness* may once have had its own distinct meaning, the word has now fallen into disuse. I suppose *witch* has a better ring to it, and the fact that our biblical wraith-raiser came to be commonly known as such is a testament to the ways in which the categories of various types of magic—divination, necromancy, spell casting, channeling, and so on—have been collapsed over time and shaken together in a grab bag marked "witchcraft."

PROPHECY AND THE mysteries of mortality are important elements in another legendary witch story: Shakespeare's *The Tragedy of Macbeth*. The three Weird Sisters are perhaps the most famous witch trio in history, and they are the catalysts for Macbeth's bloody pursuit of the crown. Like the Witch of Endor, they are also morally nebulous figures whom the protagonist is unnerved by but consults nonetheless. And, like her, they never call themselves witches, though Shakespeare does name them as such in the dramatis personae.

Furthermore, in the original edition of the play, Shakespeare didn't refer to them as "weird" but rather "wayward." However, he was pulling the story of Macbeth right out of a set of history books called *Holinshed's Chronicles of England, Scotland, and Ireland*, which does indeed refer to these characters as "weird sisters"—and so modern translators have brought the term back. At any rate, it is an apt name for them, for *weird* comes from the Old English word *wyrd,* which means "fate." And these witches are certainly agents of fate, to put it mildly.

The Sisters kick off the play by telling us that they are about to meet with Macbeth, and that plenty of ambiguity will ensue: "Fair is foul, and foul is fair. . . ." This sets up the story's prominent polarities that are woven throughout. Dichotomies such as human nature vs. the supernatural, masculine power vs. feminine power, and desire vs. destruction are played against each other over and over by Shakespeare, and his text constantly probes the spaces where these seeming opposites coexist, overlap, or invert.

When Macbeth and his companion, Banquo, first encounter the Sisters, they tell him that he will be king, and that Banquo will beget a line of kings, despite not being one himself. This (plus some expert ball-busting from his wife, the Lady of the house) motivates Macbeth to murder the current keeper of the crown, King Duncan, as well as some guards. He then hires some murderers to kill Banquo and his son, Fleance, though Fleance escapes. Banquo's ghost appears to Macbeth at a banquet later that night. Feeling rightfully spooked and insecure about his future, Macbeth seeks out the Three Sisters again in hopes that they will spill more soothsaying beans.

The play's iconic bubbling cauldron scene is their preparation for this meeting. The eye of newt, frog's toe, baboon blood, and other awful offal are ingredients for their "deed without a name," which is presumably the conjuration of four prophetic—if cryptic—visions to follow. These messages are misinterpreted by Macbeth as being somewhat reassuring, and he continues his killing spree, albeit in an increasingly paranoid state. Most notably, he believes that the witches' prediction that "none of woman borne / Shall harm Macbeth," means that he is safe from mortal danger. As he soon learns, this is not the case after all, for his enemy Macduff's birth was via a cesarean section, from a mother who most likely died in labor. It is this man who kills Macbeth, validating the Weird Sisters' words.

Ultimately, *Macbeth* is a story about fate vs. free will. Do the Sisters cause Macbeth's murderous rise and ultimate demise? Or is Macbeth's downfall simply a case of self-fulfilling prophecy— the inevitable culmination of untethered ambition spurred by the power of suggestion?

On the one hand, throughout the play, the witches definitely do things with intention: they conjure winds, they brag about inflicting harm on other people, and they purposefully seek out Macbeth to begin with. Just before they encounter him and Banquo for the first time, we're told they're doing a circular dance to cast a sort of spell:

The weird sisters, hand in hand,
Posters of the sea and land,
Thus do go, about, about,
Thrice to thine, and thrice to mine,
And thrice again to make up nine.
Peace, the charm's wound up

We also have the speech of their goddess, Hecate, to contend with (which some have suggested was actually written by Thomas Middleton and added to the play later, to further complicate matters). In it she says,

. . . How did you dare
To trade and traffic with Macbeth
In riddles and affairs of death;
And I, the mistress of your charms,
The close contriver of all harms,
Was never call'd to bear my part,
Or show the glory of our art?

In essence, Hecate is scolding the Sisters for deploying their trickery on Macbeth without her. In versions of the play that include this speech, it is she who encourages them to do the toil and trouble doubling in the first place: she tells them to meet her in the morning for a spell-casting session where they will reveal Macbeth's destiny to him.

Still, it can also be said that Macbeth interprets their prophecies in a way that suits his own desires, and that his tragic end is brought about by his own actions.

s it's a combination of both, and that through our
meet destiny halfway.

Regardless, examining the disparate ingredients that Shakespeare used to craft the Weird Sisters is worth contemplating, for
he further stretched the boundaries of our conception of witches.
They were in part inspired by the Three Fates that occur in several
traditions: the Greek Moirai and Nordic Norns were different
iterations of a similar group of three female deities who would
determine one's life and time of death. In this mythological triad,
they are sometimes depicted as a lady who spins the thread of life,
a lady who measures its length, and a lady who snips it finished
with her terrifically terminal shears. These women are the over-
seers of destiny, highly respected and formidable.

Shakespeare was also writing during the British reign of King
James I (formerly known as King James VI of Scotland), a man
who, as we've seen, was notoriously obsessed with witchcraft.
He believed witches had sent a storm in an attempt to ship-
wreck the vessel in which he and his new wife, Princess Anne,
sailed home from Copenhagen after their wedding. Witch trials
in response to this incident were held in Denmark and then in
North Berwick, Scotland (the first in the country), the latter of
which he presided over. After they'd concluded, in 1597, James
published his aforementioned *Daemonologie*, presumably also as
a refutation of Reginald Scot's *The Discoverie of Witchcraft*. In
it, he made the argument that witches were "slaves of the Devil,"
and he used many of the witches' "confessions" during these trials
as evidence of this. *Macbeth*, in this context, can be seen as evidence of Shakespeare being a bit of a royal suck-up. As Professor
Carole Levin writes, "James I's fascination with witches was well

known, and no doubt Shakespeare composed Macbeth in 1605 or 1606 . . . to please his new king." Using the king's own *Daemonologie* as a resource provided ample fodder for the development of the Sisters as well, which is probably why they are a conflation of prophesying oracles and cooks of culinarily questionable spells.

The play was also certainly relevant to audiences of the age. Beliefs that witches could use magic to retaliate against people who had wronged them were still very much held by some Englishmen and -women of all social strata during this time. Practicing witchcraft had been officially criminalized in England since the Witchcraft Act of 1542 (though this was repealed five years later, only to be replaced by several others). The 1563 and 1604 acts transferred witch trials from the Church to the courts. The 1604 act was passed shortly after King James took the throne, its full title being *An Act against Conjuration, Witchcraft and dealing with evil and wicked spirits*. It was this statute that emboldened Matthew Hopkins, the self-proclaimed Witch-Finder General, to prosecute and put to death an estimated three hundred women between the years 1644 and 1646, as well as to write his infamous treatise *The Discovery of Witches* in 1647. The last person to be executed for witchcraft in the British Isles was a Scottish woman named Janet Horne, who was burned to death in 1727.

That said, there were certainly also those like Reginald Scot who were skeptical about witchcraft being a real threat—or real in any way at all. It's not certain what Shakespeare's own beliefs were, though he continued to be interested in magic as a topic, as exhibited most notably in *The Tempest*, which many believe to be the last play he wrote entirely himself, five or six years before his death in 1616. He also penned a cheeky "hex" for his own gravestone:

Good friend for Jesus sake forbeare
To dig the dust enclosed here.
Blessed be the man that spares these stones
And cursed be he that moves my bones.

One can picture the Weird Sisters chanting such a thing them-selves. They have become quintessential witch characters, iconic because Shakespeare has done a masterful job in combining various female taboos. Not only does he use them to display the mythologized feminine connection to the supernatural, but he also writes of the putridness of their ugly and aging bodies. As we've already established, many if not most of the people who were killed in the name of eradicating witchcraft were socially unappealing, and often older, women. Shakespeare's witches reflect this too. We're told they're "withered, and so wild in their attire" and that they have "choppy fingers," "skinny lips," and "beards"—this final element most likely a winking bit of word-smithery alluding to the fact that in Shakespeare's time, the actors playing them were men.

Still, the witches of *Macbeth* have shape-shifted over the years, turning into Haitian Vodoun practitioners in Orson Welles's 1936 staging (often referred to as *Voodoo Macbeth*) as well as his subsequent 1948 film; to a single Forest Spirit with a spinning wheel in Akira Kurosawa's 1958 film *Throne of Blood*; to a group of ravers in Punchdrunk's popular immersive theater piece *Sleep No More*, which debuted in 2011 and is still running in New York City today.

Each of these retellings reflects its cultural context as well as the preoccupations and tastes of its director. But no matter the guises they come in, what makes the witches of *Macbeth* so iconic is that they are grotesque, feminine figures who are able to see something the rest of us cannot. Whether one interprets them as being fascists of fate or entities of anarchy, they are the ultimate messengers of our own Unknowing. They remind us that with each passing moment, we are grappling with how much control we actually have over our own lives. The Weird Sisters make us face the Big Questions of existence—those that we are supposed to be too polite or too practical to be asking in our daily discourse. The ones that make us peer into the bubbling brew of who and what we really are.

BELIEF IN SUPERSENSORY female powers far outlasted Shakespeare's time, and it presented itself in new skins and semantics 250 years after he penned *Macbeth*. During the Spiritualist movement of mid-nineteenth- century America, the word *witchcraft* would not be used nearly as often, but the constituent parts of femininity intersecting with phantom forces remained the same.

In 1848, the adolescent sisters Kate and Margaret Fox of Hydesville, New York, made quite a commotion when they told people of the strange rapping sounds they heard throughout their house. In the ensuing months, they began to communicate with "Mr. Splitfoot," the devilish name they gave to the spirit that they said was the source of the knocking. According to the girls, this entity later identified himself as the ghost of one Mr. Charles B. Rosna, and he told them that he had been murdered and buried in their cellar five years prior. Alarmed neighbors came to dig beneath the house. When they found some pieces of bone, an investigation commenced, and a local man was arrested for the alleged murder. Word spread of the shocking incident, and soon the Fox farm was overrun by people who wanted to meet the girls who talked to the dead. Amid the hubbub, eleven-year-old Kate and fourteen-year-old Margaret were collected by their thirty-three-year-old sister, Leah, to come live with her in Rochester. But they could not escape the rumors of their revenant-canoodling.

The girls confessed to Leah that the whole thing had been a hoax (though they would later recant). Rather than blow their cover, Leah smelled opportunity. She began having them hold paid séances and appointed herself the "interpreter" of the rappings. Their reputations quickly grew, and they attracted both the interest of curious paying visitors and the scorn of local clergy, who called them heretics and witches. Demand for their services began coming from far and wide, and soon they were traveling to places like New York City, Philadelphia, and Washington, DC, to demonstrate their miraculous mediumship. Large crowds of believers and skeptics alike came to see the supernatural sisters. But their impact was to be much larger than they ever imagined. The craze for having heart-to-hearts with the disembodied began to take hold.

The time was ripe for it. Certainly people had long attempted to speak to the dead. But mid-nineteenth-century America was a hotbed of alternative spirituality, especially throughout what came to be called the Burned-Over District of upstate New York. Some groups sought to reject the Calvinist idea that all souls were damned from the start, and that only the most pious people could be saved. A faction of radical Quakers was particularly invested in the idea that all human beings were equal regardless of race or gender—a sentiment that was beginning to catch on in more open-minded circles. Communication with the other side seemed to confirm that bodies were mere shells and that the spirit was what truly mattered. People throughout the US and Europe began holding séances in their parlors and using methods such as trance, automatic writing, and, eventually, spirit photography to try to make contact with their dearly departed. (These Spiritualist practices would then spread to Latin countries under the name Spiritism or *espiritismo*, largely due to the books of a Frenchman who wrote under the name Allan Kardec, though it's important to note that his ideas were incorporated into already existing practices of ancestor worship in these regions.)

Spiritualism was a social phenomenon. Because it was informally organized with no single governing body, estimates of the number of Spiritualists during its peak in the 1850s and 1860s vary widely, from 45,000 to 11 million in the US alone. But what *is* clear is that it was driven in large part by women. During this period, high death rates of young children and Civil War soldiers alike cast many mothers and wives into a state of perpetual bereavement. Grief became more public, thanks in part to Queen Victoria, who famously wore black during the forty years after her husband, Albert, passed away in 1861. When Willie, the favorite son of Abraham and Mary Todd Lincoln, died of typhoid fever in 1862, Mary began holding séances in the White House to contact him. Spiritualism offered comfort to the living, and consolation that their beloved family members were still with them and able to be reached, heard from, and seen in ghostly photographs.

Not only were many women followers of this faith—they were the leaders of it. The majority of mediums were female, and largely due to this fact, Spiritualism was a profoundly unique and socially progressive movement. As Ann Braude states in her landmark book *Radical Spirits*, "In mediumship, women's religious leadership became normative for the first time in American history." Spirit mediumship became one of a very small set of professions available to women. It gave them gave the ability to make money and have public influence, no matter their economic background. Unlike in the Church, one did not have to be ordained to be a medium, one merely had to have "the gift."

On its surface, Spiritualism also didn't present a huge threat to the patriarchy, because the very features possessed by the so-called weaker sex—nervousness, heightened sensitivity, and a delicate constitution—were what supposedly made them the best candidates for mediumship in the first place. Furthermore, as passive channels, mediums were not responsible for the words that flowed through them. It was often remarked that their spiritual transmissions came in the form of unhalting, eloquent speeches. The vocabulary and delivery that were used in trance were considered far too sophisticated to possibly have come directly from the medium herself.

Regardless of who authored the utterances, these ghost-hosting women found themselves in the rarefied position of getting to transmit meaningful messages to large groups of people. Because of this, Spiritualism was deeply interlaced with various social justice movements, from abolitionism to children's rights to feminism. Braude writes, "Spiritualism became a major—if not *the* major—vehicle for the spread of women's rights ideas in mid-nineteenth-century America. . . . While not all feminisists were Spiritualists, all Spiritualists advocated woman's rights."

Large Spiritualist gatherings became one of the primary ways that these radical ideas got disseminated, both through the mediums who would deliver messages from the spirit world about the importance of the liberation of all people, and via the conversation among mingling spectators. Likewise, Spiritualists would sometimes speak at women's rights gatherings. Though it's often left out of the history books, the significant overlap in the Venn diagram of Spiritualists, abolitionists, and suffragists was a critical component of such revolutionary American milestones as the outlawing of slavery and the legalization of women's right to vote.

Some of the biggest names in equal rights reform brushed up against Spiritualism, if they weren't adherents themselves. The parlor table where Elizabeth Cady Stanton and Lucretia Mott drafted their Declaration of Sentiments for the Seneca Falls Convention had also reportedly received raps from the spirits. (It belonged to two radical Quakers and Spiritualists-to-be, Thomas and Mary Ann McClintock.)

Susan B. Anthony was agnostic about Spiritualism, but she did write the following to Stanton in 1855: "Oh, dear, dear! If the spirits would only just make me a trance medium and put the right thing into my mouth. . . . You can't think how earnestly I have prayed to be made a speaking medium for a whole week. If they would only come to me thus, I'd give them a hearty welcome." Despite her reputation for being a strong orator, Anthony was nervous about public speaking, and she envied the mediums' ability to let words pour out of them extemporaneously. She would later go on to speak at the Spiritualist community of Lily Dale in the summers of the 1890s during their annual Woman's Suffrage Day, as did many other women's rights luminaries, including birth control advocate Margaret Sanger.

When abolitionist and social justice activist Sojourner Truth first encountered Spiritualism, she was skeptical. In 1851, when she attended her first séance in Rochester, New York, she reportedly brought her signature irreverence to the experience, calling out, "Come spirit, hop up here on the table, and see if you can't make a louder noise." But she came to embrace Spiritualism, eventually moving herself and her family to a Michigan Quaker-Spiritualist community called Harmonia in 1857. She was attracted to this group for their values of open-mindedness, pacifism, and inclusivity, if not their proclivities for interaction with the afterlife. However, Nell Irvin Painter writes that with time she did ". . . grow less suspicious of spirits, even coming to see her father's spirit as a protector." When Harmonia began to falter a few years later, she chose to stay in the area, moving to nearby Battle Creek, where she lived the last sixteen years of her life.

Victoria Woodhull was a medium and carnival show clairvoyant, and she contended that spirits protected and guided her throughout her life. Perhaps it was their support that allowed her to achieve so many firsts: she started the first woman-owned Wall Street brokerage house with her sister, she founded the first woman-owned newspaper in the US, and she was the first woman to address a Congressional committee when she petitioned them to give women the right to vote. But she is perhaps best known as America's first woman to run for president, which she did under the Cosmo-Political Party in 1872. She chose Frederick Douglass as her running mate, though this was more of a symbolic act than anything else, as by all accounts he didn't know about it until after it was announced. Her championing of free love, her beliefs that marriage was institutionalized slavery and that sex should always be consensual, her insistence that women wear less restrictive clothing, and her support of paid sex work were just a few of the "far-out" views that earned her the sobriquet Mrs. Satan. (Her track record of various dubious practices in both the spiritual and political arenas probably helped too.)

Suffragettes and socialists alike would come to renounce Woodhull, considering her too controversial and attention-hungry, but the American Association of Spiritualists continued to support her until its demise in 1875. She was a complicated, even contradictory individual: she was antiabortion, and when she got older she would rail against promiscuity and expose certain Spiritualists as frauds. But the fact remains that she was a pioneer in so many areas of women's liberation and light-years ahead of her time. Throughout much of her life, she insisted that her convictions and actions were directed by her guides in the spirit world. As her biographer Barbara Goldsmith writes, "Victoria's belief in spirit guidance empowered her and her followers to challenge the law, the church, and the entrenched male establishment."

Contact with the spiritual world was not just a hopeful pastime of the bereaved, then. Spiritualism may have been a soothing source of consolation when it began, but it morphed into an ethereal engine of confidence for many of the women who practiced it. The messages of self-worth and female independence missing in their mundane lives were found in the voices of the discarnate.

GRANDMA TRUDY TURNED up in a dream recently. She had a baby swaddled in her arms, and I knew it was mine. This was disconcerting on two counts. First, as we've established, I don't have any children; and second, my grandma passed away in 2001. What was she trying to tell me? Was this her message from the Great Beyond that I've made a mistake? Could it be a prophecy of what's to come, or a ghostly glimpse of what I'm missing out on? As I approached her, I saw more clearly, and ripples of relief washed over me: it wasn't a baby at all—it was a book. She handed it to me and then gestured to reveal a row of more books floating in midair: either things I'd write or perhaps a shelf of books written by others that I'd be contributing mine to. A different sort of family line.

I woke up feeling reassured. Though I'm now comfortable with my decision to make other things instead of babies, I appreciated my apparition's affirmation.

Still, as lovely as it was to see her, it reminded me that there's so much I may not ever fully understand. Was my grandma really reaching out to me across dimensions? Or was my psyche just spitting out images that I would find soothing? I have no idea.

What I do know is that, despite all scientific developments, the greatest mysteries of our existence still revolve around death, destiny, and the invisible realm: What happens when we die? Are there ghosts or spirits, and can we interact with them? Do we control our fate, or are we being pulled by celestial strings?

It is witches—Shakespearean sages and suffragist-Spiritualists alike—who remind us that, after thousands of years of asking, we still don't have any clear answers to these questions. These characters traffic in ambiguities and traverse nether zones. They know things that we don't and perhaps don't really want to. They see things that we can't or maybe shouldn't. Their secret knowledge is *sublime* in the eighteenth-century sense of the word: it inspires awe *and* terror. We cower in the wake of their abilities and feel grateful when they offer us some direction, however cryptic their insights may be. They cause us to confront the irrational, the inconceivable.

But if we're lucky, these wyrd women can deliver us moments of epiphany. They offer a glimpse of who we are, and who we might be in the future.

Chapter 6

THE DARK ARTS: MAGIC MAKERS AND CRAFT WOMEN

"Were the First Artists Mostly Women?" So asks a 2013 article on NationalGeographic.com, which reported on a new analysis of handprints in the cave-art paintings of eight Paleolithic sites. Some 75 percent of the prints were made by female hands, the study claimed, and not by male hunters, as was previously assumed. Naturally, I love this idea, and I can't help but wonder what these ancient *artistes* were up to. Archaeologists have suggested that these pictures were made by Cro-Magnon conjurors or shamans, who painted images of animals and female nudes to manifest food and fertility. The handprints may have been some sort of added manual magic, or they may simply have been in lieu of a signature: a mark to say *I made this*.

We may never know the truth. But it's appealing to think about Stone Age art sorceresses, because the annoying fact is that for most of human civilization, it has by and large been men who have been allowed to create work for public consumption, or who have at least gotten most of the accolades. And because what male artists made was often images of women, they could dictate what was considered desirable or repugnant, both aesthetically and behaviorally, in regard to the opposite sex. This is particularly clear when we delve into the topic of witches in art. As we've seen, it was men like Albrecht Dürer and Hans Baldung Grien who helped visually define witches with their drawings of naked ladies and other devilish ne'er-do-wells in the late fifteenth and early sixteenth centuries. Other prominent witch-depicters through the ages include Frans Francken the Younger, Salvator Rosa, Henry Fuseli, Francisco Goya, and John William Waterhouse. Though the artists' actual belief in witches fluctuated over the centuries in accordance with society's shifting attitudes, their visual vocabulary remained much the same: witches were shown as either old and horrid, or young and fatally attractive.

At first blush, it seems that the witch undergoes some redemption in the twentieth century. Several male Surrealists became inspired by the *femme-sorcière* archetype, thanks in large part to Michelet's aforementioned 1862 book *La Sorcière* and the 1922 Swedish-Danish silent film it inspired, *Häxan*. The idea of the free-spirited, intuitive, bewitching woman inspired Surrealist painters including Max Ernst, Paul Delvaux, Victor Brauner, and Kurt Seligmann. These men made several witch-themed works, many of which were meant to be enchanting and erotic in equal measure. But even with their supposedly more positive artistic spin on women with special powers, many of these witch pictures are faceless or nude, and often both.

Now, I must say, as an art nerd in general and a witch-obsessed one at that, I adore many of the works of these mesmerizing men, as objectifying or politically incorrect as they may be by today's standards. But an interesting thing happens when women wield the creative wands, whether in the form of pencils or paint-brushes: they materialize their own magic, and become witches of a sort themselves.

MOST ART HISTORY textbooks position Wassily Kandinsky as the granddaddy of abstract art, and his bright fields of color splotches and scribbled lines were undoubtedly groundbreaking when he began painting them in 1910. Inspired by Theosophy and other esoteric fields of study, he believed that society needed to turn away from materialism. His metaphysical image-making was an attempt to translate invisible energies into visible forms and to usher in a new age of consciousness. "Literature, music, and art, are the first and most sensitive spheres in which this spiritual revolution makes itself felt," he wrote in his 1911 book *Concerning the Spiritual in Art*. He certainly deserves some of the credit for popularizing the idea that nonfigurative art could be a means of making contact with the spiritual realm, along with other painters like Piet Mondrian, Kazimir Malevich, and František Kupka. But regarding the advent of European abstract art, two witchy women beat them all to the punch: Georgiana Houghton and Hilma af Klint.

Georgiana Houghton was born on Grand Canary Island in 1814 and lived most of her life in London. Though she trained as an artist when she was young, she gave it up for several years when her sister died in 1851 at the age of thirty-one. This was the second sibling Houghton had lost, as her younger brother had died in 1826 at the age of nine. Like many Europeans and Americans in the mid-nineteenth century, she was drawn to Spiritualism. Brokenhearted from her sister's death, Houghton took part in her first séance in 1859. The experience was so profound that she decided to become a medium herself. Ultimately she turned to spirit drawing, a method of art-making that positioned the medium as a channel through which spirits would transmit their messages and visions. In 1861, at the age of forty-seven, Houghton reconnected with her deceased sister and resurrected her own creative practice at once.

Like other artist-mediums of the day, Houghton's drawings at first came through as images of flowers, fruits, and other recognizable figures. But her spirit guides—or "invisible friends," as she called them—soon led her in an aesthetic direction that was quite dissimilar to that of her contemporaries. Whirls, swirls, and latticed patterns began to emerge on her paper. Her structures look like psychedelic spiderwebs or the wind-tossed feathers of a bird of paradise, but really, they resemble nothing familiar at all. The images weren't entirely mysterious to Houghton, though, as she had her own interpretation of what the different colors and shapes meant. According to Simon Grant and Marco Pasi, she believed that: "Yellow, for instance, represents God the Father, but also faith and wisdom. Orange is power, violet heavenly happiness. . . ." These drawings are intricate, complicated, and astonishingly beautiful by today's standards, so one can only imagine how shocking they must have been at the time. Houghton referred to them as "Sacred Symbolism," representing illuminating information from on high.

Not only did Houghton have conviction, she had ambition. In 1871, she mounted a show of 155 of these channeled works, wanting more people to see them than just her spirit-communing community. The exhibition, by most accounts, was a failure. She got panned by critics, lost most of her savings doing it, and sold only one drawing. She spent the rest of her life writing, making art, and continuing her mediumship, until she died in relative obscurity in 1884. Her spectacular, spectral works were scattered throughout the world and remained largely unknown for more than a century except in small Spiritualist circles.

That we are aware of her contribution to art history now is thanks in large part to an exhibition of thirty-five of her drawings that was curated at London's Courtauld Gallery in 2016. I was lucky enough to attend this show and was moved not only by her immense gift, but by how startlingly colorful her drawings are. I'd seen plenty of spirit photography: black-and-white images of dour-looking Victorian men and women posing with "ghosts" or skeins of gauzy ectoplasm. Houghton's images, with their radiant, rainbow plumes, could not be more of a contrast. There is something ecstatic about them. Whether her hand was guided by the dead or by the grip of angels, the feeling I got from them was euphoria.

It's a similar sensation that I get when looking at the paintings of a second female abstract art progenitor, the Swedish spirit painter Hilma af Klint. Though they were nearly fifty years apart in age and lived in different countries, af Klint's origin story has parallels to Houghton's. Born in 1862, af Klint was raised in Stockholm, where she studied art as an adolescent. Like Houghton, af Klint was drawn to Spiritualism, and she began attending séances when she was a teenager. Her interest in mediumship deepened when she too lost her sister, in 1880. She attended Stockholm's Royal Academy of Fine Arts from 1882 to 1887, where she painted—

and occasionally exhibited—the usual portraits, florals, and landscapes that women of her art school were taught to make.

By 1896, however, she began experimenting with other styles that melded her art training and her interest in mediumship. In that year, she and four other women formed a collective they called De Fem (or The Five). The purpose of the group was to make contact with spiritual beings who would deliver messages to them via pictures. During the ten-year period that the group regularly met, the women engaged in automatic writing and drawing, a means of generating work from an unconscious or trancelike state, which they believed made them more fully receptive to the entities who were contacting them. (This creative method became known as *automatism* and was eventually popularized by the Surrealists decades later.) They took turns doing the drawings, and af Klint eventually became the primary artist-medium of the group in 1903.

In 1905, at the age of forty-three, af Klint was told by a spirit guide named Amaliel that a large body of work was going to come through. This was to be, as Iris Müller-Westermann puts it, a cycle of "images of a supernatural, non-physical reality." In actuality, this project ended up consisting of 193 pieces done by af Klint between 1906 and 1915 called *The Paintings for the Temple*. As curator Tracey Bashkoff writes, "The titular temple was not one that existed anywhere in the world. She envisioned her *Paintings for the Temple* filling a round building, where visitors would progress upward along a spiraling path, on a spiritual journey defined by her paintings." And these temple works could not be more different from the genteel, easily recognizable pictures that she was originally trained to make.

The earliest of these, which she called the *Primordial Chaos* series, contain shapes that resemble amoebas, wiggly serpents, and snail shells floating in space, with curved lines, letters, and words painted in large script. The main colors used are blue, which she interpreted as feminine, and yellow, which she interpreted as masculine. Green also makes an appearance, presumably to imply a combination of the two energies. Her *Eros* series of 1907 is far softer, with pinks and whites and looping lines that resemble flowers or the orbit patterns of pastel planets. These pictures look more like diagrams than anything else, the scribblings of a frenzied professor trying to crack a secret code.

During 1907, af Klint also began working much bigger and much brighter. The title of her *Ten Largest* series is self-explanatory insofar as their scale, but the name may as well be referring to their scope too. They trace human development from childhood to youth to adulthood to old age, but they may be read as a depiction of the development of the universe as well. These images are astonishing, with a richly saturated color palette using a range of oranges, roses, violets, yellows, and blues, and ovoid, undulating spirals and rings. They look like constellations or atoms, both macrocosmic and microcosmic at once. Some of them have Roman numerals and cursive letters and words. To gaze at them is to see kaleidoscopically. Af Klint was in a transcendent state when she painted them, and that energy is infectious. It is difficult not to feel groundless when viewing them. There are few familiar footholds, no typical shapes. I don't know if it's actually the visual language of a supercelestial being, but I can imagine it so. The imagery is, to use the well-worn phrase, out of this world.

As af Klint's work progressed, more recognizable images began to appear. From 1913 on, swans, hearts, and pyramids are found next to more geometric forms such as cubes and crosses. She grew interested in the teachings of esoteric philosopher Rudolf Steiner, whom she knew (and who was critical of her spiritual and artistic methods), as well as in Rosicrucianism, Theosophy, and world religion overall—though she was also a practicing Lutheran for much of her life. And though she believed her visions were coming from an external source, as she went on she began to feel like a fully active participant in the process, rather than just a vessel for extrasensory communications.

Though her style morphs over the years, a few things remain somewhat consistent: her bold use of color and her sense of balance, if not absolute symmetry. Whether she's painting opalescent double helixes or mirrored grids or solar altarpieces, there seems to be a yearning for reconciliation. "As above, so below," the alchemical adage states. Binaries of masculine/feminine, light/dark, inner/outer, and so on are all present here, implying the presence of some sort of universal equilibrium between opposing forces, or at least a wish for it.

Several scholars have rushed to point out that it is perhaps not quite fair to say that Georgiana Houghton and Hilma af Klint are the "real inventors" of abstract art. The argument goes that though they may have been drinking from the same intellectual and spiritual waters as Kandinsky and his ilk, they didn't contextualize what they were doing as pure "art" (even though both Houghton and af Klint fully identified as artists), nor did they have the same intention or ability to evolve society's aesthetic understanding. And even if there was *some* overlap in content—after all, Kandinsky was also trying to give the viewer an experience of the divine, even if he thought his ideas came from himself rather than from external spirit guides—Houghton and af Klint were simply not part of the conversation. They couldn't influence other artists or be considered canonical because, well, very few people saw their work. The art world was dominated by men, so it was difficult for any female artist to be taken seriously. That they were creating such visionary works, unlike anything the world had seen before, made them all the more marginal—and all the more remarkable.

If most people aren't familiar with Georgiana Houghton's oeuvre, it isn't due to her lack of trying. Not only did she produce the aforementioned exhibition, she also submitted her drawings to such institutions as Britain's Royal Academy and wrote several books. Af Klint, on the other hand, believed no one would understand her own channeled artwork in her lifetime, and so she was determined not to let anyone display her 1,200 or so paintings until at least twenty years after her death in 1944. Still, she did want them to be seen eventually, and she devised a fastidious system in her journals to denote which of her pieces she felt were worthy of display once the world was ready for them.

It's taken far longer than either of them envisioned for people to learn about their creations. The first time af Klint's art was in a major exhibition was in 1985, at the Los Angeles County Museum's survey *The Spiritual in Art: Abstract Painting 1890–1985*. It took until 2013 for there to be a major retrospective of her work, at Stockholm's Moderna Museet, followed by her first major solo show in the US at the Guggenheim Museum in 2018 (the latter bearing an uncanny resemblance to the round, spiraling art temple she saw in her visions). Scholars are only now beginning to recognize her contributions, and the trajectory of modern art is undergoing reassessment. As Guggenheim director Richard Armstrong writes, af Klint's work "... does more than shift a timeline. It occasions an important and timely reevaluation of the emergence of abstraction, bringing to the fore fundamental questions about which factors shaped its formation, how we recount its development, and who is integral to that still-developing narrative."

Perhaps that sentiment will extend to Georgiana Houghton. If a solo exhibition of her drawings happened at a major museum before the one I saw in London in 2016, I'm not aware of it, and at the time of writing this, I don't know of any plans for that show to travel. I hope that this is remedied, for she too is worthy of worldwide acclaim.

Georgiana Houghton was born more than 200 years ago and Hilma af Klint more than 150. That we're being made aware of their achievements only now is bittersweet. If there is an afterlife, I hope they are watching.

THERE IS ANOTHER undersung artist who blurred the line between illustration and divination. Many are familiar with her work, but few know her name. And that's because for a century, it was left out of the title of the hugely popular Rider-Waite tarot deck, even though she was the artist who created its iconic—and now ubiquitous—imagery.

Pamela "Pixie" Colman Smith was born in England in 1878 to two American parents, though she spent a great deal of time in New York and Kingston, Jamaica, due to her father's work as a merchant with the West India Improvement Company. She grew up with a love of the arts and lived for a time with famed British actress Ellen Terry while her father went on business trips. She was also looked after by the staff of London's Lyceum Theatre, including their business manager—and eventual *Dracula* author—Bram Stoker, whose book *The Lair of the White Worm* she would illustrate in later years.

She studied art at the Pratt Institute in Brooklyn from 1893 to 1896, though she never graduated, most likely due to her mother's sudden death. Many have speculated that her mother was Jamaican, and Smith's own physical features were often described as "exotic" or perhaps of mixed race throughout her life (and to this day), though whether this is true has yet to be confirmed. What is certain is that Jamaican culture was hugely influential on her. One of her favorite forms of entertainment was to dress in island garb and tell traditional tales at salons and parties, and she was so captivating that writer Arthur Ransome described her as "goddaughter of a witch and sister to a fairy." She later released books of Jamaican folklore including *Annancy Stories*, which she both wrote and illustrated.

She enjoyed some success as a commercial artist in New York, and then moved back to London in 1900 following her father's death. Despite her grief, she went through a prolific period, writing and illustrating several books and, according to Stuart R. Kaplan, doing "miniature theater using cardboard characters and props." She also hosted a coterie of urban bohemians at her studio, and became friends with such mystically minded Irish writers as A.E. (the same man who would go on to inspire another Pamela, *Mary Poppins* author P. L. Travers) and the poet and playwright William Butler Yeats.

Her friendship with Yeats proved to be quite influential on

Smith's development, both artistically and spiritually. Through him and his family, she became interested in Celtic mythology. She would go on to state that she believed in fairies and goblins and that she could see the supernatural beings called the Sidhe, or the Shining Ones. Yeats also introduced her to the Hermetic Order of the Golden Dawn, a society of artists and freethinkers who gathered to study occult teachings and engage in magical rituals. The Order was loosely based on Masonic principles of initiation, and members gained knowledge about such topics as Kabbalah, astrology, alchemy, and astral travel as they progressed. Unlike Freemasonry, the Order accepted women as members in "perfect equality" with the men. Under Yeats's encouragement, Smith joined the Isis-Urania Temple of the Order of the Golden Dawn in the fall of 1901.

During this period, her artistic output flourished, if not her finances. She began her own small magazine called the *Green Sheaf*, which was filled with fantastical poetry, fiction, and illustrations, including much of her own. After that and her subsequent imprint, the Green Sheaf Press, folded, she focused more on her fine art. Sonic stimuli became particularly important to her, and she began a series of works based on the synesthetic images that came to her through classical music. When asked by the *Strand Magazine* to explain how these pictures were conceived, she said that they were "not conscious illustrations," but were rather ". . . just what I see when I hear music—thoughts loosened and set free by the spell of sound." Though her musical pictures varied depending on the song she was painting, they often featured mythical women wearing flowing robes in sweeping natural landscapes. These works became the first nonphotographic images that famed photographer (and eventual husband of Georgia O'Keeffe) Alfred Stieglitz would show in his New York City gallery, to much acclaim. She also began collaborating more actively with Yeats, illustrating scenery and doing costume design for several of his plays. In retrospect, all of these seemingly disparate projects prepared her well for what was to become her magnum opus.

In 1903, Smith left the Isis-Urania Temple that Yeats headed, and followed the poet Arthur Edward Waite to a new faction he created called the Independent and Rectified Order of the Golden Dawn. As Elizabeth Foley O'Connor writes, "Waite wanted to create a more spiritual Rosicrucian-Christian order, and it is possible that this focus influenced Pamela's decision to convert to Roman Catholicism . . . in July 1911." Regardless, in 1909 Smith received a fateful commission from Waite, who invited her to design a new deck of tarot cards. Already someone who infused her art with mystical aspects, and who was "abnormally psychic," as Waite called her, Smith seemed ideally suited to the task. Her images would be not only looked at, but used to elevate the viewer's consciousness and bring guidance from another realm.

Though the tarot has evolved from various card games over hundreds of years, the provenance of the divinatory deck as we know it can be traced to fifteenth-century Italy, including the Sola-Busca deck, which Smith was most likely inspired by. Throughout the sixteenth and seventeenth centuries, tarot production was centered in Marseilles, France, and it was there that the Major Arcana that we're now familiar with (i.e., the first twenty-two cards in the deck, including the Fool, the Magician, the High Priestess, and so on) became standardized and given a set order. The Marseilles deck, however, does not have full illustrations for the numbered "pip" cards of the Minor Arcana (for example, the Two of Cups or the Nine of Pentacles).

Waite wanted to create a new tarot deck that, unlike most prior sets, would have full illustrations for each of the seventy-eight cards and also incorporate astrological elements. This meant that Smith would not only have to reinterpret existing designs of the twenty-two Major Arcana cards but that she would have to invent entirely new images for the Minor Arcana, including the forty pips. She was also responsible for creating the card backs and the nameplate, eighty illustrations in total.

In a letter she wrote to Alfred Stieglitz in November of 1909, she says, "I've just finished a big job for very little cash! A set of designs for a pack of Tarot cards 80 designs. I shall send some over—of the original drawings—as some people may like them!"

Today this note strikes a chord that's both sweet and sour. The thirty-one-year-old writing it had no inkling how renowned her images would become after they were published in 1910. The Rider-Waite tarot deck, as it came to be called (after Waite and the publisher, William Rider & Son), is now arguably the most successful and recognizable deck ever made, and it is the number-one-selling deck in America and England. Her complex, symbolic artwork has been a source of inspiration and deep meaning to card readers for more than a hundred years, not to mention its numberless appearances on everything from T-shirts to coffee mugs to haute couture dresses by Dior and Alexander McQueen. One could argue that most of the thousands of tarot decks that came after the Rider-Waite are riffing on her intellectual property, if not copying it outright.

Unbeknownst to her, Smith created the sort of legacy that artists dream about. That she was paid so little for her work and received no royalties to speak of is a tragedy. Though she kept illustrating and exhibiting her art after the deck's release, she continued to struggle financially and never achieved the sort of recognition she hoped for in her lifetime. It's hard to say which is more galling: the paltry sum she received, or the repeated lack of credit for her tarot designs. To this day, the Rider-Waite deck is a household name. Pamela Colman Smith is not.

Fortunately, the historical record is starting to be corrected. U.S. Games Systems, the world's largest publisher of tarot decks, issued a Pamela Colman Smith commemorative set to mark the deck's centenary in 2009. They now have available a "Smith-Waite" deck, and tarot scholar and U.S. Games Systems founder Stuart R. Kaplan has also recently released the first full biography of her, *Pamela Colman Smith: The Untold Story*. Pratt Institute, her alma mater, held an exhibition of her illustrations in the winter of 2019. Certain occult shops will now only sell the Smith-Waite deck, and I have friends who, like me, will no longer use the one titled "Rider-Waite." If we can't pay Pixie for her work, at least we can pay her more attention.

Like many people, I have accumulated dozens of decks over the years in a wide variety of styles and themes. But my own Smith-Waite deck has a special place in my heart. Whenever I use it, I feel a deep connection to this woman, this "goddaughter of a witch." We not only share a name, we share an outlook. We were both born under the sign of Aquarius, and thus are related to the Star, a tarot card that symbolizes intuition and inspiration. And like her, I'm fortunate enough to be part of a community of inspiring magic-workers and mystically minded artists, who seek knowledge and spiritual expansion. Pamela Colman Smith believed that there is more to this world than meets the eye. She wanted her art to open us up to possibilities beyond the rational, the quantifiable, the already known. To take us further and show us more.

I shuffle her cards in my hands, flip them over one by one. I let them tell me a story: about who I am, where I've come from, and where I'm going. There are many like me who consult Pixie's pictures in this manner, as tarot reading is more popular than ever. Though she passed away in 1951, she still has much guidance to give us.

I DIDN'T LEARN about Georgiana Houghton, Hilma af Klint, or Pamela Colman Smith until I was an adult. But I was lucky enough to encounter the work of two other art witches when I was in my teens. Remedios Varo and Leonora Carrington have become more prominent in recent years, but when I discovered their paintings in the 1990s, it felt like stumbling on buried treasure.

Growing up in close proximity to New York City and having a father who commuted there each day meant that we would go on family outings to Manhattan with relative frequency. We'd meet up with my dad for a night on the town after he finished work or go in during the weekend for special occasions. My sister preferred to celebrate her birthday with a Broadway show, which is how I got to see such 1980s classics as *Cats* (terrifying), *Les Miserables* (super romantic, suuuuuuper long), and *Phantom of the Opera* (swoon-worthy: I loved the Phantom—nay, I *was* the Phantom!).

For mine, we'd usually make a pilgrimage to my favorite place on the planet, the Metropolitan Museum of Art. There we'd see whatever new exhibitions were up, and then run a circuit of my most beloved spots: a contemplative stop at the Temple of Dendur, a lunar salute to Augustus Saint-Gaudens's bronze *Diana* in the American Wing, and visits to old friends like Kiki Smith's *Lilith* and the two gauzy lovers in Pierre-Auguste Cot's *The Storm*. We'd wind things down with a special dinner in the main cafeteria with its mesmeric mosaic floor and slabs of prime rib cut right off the bone (I still mourn this restaurant's passing, no matter how elegant the Greek and Roman galleries that it morphed into may be). Then we'd cap off the whole day with a leisurely wander through the museum's heavenly bookstore. Though the whole place was a wonder palace for me, the shop was where I was struck by the lightning of true love.

I'd like to think that most of us have had at least one such encounter: a meeting with a work of art so profound that it becomes an instantaneous beacon to a bigger, more vivid world. Its effect is as much physiological as it is psychological. Pupils dilate. Pulse rushes. Flesh buzzes and blooms. It feels like a key sliding into a lock, with a click that cracks the heart fully open. The body's biochemical makeup will never be the same thereafter.

Picture this: A gold-skinned woman emerges from a rippled orifice in the wall and begins to step into a vermilion, hexagonal chamber. There is a crescent moon shining through a hole in the roof and a six-sided table in the middle of a triangular-tiled floor. Roots or moss grow in hairy tendrils from the ceiling, and branches reach through the window and walls. On the table is a chalice that holds a liquid image of the moon reflected from above. Our lady has arrived to drink this celestial elixir. To take sacrament and become initiated into this house of holy feminine mysteries.

Remedios Varo's title for her 1960 painting, *Nacer de Nuevo*, translates to "Born Again." And so I was.

I first saw this image while flipping through Whitney Chadwick's *Women Artists and the Surrealist Movement*, which I later learned was a groundbreaking survey that put female Surrealists on the institutional map. The entire book led me to a new kind of family: ancestors who may not have been genetic connections, but to whom I was spiritually linked instead. In these pages, I met Varo and many of her acquaintances and associates whom I would get to know over the coming years: women like Leonora Carrington, Leonor Fini, Ithell Colquhoun, and Dorothea Tanning who were not content to be the subjects of paintings and insisted on creating their own image-rich worlds through pigment, canvas, paper, and other ephemera. These artists dared to believe that, despite the reigning male visual narratives of their time, their lives were also worthy of exploration. They were lady psychonauts, intrepidly plumbing the depths of their minds, panning for the precious metals of myth, memory, personal history, and private fantasy.

In addition to its content, one of the greatest gifts a book can offer is a path to more books, and in this way too Chadwick's was an enormous stepping-stone for me. After reading it, I rushed to my local library to research Remedios Varo as quickly as I could. One book came up: *Unexpected Journeys: The Art and Life of Remedios Varo* by Janet A. Kaplan. They had to order it from another branch, and getting the message that it had arrived a few days later felt like an annunciation.

I spent hours upon hours with this book, soaking up Varo's pictures and learning all about her journey from her Spanish homeland to Paris and then finally to Mexico City, where she would befriend another painter, Leonora Carrington. It was a fortuitous meeting of magical minds, and they would go on to influence each other's lives and artwork immensely—not to mention my own.

Of the two, Varo's paintings are more technically rendered, thanks to her engineer father who insisted she learn mechanical drawing. Her work is full of images that blur the boundaries between magic and science: alchemists experiment with musical notes, crystals, and plants; time and space are represented as a translucent woven basket or a window overlapping with itself; strange lands are populated with clocks, wheeled vehicles, architecturally complex towers. Many of her female protagonists feel as if they are on a quest: they sail along the Orinoco River (something she did herself), climb holy mountains, visit secret locations in nocturnal forests and celestial cities. Sometimes her heroines are part animal, as is the owl-woman of her 1958 piece *Creation of the Birds*, who is shown using the light of the moon to literally bring her paintings to life. That this creature looks a great deal like the artist herself evinces Varo's belief in the magical powers of the creative process.

Carrington's art is a bit looser in its line work but is perhaps even more magically complicated. Images of horses were totemic for her, and they show up even in her earliest pieces, such as her iconic *Self-Portrait (Inn of the Dawn Horse)* of 1937–8. Many of her paintings read like maps or multiscene tableaux that seem to tell several stories at once, per one of her favorite artists, Hieronymus Bosch. She was also greatly influenced by the alchemical engravings of the sixteenth and seventeenth centuries, which used imagery of flora, fauna, and Greek and Roman deities as symbolic stand-ins for both chemical and spiritual transformative operations. Her own paintings are stuffed to bursting with goddesses, saints, beasts, daemons, and other mythic beings, the majority of them female. Later work of hers is inscribed with magic circles, incantations, and secret messages scrawled in a backward mirror-language. To look at a Carrington piece is to enter an intricately rendered magic queendom.

In addition to their already quite radical and female-centric spiritual content, the work of both of these artists presaged the feminist art movement of the 1960s and '70s by taking the domestic spaces, activities, and crafts usually associated with women and elevating them to the realm of the divine. Carrington's paintings often depict rituals and transformations taking place in kitchens or involving food. As Susan L. Aberth puts it, ". . . [S]he began to develop her own notions about kitchens as magically charged spaces used to concoct potions, weave spells, prepare herbs, and conduct 'alchemical' cooking experiments." Likewise, Varo's work often depicts textiles being spun or sewn, and she sometimes reveals them as being the fabric of the universe itself. So often the female sphere is overlooked, taken for granted, or considered banal. Carrington and Varo showed that the everyday tasks and arenas of the feminine sphere were actually sites of enchantment.

Varo was raised in Spain and Carrington in England, but they found they had much in common. Like many artists of their age, they'd both fled from Europe and the horrors of the Second World War, and in Varo's case, the Spanish Civil War that preceded it. Carrington's own wartime experiences were harrowing, and culminated in a psychiatric breakdown and a traumatic stay in a Spanish mental asylum. Though Carrington and Varo's paths had crossed at least once before in Paris, it was Mexico City in 1943 where they became close friends and part of a tight-knit community of ex-pats and artists. (Mexico's open-door policy for refugees during this time period puts America's current immigration policies in stark and shameful relief.)

The two women bonded over their shared involvement with Surrealism, the art movement pioneered in the 1920s by André Breton, which incorporated imagery from dreams, myths, and the unconscious mind. Both Varo and Carrington had painted, exhibited their art, and socialized alongside other Surrealists in Paris, though neither was ever quite fully accepted into the group on account of their gender. Most women were relegated to the role of muse within these circles, representing the *femme-enfant* or "innocent woman" archetype with which Breton and his followers were transfixed. A precursor to the "manic pixie dreamgirl" trope of today, the *femme-enfant*'s youth was to be mooned over, her naïveté aspired to, her pure countenance captured in poetry and paint. She was not a creator herself though. And so Varo, Carrington, and other women involved in the Surrealist movement found themselves relegated to the fringes of the group by the fellows, allegedly loved but rarely lauded. As Carrington's cousin, Joanna Moorhead, put it: "[Women] might have been adored, cherished, and even, occasionally, listened to, but they were not powerful and they certainly were not equal players on the stage of Surrealism." Mexico City may not have been the center of the art world that Paris or New York City was, but it provided sanctuary from war, not to mention from the male egos that dominated the European Surrealist scene. Here, Varo and Carrington could make their work in relative peace and heed the call of their own muses.

Over the course of their friendship, they realized that it was not only Surrealist sensibilities that they shared: both were raised

Catholic, and rebelled against a restrictive upbringing as children. They also discovered that they both had a deep interest in magic of all stripes, which they began incorporating into their artwork in different, albeit complementary, ways.

For each woman, a fascination with the esoteric began in childhood. Carrington grew up listening to Celtic stories and myths from her mother, grandmother, and nanny. Her grandmother was from Ireland, and she told young Leonora that their family was directly descended from a race of Irish fairy people called the Sidhe (the same beings that Pamela Colman Smith believed she could see). One of Carrington's early homes was in Lancashire, not far from where the Pendle witch trials took place in 1612, and she was influenced by those accounts as well. She also had her own supernatural experiences that impacted her worldview. According to Aberth: "Carrington remember[ed] as a small child seeing ghosts and being afraid, but also seeing 'visions' that were amusing, such as one where a wild tortoise would sometimes cross her path or a large cat would sit in an empty dog kennel." Elements of all of these otherworldly influences can be seen in her work.

Varo used fantastical stories—both the reading and the writing of them—as an escape from the strict and oppressive Catholic education that her mother foisted upon her. "She read Alexandre Dumas, Jules Verne, and Edgar Allan Poe, as well as literature of mysticism and Eastern thought," relays Janet A. Kaplan, who then goes on to describe a note Varo secretly wrote to a Hindu to obtain some mandrake root "because she had heard that it had magical properties."

In Mexico City, Varo and Carrington met up nearly every day and exchanged ideas about magic, consciousness, and spirituality.

They read widely, and over the years their esoteric interests ran the gamut, including research into alchemy, Kabbalah, the I-Ching, astrology, sacred geometry, legends of the Holy Grail, Sufi mysticism, Tibetan Tantra, and Zen Buddhism, as well as the writings of Carl Jung, Robert Graves, Helena Blavatsky, and Meister Eckhart. They also attended meetings of the followers of mystics G. I. Gurdjieff and P. D. Ouspensky.

Books about witchcraft and the occult had particular interest to them. Carrington was a friend of the Surrealist artist Kurt Seligmann, and a great admirer of his 1948 book *The Mirror of Magic.* Grillot de Givry's *A Pictorial Anthology of Witchcraft, Magic, and Alchemy* of 1958 was another influence. And the burgeoning modern witchcraft movement being led in England by Gerald Gardner was also appealing to them both. After reading one of his books (presumably *Witchcraft Today*, 1954), Varo wrote the following in a letter addressed to him:

> . . . [W]e—that is, Mrs. Carrington and some other people— have devoted ourselves to searching for facts and data that are still preserved in remote areas that participate in the true practice of witchcraft. . . . Also, and after long years of experimentation, I am now able to organize in an optimal way the little solar systems in the home, I've understood the objects' interdependence and the necessity of placing them in a certain manner so as to avoid catastrophes, or of suddenly changing their placement to provoke acts necessary for the common good.

Varo then goes on to ask Gardner's advice regarding how to use the fresh lava from a tiny volcano that has sprung up in her friend's courtyard. She closes by saying that she'd love to talk to him about other topics, including their shared interest in trying to use witchcraft to counteract the hydrogen bomb.

Both she and Carrington engaged in all kinds of creative activities that blurred the line between art and magic. Together they wrote recipes or spells for such things as "scaring away inopportune dreams, insomnia, and deserts of quicksand under the bed" and "to stimulate a dream of being the king of England." Janet Kaplan lists the ingredients Varo wrote down for a spell "to stimulate erotic dreams," which includes "a kilo of strong roots, three white hens, a head of garlic, four kilos of honey, a mirror, two calf livers, a brick, two clothespins, a corset with stays, two false mustaches, and hats to taste."

Certainly there is much humor and Surrealist whimsy imbued in these writings. But their esoteric practice was a commitment the women kept throughout their lives. Carrington created a spell for Varo to protect her against the evil eye. She also became a magical mentor to filmmaker Alejandro Jodorowsky during his artistically formative years. In his book *The Spiritual Journey of Alejandro Jodorowsky*, he recounts the rituals and spells that they did together involving sugar skulls, blood, and hair clippings, though he is an unreliable, if wonderfully evocative, narrator. (They also staged a play of hers in Mexico City called *Penelope*.) Varo's reference to the "little solar systems" of interdependent objects that she made in her home in her letter to Gardner denotes not only an intellectual interest in magic, but the practice of actual magic itself. As Teresa Arcq writes, "Magic formed a fundamental part of the daily lives of Varo and Carrington; the very practice of painting was viewed as a magical act. Varo liked to play with the notion that she was a sorceress and even came up with her own magical phrase: *gurnar kur kar kar.*" Varo also surrounded herself with special stones and crystals whenever she sat down to create. Both Carrington and Varo became involved with reading the tarot, in Varo's case scribbling notes all over each card of her deck regarding how to interpret them, and in Carrington's case creating her own painted deck, some of which was exhibited for the first time in Mexico City's Modern Art Museum in 2018. They also frequented local vendors and often went to the Mercado de Sonora (known as the Witchcraft Market), where they obtained herbs and other supplies for their magical concoctions.

The poet Octavio Paz wrote of these women: "There are in Mexico, two admirable artists, two enchanted sorceresses. . . ." As to whether or not Carrington and Varo truly considered themselves to be witches, evidence points strongly to the affirmative, though there don't seem to be first-person accounts of them using words like *witch* or *bruja* publicly as self-descriptors. (To do so would no doubt have been risky then, as it still can be now.)

Aberth suggests, in regard to Carrington at least, that her artwork speaks for itself. In *Abraxas Journal* #6, she writes, "Within Carrington's oeuvre . . . there is a distinctive strain of works that elevate art-making to magical practice, where the canvas becomes a receptacle into which she channels her fiery energy—these are what I call her 'invocation' pieces." These pieces, Aberth theorizes, are meant to be active conjuration devices, perhaps created to bring about change in the life of Carrington or in the lives of those she cared about. One such untitled 1969 painting of hers features a shrouded female apparition standing in a magic circle. Four white lemur-looking creatures stand guard at each of the four corners outside the circle, representing the four directions or four elements, which are invoked during modern witchcraft rituals. The female figure holds another of these creatures in a maternal, even Marian, embrace, and a ghostly white serpent spirals around her body, most likely symbolizing goddess power and the knowledge of Eve, and perhaps also the kundalini energy of Hindu tradition. Rings of concentric circles ripple out from her upper half, some filled with wavy lines that represent water. There are other symbols at the top of the painting: various animals both real and mythic, a black moon, and a white sun. And at the bottom is a dead white dove, its heart exposed, with its blood dripping out the phrase "2nd Oct 1968." Beneath the sacrificial bird, Carrington has scrawled in mirror-writing her own variation of Psalm 137 of the Bible, with a reference to Yggdrasil, the Norse "world tree," replacing the usual Zion.

As Aberth points out, October 2, 1968, was the day of the Tlatelolco massacre, during which hundreds of students and civilians were slaughtered in a Mexico City public square by the military and police. This event was particularly horrifying to Carrington, who had two sons who were students, and she left shortly thereafter for New York City, where this painting was made. The piece is definitely mournful and cathartic, but it also feels protective. The mother figure and her creature-child are sealed within circles of safety. The whole work can be seen as a painted spell for Carrington to shelter the young from harm.

While Varo's pieces are perhaps not as blatant as Carrington's in regard to their literally transformational intent, her magical activities and talismanic object arrangements, plus her frequent use of her own visage in depictions of magic-workers, point at the very least to her strong identification *with* the witch, if not *as* a witch. Another of my favorite paintings is her *Witch Going to the Sabbath* of 1957. It's a distinctly ovular, blue-faced female portrait, with folds of fabric arranged to evoke a vaginal opening. As such it is reminiscent of the Virgin of Guadalupe iconography that is seen throughout Mexico to this day. Varo's holy lady, however, has black-stockinged feet, a feathery familiar in one hand, and a crystalline green gemstone in the other. And most notably, this titular witch has a mane of wavy red hair, as did Varo herself.

Carrington and Varo were not only painting the *femme-sorcière*, they were embodying her. And with each picture they made of magical women, they were becoming more skilled as conjurors themselves. Neither of them had a hooked nose or stringy silver hair or a bent back. Nor do they seem to have been particularly interested in the female form as an object of desire, either in their work or in their own lives (when a young Leonora Carrington showed up naked to a Surrealist gathering in Paris, it seemed to have been more for shock value than seduction). Though they sometimes show bare breasts or, more occasionally, full nudity in their paintings, these are generally cast in an empowered light: the female form as a conductor of the divine.

It's true that neither of them publicly proclaimed to be a practitioner or adherent of any particular occult sect. Yet I consider them both witches in conduct and construct, and I believe they would be tickled to hear it. They were bewitchingly beautiful people, not just in appearance, but because they were the masters of their own lives and architects of their own creative cosmos. Their work is steeped in images of kitchens and cauldrons and laboratories and labyrinths: magical stand-ins for the metamorphic interior spaces they occupied both physically and psychically. And in putting themselves in their paintings, whether through blatant portraiture or chimeric avatars, they demonstrated that their personal stories were worthy of attentiveness and attention; their own biographies were, quite literally, works of art. Survivors of the atrocities of war, and refugees in a country far away from their homelands, they remade themselves, healed, and infused their creations with hope in turn. They were searching for enlightenment through their research, and they visualized a better existence through their work. They scaled the peaks of esoteric knowledge, and tried to reach the summit of spiritual truth. I don't know if they ever got there.

But in these two artists, I found my own witchly godmothers, who not only did spells but crafted entire worlds where their individual visions were viable and valued. I can't think of two people who have better modeled such deep devotion to wisdom, to skill, to friendship, to making the planet a more magical place. They continue to be twin stars for me, marking true north. They've touched me. And so I'm transformed.

Thankfully, I'm far from the only person who has felt this way. Carrington's first retrospective was at the University of Texas at Austin's University Art Museum in 1976, and she would witness many more such exhibitions before she passed in 2011 at the age of ninety-four. In 2016, I had the great honor of showing her piece *El Nigromante* (or *The Conjurer*) at the *Language of the Birds: Occult in Art* exhibition that I curated for NYU. As I stood in front of this magnificent magician image day after day, I contemplated its maker. It pleased me to know that she had enjoyed some acclaim while she was alive. She had survived such hardship, and alchemized it into beauty. And she lived to see her work be internationally recognized, even adored.

Sadly, Varo wasn't quite so lucky. She died of a heart attack in 1963 when she was only fifty-four, so she didn't get to see the first major exhibition of her work in the year 2000 at Washington, DC's National Museum of Women in the Arts. I was fortunate enough to visit this show later that year when it traveled to Chicago's Mexican Fine Arts Center Museum (now the National Museum of Mexican Art), and back then it felt like a once-in-a-lifetime experience. Instead, it was the start of a new chapter in Varo's story, if a posthumous one, as her work has gone on to blossom in popularity. This painter of secret chambers is obscure no more.

Today, nearly twenty years after I made that pilgrimage to Chicago, interest in both Varo's and Carrington's art has skyrocketed. The current flurry of exhibitions, publications of their writings, and spate of accompanying scholarship is wonderful to watch. It ensures that many others will be spellbound by these artists for generations to come.

EACH OF THE five women above represents a different branch on the magico-artistic family tree. They share strong spiritual roots, though, and they are part of a witchly creative lineage that has flourished despite the hardships of war, sexism, materialism, and financial duress. These visionaries read books and signs, engaged in cosmic communiqués. They didn't exist merely to inspire the men around them. They followed their own mysterious muses and hoped their art would inspire others to join them in the pursuit of the numinous. Whether we consider the phantom graffiti of

Georgiana Houghton and Hilma af Klint, the soothsaying symbolism of Pamela Colman Smith, or the marvelous crossbred mythologies of Remedios Varo and Leonora Carrington, we are confronted with art that isn't meant to merely be regarded. Their work will awaken us and rearrange us, if we let it.

These women taught me the true significance of the word *craft*. That it's used in reference to both making art and doing magic is no coincidence, for engaging in either act is to do similar things. Artists use the power of imagination to create pieces that shift consciousness, thereby changing both the maker and the viewer. By the same token, I've learned that the most potent spells are the most personal ones, with our own added artistry and symbolic embellishments.

In witchcraft, one swirls together the elements of attention and intention, discipline and devotion. The witch attempts to pull invisible forces into reality. I can't say for sure how these five artists would have felt about being called witches. I believe that, at the very least, they would be glad to know their work is being seen and appreciated as transfixing and transformative. Still, they conjure for me a new image of what a witch can be, and in crafting their magical masterpieces, they rendered themselves visible in turn.

Chapter 7

POWER IN NUMBERS: COVENS AND COLLECTIVES

Throughout my teens and most of my twenties, I was what is known in the witchcraft community as a "solitary practitioner." My magic-making wasn't hidden per se, just private—a quietly glimmering tapestry I wove between my own walls. Occasionally I would do a spell or blessing in the presence of another, but only when I felt certain that it would be received with tenderness and not put me in any sort of social danger. Having the label of "witch" was certainly far safer at the turn of the twenty-first century in coastal America than it was in prior eras or other locales; still, I kept it close to my chest.

It wasn't simply a matter of reputation or fear of people's misperceptions that kept me flying solo for so long. The idea of connecting to like-minded people unnerved me too. I worried that they would be too flaky or too corny or too serious or not serious enough.

Besides, I prided myself on not being a joiner. My life up to that point had been a string of teams I quit, clubs I balked at, gym memberships I refused to sign up for, and work meetings I gritted my teeth through. The thought of a group of people getting together to hold hands and sing earnestly in one another's faces made me want to cut my own head off. I was fine getting my witch on without anybody watching.

But what I came to realize was that all of my resistance and bluster was a mask I'd worn for most of my life, and it was growing flimsy. I was actually afraid of exposing my own soft, spiritual underbelly. Engaging in shared emotional work in any field is an exercise in vulnerability, and for metaphysical work this is especially true. Rituals entail making noise or sitting in total silence, both potentially terrifying when done in the presence of other humans. They involve doing things like swaying, dancing, or waving strange objects in the air. They have you speaking to beings or entities that can't be seen, sometimes even serenading them. If a witch chants in a forest but no one is around to hear her, does she make a sound? A group of witches *definitely* does, and they can certainly hear one another, regardless of whether or not the spirits do.

To practice in a group requires both a loosening of self-consciousness and a tightening grip on the rudder of sincerity. You have to *care*, and you have to let others see you caring. And you have to bear witness to their caring in turn.

You will most likely grow to care about *them*. And heaven forfend, you may even allow them to care about you too.

When we decide to be part of any community, we are making a commitment to literally be there for ourselves and for each other. Once you've identified a group that you may want to be part of—and that group has signaled that you are indeed invited to join them—the next step you take is to simply show up. Doing so may feel daunting. For in that moment, you are choosing to say, "Here I am," and for many of us that is a scary prospect. It means we have to be present and accountable to other people. It means admitting that we aren't getting everything we need on our own, and letting go of our postures of pretending that we know everything or that we're self-sufficient.

It may also mean that we feel we have something to contribute— and that's scary to admit sometimes too. What if we're wrong? Or even worse—what if we're right? What if people start counting on us to keep being there? We're busy, after all. Don't they know how busy we are?

And finally, showing up is a gesture of trust, no matter how tenuous. We have to trust that, even if we look foolish or uncool or seem awkward or make mistakes, it will be okay. We have to dare to believe that we are good enough as we are, and that the people we form an alliance with are good enough for us too.

I WAS TWENTY-EIGHT years old, and things were going in a promising enough direction. I had a solid corporate job, a great group of friends, and a wonderful boyfriend named Matt who, unbeknownst to me then, would become my husband. My creative life was starting to take off. I started *Phantasmaphile*, a tiny corner of the Internet where I blogged about art I dug that had a fantastical or magical bent to it. And I had just joined a Brooklyn collective called Observatory. At our humble one-room space, we took turns curating events and art exhibitions about arcane and unusual topics, and I was the resident occultist. I had no problem being public about my interest in magic as a concept.

But my belief in magic as a guiding force of my life? That felt like something one didn't talk about in mixed company. Matt and my closest confidantes were aware of my thaumaturgical thinking to some extent. But I otherwise kept it largely under wraps, my own clandestine oculus I'd peer through only when I was sure that no one else was staring back.

For a while, that was sufficient.

And then one day, it wasn't. I can't pinpoint the exact moment; I just know that one season I suddenly started shedding my skin, wriggling out of my old sleeve of being so I could better extend my limbs.

Up until that point, most everything I knew about witch-craft I'd learned from reading. Say what you will about witches, but we are a literary bunch. Witch tales often feature dusty old tomes and wordy scrolls stained by time and tea. My own library of spells and esoterica had outgrown my shelves, and my drawers were overflowing with journals and papers scribbled with notes about things I'd learned. My spiritual guides weren't just those on the ethereal plane. They were also the searching writers who came before me, and put line after line down on paper: a trail of lettered bread crumbs that I followed with gratitude.

But in the summer of 2009, I found myself pining for more: a teacher, a group, a tribe. A space where I could bloom and find belonging. I felt a call to "Find the others," as Timothy Leary famously said, though in my case I was seeking those both like me and not like me. People who knew more, who knew differently. Who would help me wind my own way through the vast, wild wood.

What I was looking for, I realized, was a coven.

Okay then. But were those even real?

How does one find such a thing? And once you do, how do you know if it's the *right* coven? And all of that is a rather moot point, to be sure, if the coven in question doesn't covet you back.

It seemed I was going to need some help.

To complete most of my spells, I usually leave an offering at a beloved tree in my neighborhood. Its trunk splits into three large branches, so it makes me think of a crossroads or triple goddess. I call it my Hecate Tree. It's relatively out in the open, on a street I don't live on, in front of a brownstone I don't live in. It is one of many trees on the block, and the usual passerby probably wouldn't single it out as particularly remarkable, other than the occasional ensorcelled remains I leave behind. But it does the job insofar as it is a beautiful bit of nature to which I feel a distinct link. I know it as a holy, friendly place, and it knows me now too.

This isn't where I found myself walking to on that summer evening though. I was asking for something that felt larger, so I needed to make a grander gesture. Spellwork is a relationship, and it demands an exchange. What you get out of it is what you put into it, and this time, I knew I had to go farther than my usual route.

And so, that July evening, I found myself on a magic mission to Prospect Park with a Tupperware full of flower petals and a batch of big wishes.

I walked past the playground and the band shell and the dog beach and the baseball fields and entered its arboreal heart. I finally stopped at a shady clearing that looks as if it's out of a Camelot tale or a Thomas Cole painting. Most people don't associate New York City with waterfalls, but there are actually a few truly lovely ones tucked away if you know where to find them. I arrived at this urban idyll, a paved bridge of a sort surrounded on all sides by old foliage and solemn stones and the sound of a great churning.

I stood in silence, matching my breathing to the air, slipping into that level of consciousness that feels rooted in the present but splendidly endless. My lids were shut, and I cast off, ready to be heard. I made my motions, gave my words over to the water, then took fistfuls of petals and let them fall too. If there is indeed a Goddess, I believe she dwells there, and was pleased by my entreaty or at least filled with sweet pity. When you send out a great call, how do you know if it is Spirit or nature that answers? Maybe there's no difference at all. Maybe grace is green.

When I was done, the park felt as if it had slid into another dimension, gentler but somehow also more alive, as if millions of tiny eyes had suddenly fluttered open. Mystics have identified some locations as "thin places"—spots that seem as if they exist between the earthly and spiritual realms. I think this sylvan sliver of Brooklyn would make their list. During those long minutes when I wandered back in the direction of home, the park felt somehow lifted, shifted, and perennially dusk-lit.

The next day I went to work, same building as always, same cubicle per usual. But something in me felt changed and expectant. I went out on my lunch break, walking through SoHo, sensing some sort of pull eastward. Past Sixth Avenue, past Thompson, past Wooster, past Mercer. Left turn on Broadway. Right on Spring.

And then I found myself entering the Open Center, an educational space dedicated to holistic healing and alternative thought.

Their small bookshop had been a great resource for me in the past, but this time, I didn't quite know what I was looking for.

"Do you have any books on witchcraft?" I asked the man working there.

"Well," he said, "we don't like to call it that here." He lowered his voice. "But we do have a teacher who I think fits the bill. You'll find her classes listed in our catalog under 'Herbalism,' but she is definitely a witch." And he placed one of her books in my hand.

This wasn't the answer that I had in mind. I tried to be thoughtful about what I put into my body, sure, but my interest in herbs was minimal at best. I barely cooked, my apartment had no outdoor space—let alone a garden—and I was hardly the Birkenstock-wearing sort. Still, I sensed that this was a message worth paying attention to. I didn't know where it would lead me. Only that I was intrigued enough to take a step in the direction I was being pointed.

And so I started studying with Robin Rose Bennett, the Green Witch of New York City.

First, it was months of classes at the center: *The Art of Herbal Medicine Making. Healing Spices. Herbs for the Nervous and Digestive Systems.* All were hugely informative regarding various plants' effects on human physiology, and each was also laced with Robin's own brand of plant spirit teachings. Her classes weren't lectures. Rather, they were interactive sessions filled with hands-on medicine making, explorations of each plant's energy, poetic riffs on tree and flower magic, and even an occasional song. I was loving what I was learning, but I was also moved by the other students, who were all different ages and from a variety of backgrounds, but who shared a desire to live in more mindful, earth-centric ways. I felt as if my seams were being stitched back together, and old, forgotten wounds got sealed back up with honey. It was a homecoming, and I knew that I was here to stay.

One day in class, Robin mentioned that she ran a private apprenticeship circle: a group of women she would take under her wing for a period of three years. "You have to write a statement of intent if you are interested in applying," she said. "I only have thirteen women per circle." It would begin in the spring of 2010. This was the coven I had been searching for. I felt it in my herbally fortified bones. The spell had worked.

I sometimes call those three years my stint in "Witch Scouts," because it felt a bit like being in a wilderness troop. We learned to forage for herbs in parks and on sidewalks. We went on long treks through the woods, and identified different flowers, ferns, and fungi. We learned how to make tinctures, infusions, and salves; which leaves stop a bug bite from itching; which herbs to drink in order to soothe anxiety or keep blood sugar levels steady.

But much of our work was also supernatural. We cast magic circles. We meditated. We communed with plant guides. We honored the moon. We did rituals to mark the seasons, as well as milestones in each apprentice's life. Robin was our leader, but every one of us got our moment to be in the center. We took turns holding space for each other, bearing witness to each woman's growth and unfolding. We shared our stories with one another, and whatever we brought to circle was received without judgment. It was a container that could hold anything, and anyone. We were a diverse group, varied in our bodies and our life experiences. But we were linked beneath it all, our own mycelial network.

Over those three years, I saw the other women change. I

watched them grow stronger, get louder, start to heal. And I began to develop a different sort of power myself: the kind that comes with letting down defenses and letting go. I broadened my concept of who I was. I could be independent and interdependent. Unique and united. I could be part of something and still be whole.

MOST DICTIONARIES STATE that the word *coven* comes from the Latin *convenire* or "to come together," and is related to the word *convene*. It was brought into popular vernacular by the infamous scholar Margaret Murray, whose 1921 book *The Witch-Cult in Western Europe* posited that many of the "confessions" of alleged witches during the trials should be taken at face value and that the accused were in fact members of an ancient fertility cult. About the word *coven* itself, Murray writes, "The special meaning of the word among the witches is a 'band' or 'company' who were set apart for the practice of the rites of the religion and for the performance of magical ceremonies; in short, a kind of priesthood."

She also wrote extensively about "the persistence of the number thirteen in the Covens," citing transcripts of various witch trial confessions and cataloging examples of thirteen-person witch groups in the appendix of her book. One of her primary resources is the transcript of Isobel Gowdie, a Scottish woman who confessed to being a witch in 1662 and supplied her accusers with many details about her practices, including the statement that "Ther ar threttein persons in ilk Coeven." As Murray saw it, Gowdie and the other accused witches were simply recounting the facts about an old religion that the Church was trying desperately to snuff out.

Murray believed that at one time, this witch religion—or

"Dianic cult," as she called it—worshipped a deity that could take on the form of women, men, and beasts. She theorized that in medieval times, it was most often a man dressed as an animal who would represent the god during the witches' rituals. He was the leader of the coven, and she surmised that it was this figure who was rebranded as "the devil" by the Catholic Church. She believed that a typical public gathering was called a *Sabbath* and this was "possibly a derivative of *s'esbattre*, 'to frolic'; a very suitable description of the joyous gaiety of the meetings." The coven, by her estimation, was made up of those thirteen individuals who led the rituals for the wider community. More private rites were carried out during what she referred to as an *Esbat*, which she described as a more exclusive meeting for the coven alone. Their chief festivals happened at the cross-quarter days, which she referred to as May Eve, November Eve, Candlemas Day, and Lammas Day. Practices included feasting, dancing, sexual rites, sacrifices, and prayers to their deity to bring fertility to their community.

In academic and Pagan circles alike, Murray has become a controversial figure, for her research has been widely discredited. Though her book is heavily footnoted, with many excerpts of trial confessions included throughout to "prove" her hypotheses, several scholars over the years have accused her of cherry-picking the examples that supported her theories and disregarding the rest. She has also been criticized for treating the trial transcripts as reliable source material in the first place, since so many of the confessions were obtained under torture and extreme psychological duress, and recorded by untrustrworthy scribes. Because of this, her ideas about the existence of real witch-cults in early modern Europe have been largely written off.

Still, her impact on the collective conception about witches and covens cannot be overstated. In 1929, she wrote the entry on witchcraft for the *Encyclopedia Britannica* and incorporated her theories into it as if they were facts. This remained unchanged until 1969, essentially defining witch history for two generations of English-speaking people based on her own imaginings. Murray's second book, *The God of the Witches*, was aimed at a more general audience when it was published in 1933. This book expanded her ideas, toned down some of the more gruesome aspects of *Witch-Cult* to make the cult's practices more palatable, and delved deeper into exploring what she called the Horned God, which she believed was a male deity that had been worshipped cross-culturally since the Paleolithic Age. Pan and the Christian devil were just two examples of this, according to her thinking.

While it's true that both *The Witch-Cult in Western Europe* and *The God of the Witches* fizzled out rather quickly when they first appeared on the scene, they each got a second life when they were republished after World War II. The concept of "reviving" or "reconstructing" British Pagan traditions had been slowly gaining popularity in the decades prior. But after the devastation of the war, appetite for books like Murray's exploded, as a reeling nation looked for ways to heal and reassert its identity and ideals. In the late 1940s, Murray's romantic vision of nature-worshipping witches found renewed interest and a much larger audience, and *The God of the Witches* became a best seller. That the inner sanctum of academia had discounted Murray's ideas didn't seem to matter, for her writing had already captured the public's imagination, including that of the man who would become the founding father of modern witchcraft, Gerald Gardner.

★   ★   ★

IF MARGARET MURRAY planted one of the witchcraft revival's largest seeds, then Gardner was one of its primary cultivators. The origin story of the modern religion of Wicca is nebulous, but there is no doubt that Gardner was its primary steward, if not its outright inventor.

Gardner was a former owner or manager of tea and rubber plantations throughout the English colonies of Ceylon, North Borneo, and Malaya. He was also fascinated with mysticism and studied the magic of local communities where he was living, as well as the various systems of Freemasonry, Spiritualism, and other occult systems à la mode. Additionally, he was an avid antiquarian and had an extensive collection of weapons and artifacts, with a preponderance of ritual knives.

He retired to London in 1936 at the age of fifty-two, but in 1938 he and his wife moved to Highcliffe, near Engand's New Forest, to protect his collection of antiques against looming war. He stated that he was inducted into the New Forest coven in the nearby town of Christchurch in 1939 by a woman he called Old Dorothy Clutterbuck (the veracity of which has since been debated, as there is scant evidence that the real Dorothy Clutterbuck, a wealthy local, was a magic practitioner). Nonetheless, his involvement with witchcraft deepened over the next several years.

One remarkable story about this time is that of "Operation Cone of Power," a ritual that Gardner's coven allegedly participated in after France fell to the Nazis in 1940. Concerned that England would be next in the line of attack, the witches gathered in the forest on August 1—the Pagan holy day, Lammas—to raise a cone of magically charged energy for the purpose of thwarting Hitler. According to Gardner, they raised a cone four times that night, and projected the thoughts *You cannot cross the sea* and *Not able to come* into Hitler's mind. He also said that the exertion of dancing and chanting for hours naked in the cold proved too much for some of the witches, causing a few of the elders to die a few days later. The operation was otherwise effective by his estimation. As he later wrote coyly in his 1954 book *Witchcraft Today*, "I am not saying that they stopped Hitler. All I say is that I saw a very interesting ceremony performed with the intention of putting a certain idea into his mind, and this was repeated several times afterwards; and though all the invasion barges were ready, the fact was that Hitler never even tried to come."

How Gardner went from a coven member to the father of Wicca is a tangled tale that's too long to recount in detail here. Suffice it to say, he was greatly influenced by other magically concerned writers of his day. His first two books, *A Goddess Arrives* (1940) and *High Magic's Aid* (1949), were witchcraft-themed novels, the latter of which included fictionalized accounts of the rituals he was doing with his own coven, many of them clear adaptations of Margaret Murray's theories into story form. Gardner also met with the controversial occultist Aleister Crowley several times in May of 1947. It seems that Gardner was considered a likely successor to lead the Ordo Templi Orientis (or OTO), the magical initiatory society of which Crowley was the head and Gardner was also a member. These plans never came to pass, however, and when Crowley died in December of that year, Gardner was otherwise preoccupied.

During the latter half of the 1940s, Gardner kept a private book in which he wrote down rituals, readings, and other instructions for his own form of witchcraft to be practiced by his coven. His Book of Shadows, as he called it, was a veritable mash-up of other texts, including "biblical verses, the Mathers edition of the *Key of Solomon*, the *Goetia*, a work on the cabbala, three different books by Crowley, the Waite-Smith tarot pack, and one or two unidentified grimoires," according to Ronald Hutton. Charles Godfrey Leland's 1899 book *Aradia, or the Gospel of the Witches* was borrowed from as well. Gardner's own contributions were an emphasis on nudity—he was a big proponent of "naturism," or being naked outdoors as a therapeutic means for keeping the body healthy—as well as the use of physical binding and flagellating to purify the coven members and induce ecstatic states, though he insisted these not be too painful. The Book of Shadows was added to and edited into the 1950s and it ultimately evolved to become more egalitarian. Where his early writings presumed a male "magus" would be initiating a female "witch" into the coven, later amendments have a high priestess and high priest conducting rites at the same level, as well as more language about goddesses and feminine power.

Much has been made of the supposedly high kink quotient in some of Gardner's mystical rites. Not only were all of the practices supposed to be done in the nude and with such accoutrements as ropes and knives, but intercourse itself was considered the Great Rite, either done literally or represented symbolically. Whether or not these practices were the personal expression of a randy senior citizen, the evolved acts of sexual liberation between consenting adults, or merely time-tested physiological techniques for raising blood flow and inducing trance states, depends on your point of view. Gardner himself wrote that he didn't "think it fair to call

witches disappointed perverts. They may truly be said to be followers of a primitive religion, already disappearing. . . ."

Thanks in large part to the Spiritualist community, England's
Witchcraft Act of 1735 and Vagrancy Act of 1824 were both
repealed in 1951 and replaced by the less harsh Fraudulent Mediums Act, which essentially legalized witchcraft and mediumship,
so long as they weren't being used to deceive paying customers.
(This is one of the reasons you'll often see any sort of spiritual
services or items sold with the disclaimer "For Entertainment
Purposes Only.") With the passing of this legislation, Gardner
felt emboldened to become more public with his interests, if not
his outright beliefs. His 1954 book *Witchcraft Today* was his first
published nonfiction work. In it, he recounts his experiences of
witnessing the modern practice of this "primitive religion" of
witchcraft. He uses the word *Wica* (spelled as such) for the first
time in print, saying it means "wise people" and refers to those
"who practice the age-old rites." (This was later adapted to *Wicca*,
though Gardner didn't use that term himself to describe his new-
old religion.) He also echoes much of Margaret Murray's writings,
saying that the concept of the satanic witch was a result of a smear
campaign by the Church: "Witches do not kiss the Devil's posterior, first because they never kiss anyone's posterior, and, secondly,
because the Devil is never there for anyone to kiss."

In regard to covens, he writes that they traditionally consist of
"twelve witches and a leader, probably because it is a lucky number and because there are thirteen moons in a year." He goes on
to state that an ideal coven consists of "six perfect couples" plus
the priest or priestess, and that the couples should be husbands
and wives or at least betrothed. Certainly by today's standards,

this comes across as jarringly heteronormative and old-fashioned. But in the 1950s, to put women on equal footing with men in any regard, whether spiritually, socially, or sexually, was quite progressive. And just as significantly, Wicca's worship of both a god and a goddess was truly revolutionary from the perspective of Western religious history.

Gardner's writings about working magic in a group are also striking. In *Witchcraft Today*, he describes a witch as someone who can stimulate or even create more of his or her aura or personal electromagnetic field. And he says that when witches work together, "their united wills can project this as a beam of force. . . ." Later in the text, he uses the anti-Hitler "Operation Cone of Power" ritual as an example of this (though he refers to it here as an operation called Sending Forth). This gathering was an exception to the thirteen-member rule, he says, because they needed as many people as possible to do such a large working.

There is much about this book I find endearing, yet it is also factually muddled. Margaret Murray wrote the introduction for it, saying that the rites therein are "a true survival and not a mere revival copied out of books." It's an ironic claim, considering that we now know that many of Gardner's practices were based on precisely that sort of cutting and pasting from a variety of sources, including Murray's own writings. Furthermore, throughout *Witchcraft Today*, Gardner assumes an objective, outsider's tone. The witches are described as "they" rather than "we," and he positions himself as a witness, rather than a participant, or even an active creator of said "traditions." Only near the end of the book does he say, "I am a humble member of a coven, I am not its head or leader in any way, and I have to do what I am told."

I bring all of this up not in order to reject the importance of Gardner's vast contribution to religious life. The fact is that he was a profoundly progressive, wildly inventive human being, and he opened a tributary of alternative spirituality that continues to inspire people, including me, to this day. While he was certainly borrowing heavily from other writers—some of whom, like Margaret Murray, were subject to their own flights of fancy—I believe that *he* believed that he was truly tapping into an ancient vein of lost wisdom. By synthesizing an impressive amount of scholarship, sentiment, and self-experimentation, Gardner and his cohorts essentially took the practices of earlier secret societies including Freemasonry, the Hermetic Order of the Golden Dawn, and the OTO, and revamped them with an eye toward an idealized Pagan past free of sexual hang-ups and patriarchal oppression.

And regardless of Gardner's original intentions, the work that he and his coven did helped catalyze a movement. The plot of the Wicca and Modern Paganism story takes many twists and turns beyond his output, and, to his great credit, he encouraged people to adapt and add to his own ideas. (In fact, his coven's high priestess, Doreen Valiente, is responsible for penning many of Wicca's most famous and divinely feminine incantations, including a rewrite of what is now commonly known as "The Charge of the Goddess." Feminist witchcraft leader Starhawk's rewrite of the rewrite from the 1970s is perhaps the best-known version.) Covens of all types popped up throughout England and America during the 1960s and '70s, with new styles and leaders following suit. Witchcraft was reframed as a practice that was alive and accessible to anyone who felt drawn to learn it.

Most significantly of all, Gardner further cemented two crucial ideas into popular consciousness: First, that witches are positive and holy beings, not diabolical at all. And second, that their powers increase when working with other like-minded—or like-spirited—individuals, and that this pooled transformative energy can be directed toward achieving a shared goal.

IT'S TRUE THAT during Gardner's time, at least, Wiccan covens seemed to be primarily concerned with honoring nature and its deities, as well as overseeing each member's individual magical development. Of more outward, politically minded rituals done by witches in his day, "Operation Cone of Power," is the one that is most usually cited, presumably because he wrote about it himself. That said, he does end *Witchcraft Today* by surmising, "I think [witches] could perform similar rites to influence the brains of those who may control the Hydrogen Bomb." It's unclear whether or not he and his coven later attempted to do such a working.

Still, Gardner's model of a group of people pooling their magical energy and directing it toward a shared political goal was adopted by the countercultural movement in the United States, albeit in a manner that was as cheeky as it was purposeful.

A demonstration in protest of the Vietnam War was planned at the Lincoln Memorial for the fall of 1967. Activists Jerry Rubin and Abbie Hoffman decided this was the perfect opportunity for an even bigger spectacle. Hoffman had already been making a name for himself as a trickster who used elements of absurdism and guerrilla theater to bring attention to sociopolitical causes and disrupt the status quo. Inspired in part by the Gary Snyder poem "A Curse on the Men in Washington, Pentagon," Rubin and

Hoffman realized that doing a magic ritual would make people sit up and take notice. They decided to oversee a mass exorcism of the Pentagon, followed by a collective working to levitate it twenty-two feet off the ground (though the government ended up giving them a permit for only ten feet). They enlisted Ed Sanders, frontman of the mystically leaning New York City protest band the Fugs, to help lead the exorcism. Sanders in turn consulted with underground filmmaker and all-around occult expert Harry Smith to craft the ritual.

Word spread about the plan, and it was certainly a draw for some of the estimated 100,000 protestors who showed up in Washington, DC, on October 21, 1967. After music and speeches, the march went from the Lincoln Memorial across the Potomac River via the Arlington Memorial Bridge, past the Arlington National Cemetery, and down to the Pentagon. There, in the North Parking Lot, Ed Sanders and the Fugs performed their exorcism from a flatbed truck. As Sanders told *Arthur* magazine in 2004: "[Harry Smith] told me about consecrating the four directions, surrounding it, circling it, using elements of earth, air, fire and water, alchemical symbols to purify the place, to invoke certain deities, and so on. So I sing-songed a whole retinue of deities past and present, imaginary and real, to summon the strength to exorcise this place. It was part real, part symbolic, part wolf ticket, part spiritual, part secular, part wishful thinking and part anger. And it had humor. You gotta have the universal humor. And, since I knew Indo-European languages, I learned this Hittite exorcism ritual. I actually put together a decent exorcism."

The entire chant was eventually recorded under the title "Exorcising the Evil Spirits of the Pentagon, October 21, 1967," its crescendo a repetition of the phrase "Out, demons, out!" As part of the ritual, Sanders also announced that there would be a "grope-in," wherein couples would engage in a "rite of love" on the lawn—which did indeed take place, if in smaller numbers than the organizers perhaps originally envisioned. Hoffman hadn't been able to get a permit for protestors to encircle the Pentagon, which was to be a crucial component of levitating the building. But other actions took place, including Mayan healers sprinkling cornmeal in magic circles and the poet Allen Ginsberg uttering mantras. Occult filmmaker Kenneth Anger was also in attendance, though by his account he thought the others were "show-offs" creating more of a circus than a meaningful antiwar gesture. He chose to do his own spells rather than participate in the group activities.

All in all, the entire scene made quite an impression. As Norman Mailer described it in the chapter "The Witches and the Fugs" in his Pulitzer Prize–winning book *The Armies of the Night*: ". . . now the witches were here, and rites of exorcism, and black terrors of the night—hippies being murdered. Yes the hippies had gone from Tibet to Christ to the Middle Ages, now they were Revolutionary Alchemists. Well, thought Mailer, that was alright, he was a Left Conservative himself. 'Out, demons, out! Out, demons, out!'"

Certainly all of this spellcraft was as sensationalist as it was earnest, arguably more so. As to its efficacy, it would take another seven and a half years for the war to end. Still, many point to the march as a key element in raising public outcry. US military analyst Daniel Ellsberg said, "The idea of levitating the Pentagon struck me as a great idea because the idea of removing deference from any of these institutions is very, very important, and this is of course the kind of thing that Abbie [Hoffman] understood very instinctively." Ellsberg would go on to release *The Pentagon Papers* in 1971, four years after the protest, adding more pressure on the US government to pull out of Vietnam.

Even though the Pentagon may not have physically levitated, the spell still brought results. As Allen Ginsberg put it: "The levitation of the Pentagon was a happening that demystified the authority of the military. The Pentagon was symbolically levitated in people's minds in the sense that it lost its authority, which had been unquestioned and unchallenged until then."

Group ritual with a shared intention had shifted perceptions, then, if not literal foundations. Perhaps that was magic enough.

DURING THIS PERIOD, the women's movement was lifting off in the States. Abbie Hoffman and his band of tricksters would go on to call themselves the Yippies (their group was the Youth International Party, or YIP), and their activist theatrics continued, if not quite as obviously occult-themed. But another collective, this time made up of all women, took a page out of Hoffman's Pentagon protest playbook and continued to combine magical shenanigans with political intent. Robin Morgan, Florika Remetier, Naomi Jaffe, Peggy Dobbins, Judith Duffett, Bev Grant, Marcia Patrick, Cynthia Funk, and other former members of the New York Radical Women activist organization found the witch to be an ideal conduit for their message about female liberation. She was a symbol they could weaponize to illustrate the chronic pervasiveness of sexism through the ages and across various social spheres. She was also in keeping with the Yippies' effective approach of creating friction while having fun. After all, who better than a witch to cause a stir?

And so, with their first public action on Halloween of 1968, the feminist activist group called W.I.T.C.H. was born. Its members donned witch costumes, replete with brooms and pointy black hats, and did a public ritual performance of hexing the New York Stock Exchange. Did it work? Well, as Gloria Steinem wrote about the incident in *New York* magazine, "A coven of 13 members of W.I.T.C.H. demonstrates against that bastion of white supremacy: Wall Street. The next day, the market falls five points." (The glue that the witches added to the locks of the NYSE doors also added a bit of whammy, no doubt.)

Another noteworthy W.I.T.C.H. action was to disrupt the first annual Bridal Fair at Madison Square Garden in 1969 to fight what they perceived as the dark forces of the wedding industrial complex. A flyer announcing the protest invited the public to "Bring posters, brooms, costumes, consciousness, anger, witches' brew, love, bridal gowns, tambourines, hexes, laughter, solidarity, and alternatives. . . ." Several of the women infiltrated the convention, where they hexed the vendors and sponsors and let loose a flurry of white mice on the showroom floor.

W.I.T.C.H.'s activities gained traction thanks to its mix of witchy wit and gutsy political theatrics (as cofounder Robin Morgan wrote of the collective ". . . its insouciance was undeniable"). Soon, other W.I.T.C.H. groups sprang up around the country— and even as far away as Tokyo—though their operations varied. The acronym's meaning fluctuated, initially standing for "Women's International Terrorist Conspiracy from Hell," a tongue-in-cheek title created before the word *terrorist* held the weighty connotation it does now. Later iterations included "Women Incensed at Telephone Company Harassment," "Women Interested in

Toppling Consumption Holidays," and "Women Inspired to Tell their Collective History."

They were mischievous in their approach but dead serious in their goals. And while they were more interested in playing with the provocative power of symbols than they were in doing "actual" witchcraft, their manifesto left room for both: "W.I.T.C.H. is an all-woman Everything. It's theater, revolution, magic, terror, joy, garlic flowers, spells. It's an awareness that witches and gypsies were the original guerrillas and resistance fighters against oppression—particularly the oppression of women—down through the ages."

Furthermore, there was no governing body or gatekeeper of the group, and any woman who shared their values could be a member and take part in the W.I.T.C.H.craft: "There is no 'joining' W.I.T.C.H. If you are a woman and dare to look within yourself, you are a Witch. You make your own rules. You are free and beautiful. You can be invisible or evident in how you make your witch-self known. You can form your own Coven of sister Witches (thirteen is a cozy number for a group) and do your own actions. . . . Your power comes from your own self as a woman, and it is activated by working in concert with your sisters. The power of the Coven is more than the sum of its individual members, because it is *together*."

Arguably, this spirit of togetherness is what made women's lib so vital overall. The women who took part in the second-wave feminist movement were certainly sparked by reading books like Simone de Beauvoir's *The Second Sex*, but it was in-person conversations via consciousness-raising groups that proved to be truly transformative. For the first time, many women were realizing that their feelings of frustration, oppression, and pain were not abnormal. They got together to share personal stories about their own experiences of womanhood, including discussions about usually hushed-up topics like abortion and rape. Participants in these groups realized that they weren't alone, and they began to let go of the secrecy and shame that surrounded the truth of their own lives.

While not every feminist consciousness-raising group would have called itself a coven the way the members of W.I.T.C.H. chose to, it's a word that is apt nonetheless. These women learned that by convening within a circle of trust and freely sharing their beliefs, they could become stronger and more liberated individuals. Moreover, they proved that by joining forces and aiming their combined focus at an intended objective, they could make significant change in the wider world.

IF W.I.T.C.H. IS an example of feminist politics borrowing from the realm of mythos, then it should come as no surprise that feminist spirituality began to get more civic-minded in turn. Though there is evidence that some American Pagan covens existed as early as the 1930s, and Gardnerian Wicca had reached the States by the 1960s, the 1970s brought about a new style of witchcraft that was intent on "combining political and spiritual concerns as if they were two streams of a single river," as Margot Adler put it. It took the framework of Wicca but gave it a much fuller emphasis on worshipping goddesses and honoring the female body. It also more blatantly reclaimed the witch as an icon of resistance against the patriarchy, following the sentiments of earlier pro-witch thinkers like Matilda Joslyn Gage and Margaret Murray, and the writings of radical feminists like Mary Daly and Andrea Dworkin.

Zsuzsanna "Z" Budapest is a Hungarian-cum-Californian witch who founded the Susan B. Anthony Coven No. 1 in 1971, with magical aims to match its political name. She deemed her brand of witchcraft Dianic Wicca and she became both beloved and notorious for excluding men from her coven entirely. (She later came under intense criticism for stating that transgender women were not "real" women, and therefore could not be part of her practice—a stance that many people including myself consider wrongheaded and reprehensibly transphobic.) Her vision of a coven also had thirteen members, and anything larger she deemed a "grove." Budapest sought to create a religion where the feminine experience was lauded above all else, her goal being to restore a matriarchal way of life across the globe. Though she is a very controversial figure—and with good reason—her influence on the development of modern witchcraft has been vast. Through her teachings and best-selling books including 1979's *The Holy Book of Women's Mysteries*, her ideas captured the imagination of second-wave feminists, and helped shape the concept of witchcraft as an attractive alternative to the male-centric major religions.

Another Californian named Miriam "Starhawk" Simos would evolve this approach even further. She too has written that the Goddess is crucial for women to embrace in order to see themselves as holy and worthy. Unlike Budapest, however, Starhawk believes that the inclusion of men in this paradigm is essential. As she wrote in her best-selling 1979 book *Spiral Dance*, "The symbol of the Goddess allows men to experience and integrate the feminine side of their nature, which is often felt to be the deepest and most sensitive aspect of self. The Goddess does not exclude the male; She contains him. . . ." Where Budapest has remained staunchly separatist regarding gender, and continues to insist that Dianic Wicca is only for cisgender women, Starhawk has become more inclusive over the years, writing in the introduction to the tenth anniversary edition of *Spiral Dance* that her feelings about the absolutism of gender had changed, and that "we . . . must be willing to examine how our own interpretations have been shaped by the limits of our vision." In 2009, she also wrote, "Lately all our transgender folks and their friends have been noisily challenging our nice two by two assumptions. Those kind of challenges are great—they make us look at the world in a new way, examine our assumptions, deepen our understanding of Mystery." This embracing of diversity is a necessary improvement, as LGBTQ+ witches are not only part of the modern witchcraft movement, they are often its leaders. Musician Anohni has stated, ". . . I'm a witch. I actually de-baptized myself. And what's great about being transgender is you're born with a natural religion. It applies almost across the board no matter what culture or economic group or nation that you're from—you're almost automatically a witch. None of the patriarchal monotheisms will have you."

In Starhawk's view, the witch is a being who honors all of life; therefore activism is a large component of her practice. As she sees it, witchcraft is a process of dissolving estrangement—or rather, the false idea of estrangement—from other living beings. And once you do that, you realize that taking care of others is a holy responsibility, because everything is interconnected. Involvement with ecology and environmentalism, civil rights discourse, and antiwar efforts are all included in Starhawk's spiritual system, which she now classifies as "modern earth-based spirituality and ecofeminism," according to her website. Her books after *Spiral*

Dance explore the relationship between magic and activism in more overt terms. In *Dreaming the Dark: Magic, Sex, and Politics,* she writes "If magic is 'the art of causing change in accordance with will' then political acts, acts of protest and resistance, acts that speak truth to power, that push for change, are acts of magic."

She also evolves the concept of the coven. In *Spiral Dance,* she describes it as ". . . a Witch's support group, consciousness-raising group, psychic study center, clergy-training program, College of Mysteries, surrogate clan, and religious congregation all rolled into one." And in *Dreaming the Dark,* she writes about how typical models of power are hierarchies or ladders that cause oppression and disconnection. Covens, however, are structured in circles or webs: "In a circle, each person's face can be seen, each person's voice can be heard and valued. All points on a circle are equidistant from its center: that is its definition and its function—to distribute energy equally." The coven is not only a sanctuary for kindred outliers, then. It's also an aspirational paradigm for society at large.

BY 2012, I was teaching my own magic workshops at Observatory. My classes were a combination of lecture, ritual, and hands-on spell crafting, with names like *Autumn Descent and the Eleusinian Mysteries* and *Full Moon Fire Magick.* Instructions beforehand would vary regarding how students might prepare, though they were always encouraged to bring whatever special items they wished to place on the altar to get energetically charged, as well as to honor the deities of their choosing.

I began class by asking each student to state their name and their intention for being in circle that day. Then I would go around

and purify each person with song and sacred smoke. They closed
their eyes and surrendered, letting stresses of the day drift away
with the sound of my voice and the scent of burning herbs. We
then called circle in the order that I learned from my own teacher:
the Spirit of Air in the East, the Spirit of Fire in the South, the
Spirit of Water in the West, the Spirit of Earth in the North, the
Spirit of the Ancestors Below, the Spirit of the Guardians Above,
and the Spirit of the Center which holds Love and all of the great
mysteries that transcend language. Then I would speak for a bit
about the topic of the class, weaving together historical information with mythopoetic interpretations, in order to give context
for our gathering. The group would share thoughts and engage
in loose discussion about whatever the workshop's theme brought
up for them. And then, a participatory activity would commence,
in the form of making a magical object, doing a meditation, or
going through a more complex ritual to honor the season or elicit
a personal alteration. We would end by calling the spirits in the
direction opposite of that in which we had cast the circle, starting
with the Spirit of the Center. Our last action was to cast blessings
up and out into the universe, and then replenish our own well by
wrapping our arms around ourselves. Sometimes we'd then have
food or wine if we were marking a celebratory occasion. And often
students would linger after class, asking questions of me and chat-
ting with one another.

Though the workshops were open to anyone, several of the
participants began showing up repeatedly, and in doing so, they
formed their own ties of trust and familiarity. But even those who
turned up sporadically—or just only once—would find a ring of
welcoming witches, ready to hold whatever they had to bring to

the evening. Each session would be filled with different stories: someone trying to conjure a new job, to reconnect to nature, to grieve a recently lost relative, to gain focus for a new creative project. People brought down their walls and opened their hearts. And no matter how stressed-out we might have felt at the beginning of the session, afterward we shared a sense of peace and release.

After Observatory closed, my teaching mostly took the form of lecturing, writing, and putting together magic-themed public events and exhibitions. Several of my students became friends and collaborators who took part in my various endeavors, and they continued to be teachers to me as well. Our community may have taken a different form, but many of us remained tied to one another. And for a time, that was plenty for me. Finding these kind and insightful people and creating a connection to them was the culmination of its own sort of love spell. I had found another family, bonded by belief, if not blood.

THE CONCEPT OF the coven is one that, like witches in general, has grown in recent popularity. The 2013 FX TV show *American Horror Story: Coven* helped reintroduce the word into pop culture, and online conversation soon followed suit. The #covengoals tag on Instagram began getting applied to photos by some users in place of #squadgoals, as people got swept up in the semantics of a new kind of social sorcery. "Forget Squads—2017 Is the Year of the Coven" proclaimed a headline on Refinery29.

The Wing, an all-women coworking space, is probably the aesthetic opposite of what one might picture when envisioning a coven, with its millennial pink couches, bright lighting, and trendily dressed ladies quietly typing away on a sea of MacBooks.

"Your coven awaits" was the subject line of the welcome e-mail I received after I joined—and the application was found at the URL witches.the-wing.com. The allusions are carried through inside their spaces as well. Sandwiches are simply called "'witches" on their café menu, and their shop carries WING COVEN MEMBER shirts with pentagram designs and Wing Coven beanies that say INCANTATIONS, SHOUTS, & CHANTS. While this language is used in a playful way, it implies that members are meant to feel as if they're part of a special society of powerful women.

The word *coven* is also being more frequently applied to groups of people who have shared political goals—and usually progressive feminist ones. Pro-choice nonprofit Lady Parts Justice League describes itself as "a coven of hilarious badass feminists who use pop culture to expose the haters fighting against reproductive rights" on their website. Satirical news show *Full Frontal with Samantha Bee* regularly invokes the language of witches when talking about left-leaning women, such as describing a group of female lawmakers who introduced legislation to end forced arbitration as "a bipartisan congressional coven." In a sketch on its debut episode, Bee is shown being asked by reporters what it took to be the first female late-night talk show host. "Hard work, a great team, and maybe just a little bit of magic," she answers. Cut to a montage showing Bee screaming in a ring of candles, surrounded by a group of spooky characters with lightning coming out of their hands. "It's true, we're all witches," she says to camera with a wink.

These jokes have perhaps a more personal layer too, as Bee grew up with a Wiccan mother, though she herself does not identify as such. As with the resignified phrase *nasty woman*, which Bee is also a fan of, her use of these witchly terms is an act of subversion, poking fun at the image of a raging feminist harpy while proudly wearing these so-called pejoratives as badges of honor. As Bee told the *Guardian* in January 2018, "I'm leaning so hard into feminism that I've gone full witch." Her fans tend to share her values, and so can feel included in the *Full Frontal* satirical coven by extension.

The link between groups of outspoken feminists and covens was fortified during the 2017 Women's March immediately following Donald Trump's inauguration. Among the most popular protest signs were those emblazoned with phrases like HEX THE PATRIARCHY, WITCHES AGAINST WHITE SUPREMACY, and WE ARE THE GRANDDAUGHTERS OF THE WITCHES YOU WEREN'T ABLE TO BURN. My sign for my own group of marchers was an homage to W.I.T.C.H. of the 1960s, and read C.O.V.E.N.: CITIZENS ORGANIZING A VIABLE, EQUAL NATION.

It seems I wasn't the only one with those tricksy W.I.T.C.H. foremothers on the brain after the 2016 election. In Portland, Oregon, a new W.I.T.C.H. group popped up, staging protests in the form of choreographed rituals. They wore witch outfits with black veils covering their faces to remain anonymous, in the style of preceding masked activist collectives including the Guerrilla Girls, the Zapatistas, and Pussy Riot. As with the original group, W.I.T.C.H. PDX encourages other chapters and has open membership, provided the following values are upheld per their website's manifesto:

ANTI-RACISM—ANTI-FASCISM—
ANTI-PATRIARCHY—INDIGENOUS RIGHTS—
GENDER SELF-DETERMINATION—WOMEN'S
LIBERATION—TRANS LIBERATION—

ANTI-RAPE-CULTURE—REPRODUCTIVE RIGHTS—SEX
WORKER SUPPORT—LGBTQIA RIGHTS—ENVIRONMENTAL
PROTECTION—RELIGIOUS FREEDOM—IMMIGRANT
RIGHTS—ANTI-WAR—ANTI-CAPITALISM—DISABILITY
JUSTICE—PRIVACY RIGHTS—WORKER'S [*sic*] RIGHTS
WE DISAVOW ANY INDIVIDUALS OR COVENS CLAIMING
THE NAME OF "W.I.T.C.H." AND FAILING TO UPHOLD THESE
VALUES.

ANYONE PUBLICLY CLAIMING TO BE ONE OF US IS NOT
ONE OF US—WE ARE ANONYMOUS.

There are now online presences for W.I.T.C.H. chapters throughout the US, including in New York City, Boston, Minneapolis, Denver, Detroit, and Austin, and internationally, including in London, Paris, Mexico City, and Tokyo. Their activist covens have been seen both at large marches and doing their own group actions, and their signage has made mention of such issues as immigrant rights, gun control, and solidarity with Black Lives Matter, to name but a few. Though their concerns are serious, they also embrace the subversive humor of the 1960s group. I've seen placards with declarations like EVEN A W.I.T.C.H. BELIEVES IN SCIENCE and WE SHALL NOT SUFFER THE PATRIARCHY TO LIVE on them. One of my favorite photos from the @witchpdx Instagram feed shows two W.I.T.C.H.es with a pair of signs that say HEY PAUL RYAN … MISSING SOMETHING? and holding a life-size spine between them. It's an image that's both wickedly funny and perfectly macabre, given that the bones look like an ideal ingredient for a spell. Jinxing for justice, perhaps.

A similar thing is happening specifically in communities of color, with the Spanish word for witch—*bruja*—being reclaimed not only by magic-workers, but by groups of artful activists. The Bronx-based Brujas began as a tribe of female skateboarders who wanted to claim space in a community that was dominated by white men. They soon evolved into a full-blown radical organization, producing events and street wear that raise awareness about important issues such as mass incarceration, gentrification, and mental health. And the B-Side Brujas is a four-woman DJ collective based in Oakland, California. They banded together to spin records and combat sexism and racism in the club scene, and their sets incorporate healing blessings. They have also been known to put up altars in front of their DJ booth honoring people of color whose lives were taken by police violence, such as Alton Sterling and Philando Castile. To those in attendance, it may seem like any other night out dancing. But these women are bringing some true *brujería*: they light candles, make music, and honor those who have departed far too soon. Each performance is a ritual of remembrance and a public offering of release and rejuvenation.

THE LINE BETWEEN collective actions and actual spells is a fuzzy one, which is one of the reasons the word *coven* is now applied to a variety of intentional gatherings. Likewise, in the digital age, these groups can be formed online with their workings shared across a web of screens. Thanks to social media, one needn't gather with others in a forest or in front of the Pentagon to do a collaborative conjuration. Covens can now be virtual and can occupy public and private spaces at once.

In February 2017, magic practitioner Michael M. Hughes shared his "A Spell to Bind Donald Trump and All Those Who Abet Him" on Medium.com. As with most spells that circulate, it has a list of ingredients (his suggestions include an unflattering photo of Trump, a Tower tarot card, and a tiny stub of an orange candle—though a baby carrot can be substituted, he states). It also has an incantation to be read out loud. An excerpt of Hughes's spell includes the following language:

> *I call upon you*
> *To bind*
> *Donald J. Trump*
> *So that his malignant works may fail utterly*
> *That he may do no harm*
> *To any human soul*
> *Nor any tree*
> *Animal*
> *Rock*
> *Stream*
> *or Sea*
> *Bind him so that he shall not break our polity*
> *Usurp our liberty*
> *Or fill our minds with hate, confusion, fear, or despair*
> *And bind, too,*
> *All those who enable his wickedness*
> *And those whose mouths speak his poisonous lies.*

All of Hughes's instructions, however, are just recommendations and can be adapted or modified entirely. The most crucial component is that the spell be done by everyone at the same time, in this case, "at midnight on every waning crescent moon until he is removed from office." As he states, ". . . the critical elements are the simultaneity of the working (midnight, EST—DC, Mar-a-Lago, and Trump Tower NYC time) and the mass energy of participants."

Though the binding spell began with Hughes and a few of his friends, it quickly went viral, and became a monthly virtual working that anyone can participate in. It got the inevitable press coverage, though most articles mislabel it as a hex, not a binding, and there's a crucial difference: a hex is curse, but a binding is *not* intended to harm the target—rather, it's a means of preventing them from doing harm to others. At any rate, the spell also got attention from high-profile participants including musician Lana Del Rey, who told *NME*, "Yeah, I did it. Why not? Look, I do a lot of shit . . . there's a power to the vibration of a thought. Your thoughts are very powerful things and they become words, and words become actions, and actions lead to physical changes. . . . I'm a bit of a mystic at heart." The "Official Bind Trump" Facebook group has 3,763 members and counting, and anybody who follows Hughes's posted schedule can participate in the binding with friends or by themselves.

Though Hughes's group spell has been perhaps the most popular, other online witchcraft actions followed. In June 2016, after Stanford University student Brock Turner was given a shockingly short six-month sentence for rape, a Facebook invitation went out from witch Melanie Elizabeth Hexen and her coven. This *was* a hex, make no mistake, as it called for Turner to be rendered impotent, hounded by nightmares, and feel the "constant pain of pine needles" in his guts. (I don't condone this sort of working myself, it must be said, but the author gets points for imagination.) More than six hundred people RSVPed to the invite, and photos circulated online of participants' altars and spells.

And in October 2018, the Brooklyn occult shop Catland

Books held a public "Ritual to Hex Brett Kavanaugh," as an act of magical and political protest against his contentious Supreme Court appointment. According to their invite, the ritual was also intended to hex "all rapists and the patriarchy which emboldens, rewards, and protects them." The ten-dollar tickets sold out quickly (with 50 percent of proceeds going to Planned Parenthood and the Ali Forney Center for homeless LGBTQ+ youth), but more than fifteen thousand people marked themselves as "Going" or "Interested" on Facebook, with people participating in their own ways remotely.

I know some witches who have expressed skepticism at the efficacy of such large, public spells. One longtime witch told me that she thinks that the more variables you have in a working, the less focus the spell has. In other words, when you add more people, you risk muddling the energies and intentions—everybody brings their own baggage. Furthermore, she insists, "real" protection spells are done in private, under cover of night; the "target" shouldn't know about the spell, nor should anyone else, for that matter.

I can see her point. But I would offer that what public protest spells definitely do is build a sense of solidarity. Gathering in a group that has a shared goal reassures people that they are not alone, and that is consciousness-shifting in itself. Collective castings like these allow the disenfranchised to feel proactive and affirmed. They mobilize those who might otherwise be overwhelmed by despair, and they manifest catharsis and renewed strength. Group spells like these also put focus onto very real concerns about the dwindling safety of women, queer people, and people of color. Whether this magic "works" is subjective, but it certainly amplifies the voice of resistance in its own cone of power.

★   ★   ★

AFTER OBSERVATORY DISBANDED, and my apprenticeship in Robin's circle was complete, I was back to my solitary witch ways for a while. I had occasional get-togethers with practitioner friends over those years and would cast one-off spells for those who asked, but my regularly scheduled reverence was something I did on my own. For a time, this was fine. I was traveling like crazy for work, and when I was back home in Brooklyn, I was kept busy with projects and plans. Witchcraft was a haven then, a place for me to retreat from the dizzying demands of my day-to-day. I would light my candles, check in with my deities, mark lunar and solar occasions in quiet, private ways. I'd buy bouquets of flowers to decorate my cubicle on the Pagan holy days, and save up more elaborate ritual sessions for nights and weekends when I had the energy or the need. All of this sustained me through family hardships and health woes and the stress and strain of city living.

But in the winter of 2018, I felt called once again to be part of a more formal coven. I had just quit my corporate job of fourteen years, which was exciting but also nerve-racking. The political atmosphere felt poisonous, each day bringing more horrifying news than the one before. I had just started my podcast a few months earlier, which was thrilling, but at that point it was primarily a solo gig, and putting each episode together took many hours of isolated work. I longed to be in the presence of other seekers and to rediscover a sense of communion and support.

However, I also knew I didn't have the bandwidth to organize each meeting—and frankly, in becoming more of a public teacher of witchcraft over the years, I was missing the feeling of being led by others sometimes. I also found myself desiring a strengthening of sisterhood specifically. While I'm of the belief that witches can be any gender, and I've both led and taken part in covens where anyone was welcome, conversations about fourth-wave feminism, women's rights, and the #MeToo movement were at fever pitch. I needed a place where I could speak in shorthand about my own experiences and know that others could not just sympathize, but relate. Most of the active covens I knew of were working in formats or styles that weren't resonating with me, or else they were too far away. I was going to have to start my own.

So that winter, I invited an eclectic group of spectacular women and femmes over to kick off what I hoped would be a regular circle. Some of them were dear friends, but several were people I had met only once or twice but whom I admired and hoped to get to know better. They came from a variety of backgrounds and spiritual experiences but shared an interest in witchcraft, self-development, and intersectional feminism. And most importantly, they each struck me as kind and inspiring—the sort of people who made me feel better about the state of the world and who gave me hope for the future.

Our first meeting was on the spring equinox. There was a giant snowstorm that night, so only five of the witches ended up making it. But we feasted and talked and made our magic. We each shared intentions for what we wanted the group to be, and we talked about visions for ourselves and the world that we were trying to manifest into reality. We didn't all know one another very well, but we felt a shared recognition. We were people who wanted to grow our power and use it to make the world a fairer, more magical place. Though it was frigid outside that night, inside my apartment it was true spring, with all of its efflorescent promises of rebirth and renewal.

As I told the coven, even though I was holding the first meeting, I wasn't looking to be the group's leader. I envisioned each gathering being organized by a different member, so that no one person had to bear the burden of always hosting or guiding. People were welcome to bring guests or skip sessions whenever they needed to. And I wasn't concerned about the number of members, as long as the group didn't get too unwieldy. I trusted that whoever showed up at a gathering was meant to be there at that time, and I hoped that by each of us relinquishing full control, the coven would be fluid, communal, and hierarchy-free.

It was an experiment for sure, but so far it's been a fruitful one. We've met in backyards, kitchens, living rooms, an office, a shop, an indoor yurt. Each person brings something to contribute: food or wine or poems to read. Our altar looks different every time, but it is always teeming with candles and flowers, as well as precious objects that each witch has brought to honor the occasion or get charged up with magical energy. We're a mix of people of color, white people, queer people, and straight people, though all of us identify as female or femme. Some of us have been practicing for decades, and some are new to witchcraft. Some bring home steady paychecks, some are scraping by, and some of us are somewhere in the middle. Inside the circle, we discuss matters that are personal and political, and we each bring a different perspective. We talk about racism, sexism, family, money, work, lust, and love. We give voice to our fears and ambitions. We speak about our struggles, our anger, and our grief, and we celebrate our successes, sharing accomplishments big and small. We do rituals and spells. We drink wine and eat snacks (lots). We cry and croon and cackle our asses off. We work on healing ourselves and holding one another's hearts with softness, so we can fight more ferociously against insecurity and injustice when we leave. We honor the holiness of nature, and in doing so we honor our own sense of worthiness, for we witches are part of this world. Our coven is a cauldron, and together we brew up a better way of being.

Chapter 8

WHO IS A WITCH?

Things have come a long way since my nights of secret suburban spell casting in the 1990s. Public interest in witchcraft has gone from niche to a full-blown phenomenon. In 2017, teencentric social sharing platform Tumblr saw #witchblr enter their top community rankings for the first time, coming in at number eleven. By the end of 2018, Meetup.com had nearly six hundred witchcraft groups listed around the world, and Instagram's #witchesofinstagram hashtag had more than two million posts, its feed filled with photos of tarot spreads, altar tableaux, and portraits of fashionable folks decked out in silver amulets, daggersharp manicures, and a proliferation of black frocks. Today's Witch Wave is showing no signs of stopping anytime soon.

But while the witch may be getting more attention than ever before, she still leaves a long shadow. For if the Trump era is marked by an increased love of witches, it must also be noted for its resurgence of the term *witch hunt*. Not since the McCarthyism period of the 1950s has the phrase been applied with such regularity, only this time it's being used to describe a variety of issues at once.

The #MeToo movement has largely been considered revolutionary, as woman after woman has come forth to share stories of being assaulted and harassed by powerful men. It's sparked a public conversation about consent, as well as the corrosive by-products of male power. More importantly, it's given voice to the victims who had previously kept silent out of shame or fear of reprisal. And it's not only cathartic, it's consequential (if not nearly as often as it should be). A male chauvinist who likes to "grab her by the pussy" and pay off his mistresses with hush money may have gotten elected as commander in chief, but other abusive men are having to answer for their actions and are falling from lofty heights. Media mogul Harvey Weinstein, Fox News founder Roger Ailes, celebrity chef Mario Batali, *Today Show* anchor Matt Lauer, conservative pundit Bill O'Reilly, Democratic senator Al Franken, actor Jeffrey Tambor, and comedian Louis C.K. are just a few of the litany of powerful men who have been accused of sexual misconduct and who lost their jobs or companies outright because of it. And then there's Bill Cosby, who was convicted on three counts of sexual assault, following years of accusations by more than sixty women. He was sentenced to three to ten years in prison in 2018 (he is currently appealing his sentence).

All of this has understandably made a lot of men very, very nervous. There are those who have expressed discomfort with #MeToo, saying that it encourages punishment without due process. After all, sometimes misunderstandings can be misconstrued as transgressions, can't they? And couldn't some of the accusers be lying? Critics of the movement often point to its "mob mentality." Inevitably, the phrase *witch hunt* is invoked.

"This new puritanism imbued with a hatred of men that comes in the wake of the #MeToo movement worries me. . . . This has nothing to do with the fact that every sexual assault and all violence—whether against women or men—should be condemned and punished. But the witch hunt should be left in the Middle Ages," filmmaker Michael Haneke told the German-language newspaper *Kurier* in February 2018. *Rolling Stone* publisher Jann Wenner and actor Liam Neeson have both referred to the #MeToo movement as "a bit of a witch hunt." Woody Allen, no stranger to abuse allegations himself, warned that the backlash against Weinstein might bring about "a witch hunt atmosphere, a Salem atmosphere." And Bill Cosby's defense attorney, Kathleen Bliss, also brought up the Burning Times when she implied that the #MeToo movement was largely responsible for the accusations against him. In her closing statement to the court, she is quoted as saying, "Mob rule is not due process. And just as we have had horrible, horrible crimes in our history we've also had horrible, horrible periods of time where emotion and hatred and fear have overwhelmed us. Witch hunts. Lynchings. McCarthyism. . . . When you join a movement based primarily on emotion and anger, you don't change a damn thing."

Defenders of #MeToo have shot back, stating that this use of the term *witch hunt* is another example of the ways in which we're primed to disbelieve women and to focus on the feelings of the accused rather than those of the victims. "Yes, This Is a Witch Hunt. I'm a Witch and I'm Hunting You," was the headline of Lindy West's blistering October 2017 *New York Times* op-ed.

In the piece, she skewers men like Woody Allen, who insist on positioning themselves as the hapless targets of a conspiracy led by lying women. She ends the article by saying: "The witches are coming, but not for your life. We're coming for your legacy." By flipping the script of the hunters and the hunted, she admonishes those who have expressed any doubt about the women's stories, while simultaneously recasting the witch as a vigilante against sexual predation.

Amy Schumer has also taken issue with the people who call the #MeToo movement a witch hunt, though her quibbles are about semantics as much as sentiment. "You mean when you burned us at the stake for no reason? You don't have to support us, but come up with a better fucking example," she quipped onstage at the BlogHer18 Creators Summit. Powerful men using the phrase *witch hunt* about women persecuting *them* is pretty rich, given the term's origin story.

President Trump's fondness for the phrase is also problematic, to say the least, let alone excessively applied. He's been a fan since at least 2011, when he used it to discredit the allegations of sexual misconduct against then–presidential candidate Herman Cain, saying, "I think it's a very ugly witch hunt and I think it's very unfair." As a candidate himself five years later, Trump used it in response to press coverage about the fraudulent financial activities of his now-defunct for-profit "business school," Trump University: "The media is really on a witch-hunt against me. False reporting, and plenty of it—but we will prevail!" he tweeted on May 15, 2016.

Since then, he has used *witch hunt* more than 140 times on Twitter, the majority of them in 2018 and mostly referring to the Robert Mueller investigation of his administration's involvement with Russia. In fact, he's been crowing "witch hunt" with such frequency that the Twitter account @WitchHuntTweets has begun tabulating each occurrence. An August 14, 2018, example of one of their tweets reads: "WITCH HUNT ALERT. This is the 106th time President Trump has invoked the phrase 'Witch Hunt' in a tweet, the 86th time in 2018. This is the 11th time in August." But Trump is not the first person to hold the highest office in the land and think he is being subjected to a witch hunt: Richard Nixon also used the phrase when speaking to confidants about Watergate.

That the male captains of industry and institution are the ones who tend to use the term the most is ironic to say the least. During the witch hunts of Western Europe and the New England colonies, tens of thousands of people—most of them female—were persecuted for witchcraft they almost definitely didn't practice by citizens who usually had far more power than they did. These so-called witches were in fact victims of religious propaganda, paranoia, and scapegoating, not to mention they were usually of lower social and economic status than the magistrates and religious leaders who put them on trial and, in many cases, condemned them to death on entirely false charges. In contrast, there is ample reason for legitimate suspicion, if not outright conviction, of many of the very powerful men who are now acting like aggrieved Salem villagers. And while their livelihoods may be at stake (pardon the pun), their lives are not.

TODAY, "WITCH HUNT" is not just a metaphor that refers to anachronistic events. There are still many parts of the world where being labeled a witch is a matter of life and death, and the numbers of murders of accused witches every year are estimated in the thousands. Sadly, and unsurprisingly, the victims are usually women. Often they are widowed, elderly, or disabled, though it is a tragedy that befalls people of all ages. And the pattern of events is remarkably similar to those that occurred during the European and New England witch craze: someone in the community gets sick or dies of a "mysterious" illness, or else some other natural disaster or misfortune strikes, and a "witch" is to blame. The witch is almost never someone who identifies as such, but her denials are futile: the accusation *is* the proof. Often there is no trial, as usually the punishments are carried out by private actors in isolated villages rather than by government-sanctioned agencies. The supposed witch is expelled from the community in the best of cases, or subjected to brutal acts of violence or homicide in the worst. Mutilation, beating, stoning, burning, and beheading are just some of the gruesome repercussions that the accused may face.

A rising number of these witchcraft-related attacks have been reported since 2009, with occurrences throughout sub-Saharan Africa including the countries of Angola, Benin, Cameroon, Nigeria, Kenya, the Central African Republic, Tanzania, Gambia, Uganda, Swaziland, Zimbabwe, and South Africa. When not met with extreme bodily harm or execution, the accused are often exiled. In 2009, UNICEF estimated that there were fifty thousand street children in the Congo, and that as many as 70 percent of them had been accused of witchcraft and cast out because of it. Complicating matters is the fact that it's not only indigenous beliefs that cause this: the spread of Christianity is also a factor. As Special Rapporteur of the UN Human Rights Council Philip

Alston has written: "While traditional healers are often involved in the victimization of such children, recent reports also emphasize the growing role of churches and cults that encourage exorcism of 'evil spirits.'" Too often parishioners take matters into their own hands and banish those they believe to be "possessed," even the youngest among them.

In other countries, it's older women who are most often accused. Some theorize that it's usually widows who are called witches by their relatives who then take their late husbands' possessions or land. A misinterpretation of dementia or geriatric mental illness as being symptoms of witchcraft is also a factor. Regardless of cause, these women have no choice but to leave their communities. The problem is so rampant in Ghana and Zambia that these countries have "witch camps," which offer refuge to accused witches who might otherwise be beaten or lynched.

The 2017 magical realism film *I Am Not a Witch* was based on director Rungano Nyoni's visit to some of these camps, and she has expressed her hopes that it will "point out the absurdity of something that is misogynistic." Some of the images of the film are invented, such as the women being tied to giant spools of ribbon to prevent them from flying away. But this is intended as a metaphor for how tethered to the camps these accused witches are in real life. To leave is to invite violence from their family members or communities. These women have nowhere else to go.

Other countries with recent reports of witchcraft–related attacks include India, Nepal, Indonesia, Peru, and Colombia. In Saudi Arabia, the police force has had its own Anti-Witchcraft Unit since 2009, and sorcery is deemed worthy of capital punishment. Between 2009 and 2012, the force reportedly processed

801 cases of "magical crime," with sentences including lashings and lengthy prison terms, and at least four people were put to death. As of March 2018, five Indonesian migrant workers are currently on death row in the country for the possession of *jikat* or good luck amulets, which Saudi officials consider to be a form of evil magic.

In Papua New Guinea, there is a widespread belief in malevolent sorcery—or *sanguma*, as it's known there—and violence against alleged witches has reached epidemic proportions. Several NGOs have begun local campaigns throughout the region to educate citizens about the medical causes of illness and death, in hopes that it will mitigate the attacks on those who are currently believed to be responsible for hexing the unwell. Still, only in 2013 was the country's 1971 Sorcery Act repealed and witch-hunting made illegal. This was largely due to international outcry that resulted when a story broke about Kepari Leniata, a twenty-year-old woman who was accused of using witchcraft to kill a neighbor's boy and then stripped naked, cut with machetes, and burned alive on a busy street corner in Mount Hagen as hundreds of people looked on. To make matters even worse, not one of the men who tortured and killed Leniata was charged, even though police were present during the incident.

The subsequent repealing of the Sorcery Act hasn't seemed to change things much, on account of the country having a police force that is far outnumbered by its citizens, as well as a very low rate of perpetrators actually being prosecuted. In 2017, five years after Leniata's death, her surviving six-year-old daughter was also violently attacked after a man in a nearby village fell ill. It was believed that he was cursed with *kaikai lewa* ("to eat the heart"), an act of sorcery whereby a witch remotely removes and eats the victim's heart in order to gain his virility. Since the girl was known as a witch's offspring, she was held responsible, and her skin was flayed with hot knives by her accusers over a period of five days. If not for the rescue efforts of the Papua New Guinea Tribal Foundation and Lutheran missionary Anton Lutz, she most likely would have lost her life. The young girl is currently in hiding under an assumed name far away from her home.

IN THE US, there have been, thankfully, relatively few reported incidents of physical attacks on witches or alleged witches since the seventeenth century. The Satanic Panic of the 1980s and early '90s is probably the most recent example we have of a large-scale persecution of people who were believed to have been engaging in heinous occult activities. Three high-profile cases marked the panic at its peak.

In Kern County, California, thirty-six people were convicted and most were imprisoned after being accused of taking part in a pedophilic sex ring. It was said to have incorporated satanic ritual abuse. Thirty-four of the thirty-six Kern County convictions were eventually overturned, though two of the accused died in prison.

In Manhattan Beach, California, four members of the McMartin family and three teachers were put on trial for abusing children at the day care center the family ran, and testimonies from the kids stated that they saw witches fly and that much of the abuse took place in a series of underground tunnels. The McMartin case was eventually dismissed in 1990, after criminal trials had gone on for six years—the longest and most expensive case in US history up until then.

And in West Memphis, Arkansas, three teenagers were accused of sexually assaulting and murdering three boys as part of a satanic ritual. Damien Echols, Jessie Misskelley Jr., and Jason Baldwin—or the West Memphis Three, as they were dubbed by the media—were convicted, with Misskelley and Baldwin both sentenced to life in prison, and two 20-year sentences added on for Misskelley. Echols was sentenced to death. After serving 18 years and 78 days, the three men entered an Alford plea, meaning that they claimed they were innocent of the crime, but admitted that there was enough evidence to prove that they were guilty beyond a reasonable doubt. They were retroactively sentenced to the amount of time they served, and levied suspended sentences of 10 years. While they were not technically exonerated, they reached the plea deal so that they would be released from prison. Lawyers for the men vowed to pursue full exoneration.

In each of these cases, the accused lost years of their lives to trials and/or prison—not to mention the massive damage incurred to their reputations. Of course, these convictions are extreme examples, and all were litigated through an official court system, not carried out via bloodshed in a village square. But they are relevant in the discussion of the ways in which public fear of magic can exact great cost from individuals who are believed to be the conjurors of it.

TODAY, BEING CALLED a witch by someone else may not be life-threatening in every community, but it is still a word that is used as a means of attack. During Madonna's acceptance speech as Woman of the Year at the 2016 Billboard Awards, she stated that when she released her *Erotica* album and *Sex* book, she was dragged through the mud, even though male music star Prince was doing equally risqué things at the time without penalty: "Everything I read about myself was damning. I was called a whore and a witch."

And therein lies the rub: the witch identity takes on very different meanings depending upon whether it's self-ascribed or bestowed by another. More often than not, when the word is used about someone else, it is with the intent to insult, blame, frame, or shame. And as we've seen time and time again, the target of such an attack is usually a woman.

Among those who are frequently on the receiving end of the negative *witch* epithet are female politicians. In one particular case, it was meant literally: when Tea Party–backed Delaware Republican Christine O'Donnell was running for US Senate in September 2010, talk show host Bill Maher released footage of her appearing on his show in 1999, during which she talked about experimenting with the occult when she was younger: "I dabbled into witchcraft—I never joined a coven. But I did, I did. I dabbled into witchcraft. I hung around people who were doing these things. I'm not making this stuff up." She then described a date she went on during which they had a midnight picnic on a satanic altar with "a little blood" on it.

Maher threatened to keep showing more embarrassing clips of O'Donnell until she appeared again on his show. "It's like a hostage crisis," he said. "Every week you don't show up, I'm going to throw another body out." The witchcraft clip did enough damage on its own, however, circulating on all of the national news programs and making headlines. She canceled talk show appearances to regroup, and questions about whether or not she was a witch dogged her throughout the rest of her run.

Her campaign decided to try to diffuse the situation by releasing one of the most notorious political ads in US history a few weeks later. In the video, O'Donnell stands in front of what appears to be a wall of purplish-black fog, looks into the camera, and says "I'm not a witch. I'm nothing you've heard. I'm you!" as piano music tinkles in the background. Rather than doing damage control, it sparked a further barrage of hand-wringing from the right and mockery from the left. *Saturday Night Live* lampooned the spot, with Kristen Wiig playing O'Donnell in full *the lady doth protest too much* mode: "Just like you, I have to constantly deny that I'm a witch. Isn't that what the people of Delaware deserve? A candidate who promises first and foremost that she is not a witch? That's the kind of candidate Delaware hasn't had since 1692!" The sketch ends with the camera panning out to reveal Wiig standing in a room full of ghosts and wearing a witch's costume. O'Donnell lost the race to Democratic opponent Chris Coons, who received nearly 57 percent of the vote to her 40 percent.

I remember watching the O'Donnell debacle with mixed feelings. On the one hand, I was glad not to see her elected, as her political positions and campaign strategy decisions were objectionable to me. On the other hand, I hated that someone's experience with modern witchcraft was used as a reason to invalidate her legitimacy as a potential leader (even if the "satanic" goings-on she originally spoke of were a highly sensationalized and most likely misrepresented version of what most witchcraft tends to actually be). She didn't need to be vilified as a witch; I thought her policies were scary enough.

Watching Maher's glee at playing the clip of O'Donnell describing her dark dabblings also makes me deeply uncomfortable. He's bullying and blackmailing her, literally using the language of hostages and dead bodies. And in choosing to focus on her witchy past as the reason to humiliate her in the public arena, he's echoing the rhetoric of witch persecutions throughout history: *If you don't stand in front of me and confess, then you'll suffer the consequences.*

To Maher's credit, he eventually apologized. When O'Donnell finally appeared on his show two years later in 2012, he said, "I know when I brought out the witch tape, I made your life hell, and I'm sorry about that. . . . I don't agree with your ideas, but it shouldn't have hung on that stupid witch thing." She was conciliatory and admitted that some of it was "a self-inflicted wound" and that the "stupid ad" was a mistake. Her political luck didn't improve much after that, as she became mired in financial woes with the IRS. In 2011, she released a book that cataloged her frustrations entitled *Troublemaker: Let's Do What It Takes to Make America Great Again.*

Most female public servants needn't have "dabbled into witchcraft" in order to be depicted as witches by their opponents. Women across the political spectrum have been caricatured as witches in cartoons or Photoshopped memes. A quick online search shows Nancy Pelosi, Michelle Obama, Theresa May, Margaret Thatcher, Angela Merkel, Julia Gillard, Sarah Palin, Ruth Bader Ginsburg, Condoleezza Rice, and Michele Bachmann all as recipients of macabre virtual makeovers. They're given glowing yellow eyes and lurid green complexions, or shown casting evil spells from beneath pointy black headwear.

It will perhaps come as no surprise to learn that the public figure who appears in the highest number of witch-related search results is Hillary Clinton. Referred to as the Wicked Witch of the Left and the Wicked Witch of the West Wing, Clinton has had a decades-long association with the archetype's most negative aspects. Searching for "Hillary witch" pulls up page after page of depictions of her looking every bit the evil enchantress. She's shown riding brooms, stirring cauldrons, and snatching ruby slippers. Her face is made grotesque, manipulated to look as if she's shrieking, melting, plotting nefarious schemes, or possessed by demons.

There was even an attempt to rebrand her as a better witch: Hermione Granger. After all, both were considered rather bossy by the boys, yet could also be framed as highly intelligent overachievers who fight for goodness. As Nerds for Her site creator Paul DeGeorge told *Time* magazine, ". . . Hermione is always the smartest person in the room but gets talked over, so is Hillary." And in *Harry Potter and the Cursed Child*, Hermione grows up to become Minister of Magic, a connection that some Hillary and *Harry Potter* fans were quick to point out. Still, the "bad witch" Hillary image far eclipses the "good witch" one. A Google search for "Hillary Hermione" brings up 850,000 results. "Hillary witch" brings up more than *nine million*, many with hideous images to match.

And the pictures are just the tip of the iceberg. Though Clinton has been subject to horrific disparagement throughout her forty-year tenure in the public eye, both of her presidential runs brought a whole new barrage of pernicious personal attacks from both sides of the aisle. BROS BEFORE HOES declared one 2008 T-shirt with Obama's and Clinton's faces on it. LIFE'S A BITCH: DON'T VOTE FOR ONE proclaimed another eight years later. There were Hillary Clinton nutcrackers with stainless steel blades between her legs, and campaign buttons that said KFC HILLARY SPECIAL: 2 FAT THIGHS, 2 SMALL BREASTS … LEFT WING.

Smearing her as a witch became part of this rhetoric.

During the 2016 primaries, some of her opponent Bernie Sanders's more virulent supporters chanted for their candidate to "Bern the Witch," and unofficial Bernie merchandise with that phrase featured a picture of Clinton on a broomstick in front of a full moon. A "Bern the Witch" debate-watching event was hosted by one of his supporters and ended up on Sanders's official home page—though it was removed by his campaign staffers when they got wind of it. Sanders tried to distance himself from this segment of his base, telling CNN in February 2016 that "[a]nybody who is supporting me and who is doing sexist things, we don't want them. I don't want them. That is not what this campaign is about." But he couldn't quite put the misogyny back in the bottle, at least from Clinton's perspective. As she wrote in her election memoir, *What Happened*: "Because we agreed on so much, Bernie couldn't make an argument against me in this area on policy, so he had to resort to innuendo and impugning my character. Some of his supporters, the so-called Bernie Bros, took to harassing my supporters online. It got ugly and more than a little sexist."

Whether or not she's right that this was a big factor in her loss, it certainly didn't help.

While Sanders may have denounced character assassinations of Clinton, especially gendered ones, her Republican opponent Donald Trump encouraged his supporters to paint her with a personally damning brush. His usual name for her, Crooked Hillary, is but one of many insults he's used to associate her with malevolence. During his campaign he consistently portrayed her as a villain deserving of punishment (and he continues to do so throughout his presidency). "Lock her up" became one of the most frequently used chants by supporters at his rallies and with such a frenzied air that pitchforks could easily be imagined in the speakers' hands. As Trump's campaign went on, he warmed to the idea himself. On October 12, 2016, despite lacking any evidence to support his claims, he told a crowd in Florida that Clinton's "corruption and collusion is just one more reason why I will ask my attorney general to appoint a special prosecutor. . . . She has to go to jail." He also hinted that gun owners could perhaps take matters into their own hands, which some interpreted as a veiled suggestion of assassination: "Hillary wants to abolish, essentially abolish, the Second Amendment. . . . If she gets to pick her judges, nothing you can do, folks. Although the Second Amendment people, maybe there is, I don't know."

During the final presidential debate on October 19, 2016, Clinton declared that, as wealthy Americans, both her own and Donald Trump's tax contributions should go up, "assuming he can't figure out how to get out of it." "Such a nasty woman," he retorted with a head shake. He may have intended it as a derogatory comeback, but the words became a rallying cry for left-leaning women, who turned it into a slogan of feminist defiance. Soon the Internet became flooded with NASTY WOMAN T-shirts, hats, mugs, and bumper stickers. Celebrities including Jessica Chastain, Katy Perry, Julia Louis-Dreyfus, and Will Ferrell were seen sporting gear with the phrase on it.

This transfiguration of invective into words of honor is something that oppressed groups have done throughout history. Many slurs get turned around and reappropriated by the very people they are aimed at. Those targeted by verbal violence often voluntarily apply these malignant epithets to themselves as a way of detoxifying the language and reinforcing their own agency and dignity. Often humor is an important ingredient of this conversion. If you can laugh at something or learn not to take it seriously, its power over you will be diminished, and its lacerations won't cut quite so deep.

In current Western vernacular, "nasty woman" and "witch" are perhaps relatively mild compared to some other examples of hate speech, but those names are nonetheless still used by many to shame or scare women and certainly to shut them up. When these terms are turned into a joke, insider's lingo, or a valiant identity by the recipient, the attacker's original intent is nullified.

In occult-speak, there is a term I love called *apotropaic magic*. It describes workings or magical items that are administered to ward off evil. Sometimes a special amulet is used, such as a piece of obsidian; or an object like a mirror is employed to reflect bad energies back out and away. More often than not, the protective devices use aspects of the very terrors they are averting as part of their design. Grotesque creatures like gargoyles and hunky punks are placed on churches to frighten away malicious beings. In Greek mythology, Medusa's severed head was given to the goddess Athena, who affixed it to the centerpiece of her shield, and it is still a motif used in jewelry design and architecture—not to mention in the Versace logo—that is associated with protection and divine female power. Likewise, the glowering blue *nazar* charm is a symbol thought throughout the world to divert the evil eye, and ghoulish Halloween masks were originally meant to frighten away the unwelcome undead. By embodying the things we think will hurt us, somehow we feel safer: a creepy costume, a scary statue, intentionally dreadful décor. Sometimes all it takes is an utterance: addressing yourself with a monstrous name.

AS WE'VE SEEN, when someone describes themselves as a "witch," it can mean any number of things, since the term has now expanded beyond spiritual descriptor. But no matter the fluid intentions behind it, when a person uses it to refer to herself, these days it's more likely to be an act of self-fortification. One knowingly takes on the word with all of its terrifying history and becomes stronger and braver in doing so.

Often this magic trick happens in two stages: first a reclamation, and then a redefinition. The reclamation of the witch as a positive figure can be seen everywhere now, with stores like Urban Outfitters selling WITCH DON'T KILL MY VIBE T-shirts, Starbucks brewing up Crystal Ball Frappuccinos, and more than three thousand witchcraft-related items now available on Walmart.com, including pentagrams, spell books, and a travel mug printed with the words YES, I'M A WITCH. DEAL WITH IT! L'Oreal has had a witchy Wise Mystic makeup line in collaboration with *Project Runway*, and Charlotte Tilbury's first perfume, Scent of a Dream, debuted with a commercial that featured Kate Moss casting a fragrant spell over a crowd of black-clad, glittery dancers. New witchcraft magazines like *Sabat*, *Ravenous Zine*, and Catland Books's *Venefica* have arrived on the scene, and each has a luxe, editorial aesthetic that gives mainstream fashion publications a run for their money. Likewise, new media platforms including The Hoodwitch, Sanctuary, and The Numinous have emerged to provide astrological guidance, spell casting how-tos, and witchy style tips to hordes of devoted readers. Witchcraft is *en vogue*.

Witch memes have also run rampant among my mystical and Muggle friends alike. "WITCH BETTER HAVE MY MONEY," flashes one highly circulating gif. "IT'S BRITNEY, WITCH," says another, with a looping clip of Britney Spears riding a broom in front of a giant full moon. My politically minded pals keep posting an image from the 1971 Disney film *Bedknobs and Broomsticks* with the words "This is Eglantine Price. Eglantine learned Witchcraft to fight the Nazis. Be Like Eglantine. Hex the Fascists." (I wonder if author Mary Norton knew about Gerald Gardner's "Operation Cone of Power" when she was writing the books that the movie was based on.) My personal favorite is an animated gif by Winona Regan that shows three zaftig witches grinding raunchily in a graveyard. It has come in handy in a variety of situations, let me tell you.

Not only is being a witch now considered a good thing by many, but the definition of what a witch actually *is* is also undergoing a revamp. The word is now being used to refer to any woman who is deemed a rule-breaker, world-shaker, or no-shit-taker. Feminist design brand Modern Women sells a FAMOUS WITCHES T-shirt with the faces of such trailblazers as transgender activist Marsha P. Johnson and artist Yayoi Kusama. Lena Dunham referred to her inclusion in Taylor Swift's social circle of female celebrities as being in a "witches' coven." When I asked my own Twitter followers who their favorite witches of color were, "Oprah" was one much-liked response. (On this last point I'll add that Oprah herself has channeled the archetype, having publicly professed her love for Glinda the Good Witch while promoting her own role as Mrs. Which in the 2018 film adaptation of *A Wrinkle in Time*. Furthermore, her frequent talk of manifestation and vibrating on a higher frequency has more than a witchy tinge—but I digress.)

Pop culture has both commented upon and catalyzed this word application. *Broad City*'s "Witches" episode from October 2017 beautifully encapsulates the trend of young women using the word to describe independent, accomplished women. It aired to rave reviews from critics and viewers alike, who saw that embracing one's inner witch is a meaningful metaphor for the need to reinforce female sovereignty in the face of sexism. Though the show is a comedy, the spirit of "Witches" is one of sincerity and irreverent inspiration.

As the episode begins, the series' main characters, Abbi and Ilana, are each struggling with an aspect of their lives. Abbi is unemployed, broke, and coming to grips with getting older. Her apartment is freezing because she can't afford the space heater she wants, and she laments about finding her first gray hair. When she tries selling her handmade Christmas cards on the street, similarities between herself and a witchy old crone named Margot at the table nearby (played by comedic legend Jane Curtin) makes her feel even more worried about her future. It's not simply that she's feeling less attractive, but that these are all external markers of the fact that she isn't where she hoped she would be at this point in her life. Ilana's challenges are also corporeal: the usually sexually robust character hasn't been able to have an orgasm ever since Trump got elected. As she later reveals to her sex therapist, upping her depression meds to cope with the state of the world has made her feel less in tune with her body, and besides, every time she's aroused, her thoughts stray back to the horrors of the presidency—a total buzz kill.

Both of their issues are resolved by embracing their own inner witches. Ilana is reminded by the sex therapist that she is part of a legacy of powerful women. As she masturbates, images of Maya Angelou, Sally Ride, Malala Yousafzai, Dolly Parton, Rosa Parks, Frida Kahlo, Harriet Tubman, and many more flash in her mind's eye until she finally climaxes, her dry spell broken at last. Abbi, halfway through getting her first round of cosmetic injections, realizes that she's made a mistake: usually she finds herself attractive just the way she is, and besides, the dermatologist herself can't laugh without panicking that her own Botoxed face will suffer consequences. She flees from the doctor's office without finishing the procedure.

When the two women meet up, they share their new revelations with each other. Ilana tells Abbi about her explosive vision of historical heroines, and her realization that ". . . witches aren't monsters, they're just women. They're fuckin' women who cum and giggle and play in the night. And that's why everybody wants to set 'em on fire, 'cause they're so fucking jealous!" The episode ends with a coven scene set in Central Park: a group of women including Abbi, Ilana, the sex therapist, Margot the crone, and even the dermatologist gather in front of the fire to dance and drum and howl at the moon. The experience of being in such a powerful gathering of women gives Ilana another orgasm: this one is so strong it puts a crack down the middle of Trump Tower.

As a practicing witch, and a fan of smart, feminist comedy, I howled right along with them. If the word *witch* empowers more people to embrace their self-worth, build community, and fight fascism at the same time, I'm all for it.

* * *

THE CURRENT SURGE of on-screen witches is evolving popular thought about who witches are and what they look like. Not only has there been a marked increase in witch TV shows and films over the past decade, the faces they are reflecting are more diverse.

Several of the witches on the HBO series *True Blood* were played by actors of color, Angela Bassett took on the role of voodoo queen Marie Laveau in *American Horror Story: Coven*, and *The Vampire Diaries'* lead witch character, Bonnie Bennett, was played by Kat Graham, who is of Liberian and Russian Jewish descent. And more recent programs are consciously increasing the number of black and brown magic-makers. Netflix's *Chilling Adventures of Sabrina* features black actors in several witchly roles, including Sabrina's warlock cousin, Ambrose, and her magical frenemy Prudence. The company also has a new show called *Siempre Bruja*, about a time-traveling Afro-Colombian witch. The 2018 reboot of *Charmed* has actors of color playing the three lead sisters, the witch camp counselors of the cartoon series *Summer Camp Island* have a range of skin tones, and there are reports that ABC will be bringing back *Bewitched*, this time featuring a black actor in the role of Samantha.

Likewise, things have come a long way since the nineties when the only queer witchy characters in pop culture were Willow and Tara on *Buffy* and Foxglove and Hazel in the *Sandman* comics series. *Salem*, *Brujos*, and *A Discovery of Witches* are just a few of the recent shows that feature same-sex relationships among the magically inclined, and *Chilling Adventures of Sabrina* has also had several scenes across the sexuality spectrum.

Another groundbreaking show, this time reality TV, has flirted with queer witchery. Emmy Award–winning juggernaut *RuPaul's*

Drag Race has captured the world's heart—and mine—with its celebration of self-acceptance and audacious creativity among the drag community. The competition show has also seen its fair share of gay men channeling the spirit of the witch. Season four winner Sharon Needles first came snarling onto the screen dressed in a pointy black hat and tight black satin sheath dress with the declaration "I look spooky, but I'm really nice!" Season nine winner Sasha Velour wore a MAGICAL BITCH nameplate necklace throughout her season, and as she told *HISKIND* magazine, "I really just want to look like a magical vampire witch all the time. . . ." She also tweeted: "I'm an actual witch. Who's next?" in response to the rumor that every queen she touched was cursed and would be eliminated shortly thereafter.

Another season nine contestant, Aja, is an adherent of Santería, the Afro-Caribbean religion that involves the worship of ancestors and deities or *orishas*. In the 2018 music video for her song "Brujería," Aja pays homage to Yemayá, the orisha of the ocean and motherly love, as well as to Santería priestesses and *brujas* across various cultures. The song is full of witchy swagger, with line after line proclaiming Aja's vast power: "Straight from the coven, I conjure, I summon / Shook, they runnin' 'cause, yes, I bludgeon," she raps, though later assures us that she is ". . . so delicious / but never malicious."

RuPaul himself is no stranger to the witch archetype. He has often said that *The Wizard of Oz* is his favorite film, and on his podcast he's discussed how *Bewitched* is meaningful to him because it is about "spiritual beings having a human experience." According to Ru, Samantha Stephens's character, a witch who must pretend to be "normal" to fit society's standards, is a metaphor for having to dumb down one's capabilities in order to make oneself more acceptable to small-minded people—something he and the drag community overall can relate to. In an interview in 2017, RuPaul told Oprah Winfrey about a favorite scene in *The Witches of Eastwick* ". . . where all three women start levitating because of laughter. That's the most powerful spell you can cast." And in a fun bit of trivia, Ru also had a cameo on nineties sitcom *Sabrina the Teenage Witch*, playing the part of a female hairdresser who was revealed to be a male witch judge.

It makes sense that someone who has made a career out of the art of illusion and glamorous shape-shifting so often feels a kinship with witches. I don't know that he has ever outright referred to himself as one, but as a black gay man who regularly bends the rules of gender and identity, and whose show's primary message is about turning pain into pride, RuPaul is an honorary Grand High Witch as far as I'm concerned. As he told *Vulture* when asked about the function of drag in 2016, "It's been the same since the beginning of time when shamans, witch doctors, or court jesters were the drags. Which is to remind culture to not take itself seriously." On a similar note, both drag queens and modern witches take identities that have been considered shameful, and craft them into new beacons of beautiful disobedience.

All of this is an exciting course correction because it heralds an age of more inclusive storytelling in general, and also because viewers who are queer, of color, or both are able to see themselves in a powerful archetype that is so often depicted as straight and white. And it's truer to life, as marginalized people have long gravitated to witchcraft because it enables them to have access to power and to be celebrated as sacred in a society that questions their worth and threatens their well-being on a daily basis. Increased visibility of queer witches and witches of color shows that magic comes in all shades and orientations.

WHILE PUBLIC INTEREST in witches is soaring, and the wider application of the word *witch* may occur with the best of intentions, things get further complicated when we consider those who self-identify as witches for religious reasons. Pop-culture depictions and political statements aside, *witch* is a word that can now refer to some of the hundreds of thousands, if not millions, of Wiccans, Pagans, and other practitioners of modern witchcraft, and it seems to be a quickly growing number. Not all of these people use the word *witch* to refer to themselves, mind you, but many of them do. Furthermore, some of these adherents insist on spelling it "Witch" with a capital *W*—in the same way that "Christian," "Muslim," or "Jew" is capitalized—an indicator of how hard they have fought to have their beliefs recognized as a valid religion, and therefore protected by law. In 2007, the Wiccan pentacle (a five-pointed star enclosed by a circle) became an officially approved symbol for military-issued gravestones of deceased veterans, and the US Army has included Wicca in its chaplaincy handbook, *Religious Requirements and Practices of Certain Selected Groups,* since 1990.

In 2008, the American Religious Identification Survey estimated that there were around 682,000 Wiccan and Pagan adults in the US alone, and that figure goes up when teenagers are included. This number more than doubled in just seven years since the survey was first conducted in 2001, and there are multiple articles that have stated that Wicca is "the fastest-growing religion in America," though it's unclear which stats these claims are based on. Still, it's a narrative that has taken hold. "Witches Outnumber Presbyterians in the US," a ChristianPost.com headline from October 2018 proclaims. And Ross Douthat's "The Return of Paganism" Op-Ed in the *New York Times* on December 12, 2018 states, "... there may soon be more witches in the United States than members of the United Church of Christ." Many of these types of claims point to an article on Quartzy from October 2018 which itself cites a Pew Research study from 2014 and declares "... 0.4% of Americans, or around 1 to 1.5 million people, identify as Wiccan or Pagan." In fact, the 2014 Pew Religious Landscape Study to which they are referring shows 0.3 percent, but this would still be around 1.3 million Americans.

Presumably with witchcraft growing in popularity since the time of that survey, that number has risen even higher since then. It also must be noted that this is an international community, loose-knit as it may be. In 2011, census data showed that there were more than 56,000 people who identified as Pagan in England and Wales, and more than 32,000 in Australia, and I'm guessing those have increased over the ensuing years as well.

That said, it's very difficult to quantify the number of people who are adherents of some form of Pagan spirituality and/or do some type of witchcraft, for several reasons.

First, the practice of witchcraft is decentralized, which is one of the reasons that so many are attracted to it in the first place. There is no one governing religious body to keep track of the number of congregants (in fact, as we know, many people practice witchcraft privately, thus are not "congregating" at all). There are no dues to pay and relatively few officially Pagan-designated buildings: most rituals take place either outside, in temporary spaces, or in people's homes. A grove of trees, a statue in an art museum, and a makeshift bedroom altar can all be sacred sites, according to the Pagan perspective; thus there are no records of attendance to tally.

Second, the verbiage of Paganism is rather loose: while all Wiccans may technically be considered Pagan, not all Pagans are Wiccan. There are Druids, for example (or Neo-Druids, as they are sometimes called), as well as followers of various Reconstructionist religions who adhere to any number of pre-Christian polytheistic traditions. Even more confusingly, there are also modern witches like myself who refer to themselves as Pagan, but not Wiccan. And I know there are many who don't use either word, yet still consider themselves to be witches in the spiritual sense. The authors of religious surveys are often shoehorning a vast and variegated spiritual orientation into a highly limited descriptive lexicon.

Lastly, there are many people who practice some form of witchcraft but who don't disclose their beliefs out of fear of prejudice or discrimination from family members, friends, employers, or society at large. Using the word *witch* as a personal identifier may be in fashion now within progressive-minded spaces, but as we've seen, it is still a term that is widely misunderstood and erroneously associated with literally diabolical behavior.

Applying the word to oneself in order to make a subversive statement is a totally valid and even liberating act. But that is different from when a person uses it to mean that they do indeed practice some sort of magic, or follow a path of Pagan-related spirituality. There are still many contexts here in the West where declaring actual belief in witchcraft is to open oneself up to mistrust or mischaracterization at best, or accusations of blasphemy, mental instability, or evil-doing at worst. I know people who practice witchcraft only in private, out of fear that they will lose their jobs or custody of their children, or be shunned by friends and family. Those of us who choose to share our magical lives do so with caution, whether in our day-to-day interactions at work or social gatherings or when answering a seemingly simple survey question about our religious affiliation. While I myself have grown more comfortable with being an out-in-the-open witch as I've gotten older, I can understand why many have continued to keep this part of their identities under wraps. Shadows may seem frightening, but they can sometimes feel like the safest places for those who live within them.

AND SO, ALL of this widespread bewitchment begs the question: Who gets to use the word *witch*? Well, as we've seen thus far, the short answer is: anyone who wants to. But as with the scaling up of any niche, there are mixed results, and lots of conflicting opinions around ideas of authenticity and ownership.

I know several practitioners of witchcraft who bristle at the ever-expanding commoditization of their beliefs. As one friend wrote on Twitter: "How to become a witch in one easy step: Go actually practice some witchcraft."

I've also seen people cringe at seeing an archetype that's so deeply linked to outsiderism being adopted by those who seem to represent the very privilege and status to which witches are in direct opposition. Another friend of mine recently posted a picture on her Facebook wall with the words "When you come across the vanilla girls from high school calling themselves witches," alongside a disparaging image of Fairuza Balk's face.

On the other hand, there are plenty of old-school Pagans and Wiccans I know who have a healthy sense of humor around it: having lived through peaks and valleys of the so-called witch trend over the years, they get a kick out of seeing "new" discoveries or reinterpretations of a practice that they have been engaging in for decades.

I understand this range of attitudes because I have felt many of these things myself at various times in my life, and especially now that talk about the witch is reaching fever pitch.

In 2013, I wrote an article declaring it to be "the Year of the Witch." I was riffing off the number thirteen and its association with unruly women, as well as marking a moment when it seemed that witch imagery was everywhere, and its associations with feminism were being more prominently linked. Seemingly overnight, this lifelong preoccupation of mine had gone fully pop again, and a large part of me was excited about it. It boded well for us as a society to spotlight strong and complicated women, I thought. Plus, it was good fun. Superheroes and zombies and vampires had gotten plenty of attention up until that point. It was high time we witches got thrown a bone—or a whole skeleton, even. I reveled in the newest books and films featuring maverick magiciennes who thought freely, worshipped openly, and navigated the choppy waters of being a person with powers that others deem threatening.

I was also, it must be said, a little bit wary. It reminded me of the time my favorite college rock band, the Yeah Yeah Yeahs, had suddenly become very, very famous. I was happy for them, because it meant that they were being appreciated and compensated, and that mattered to me. But I was also afraid that their music would become watered down. That more people loving them would somehow make their magic leak away as they catered to larger audiences and record label directives. And if I'm honest, I worried that I and other "true" devotees would be forgotten. After all, it was our love and attention that had helped give the band their start in the first place.

Fears aside, in a very real way, I could no longer see them perform in sweltering dive bars to a crowd of sixty people. My recognition that they were special made me feel special right back. And when millions of others discovered my discovery—well, then they no longer belonged only to me.

I see spiritually identified witches in this defensive crouch from time to time, and I hear them expressing displeasure about how something that means so much to them is getting commercialized and co-opted. When Sephora announced it would be selling a Starter Witch Kit from beauty brand Pinrose that was to contain a deck of tarot cards, a rose quartz crystal, a bundle of white sage, and various perfumes, some practicing witches got so up in arms that the plans were scrapped entirely. Pinrose issued an apology:

> First and foremost, to those who have shared their disappointment or taken offense to this product, we apologize profoundly. This was not our intent. We thank you for communicating with us and expressing your feelings. We hear you; we will not be manufacturing or making this product available for sale.
>
> Our intention for the product was to create something that celebrates wellness, personal ceremony, and intention setting with a focus on using fragrance as a beauty ritual.

WAKING *the* WITCH 259

Between the kit's inclusion of white sage (which is said to be overharvested, and which many find an offensive appropriation of Indigenous American practices), the name's implication that anyone can become a witch overnight; and the fact that corporate entities, rather than actual witches, were perceived to have designed the product, there were several strikes against it. I totally get it, and I can absolutely see why some people were upset. It could certainly have been handled more thoughtfully on the part of the manufacturers.

But let's be clear: plenty of other mainstream stores sell all kinds of witchcraft items, as they have for decades, and I am certain that not every single one has been produced or vetted by actual practitioners. And that's where things get confusing, and it can seem as though the goalposts for what a "real witch" is are constantly moving. In truth, no one owns witches, in the same way that no one fan owned my favorite band. My identity as a member of their community—their coven, if you will—is personal and indelible and nobody can take that away from me. But I also know that their music is here for anyone to dance to.

I've also come to realize that the witch has a tendency to reach the ones who need to be reached, and there's a reason her drumbeat is growing louder. I believe people need her more than ever, whether as a holy figure, a feminist statement, or a bit of frenetic fun.

BESIDES. AS WE'VE seen, our love affair with witches is nothing new. She is a figure that unorthodox people have been reclaiming for the past several centuries, spiritually, culturally, and politically. Hers is an identity that unconventional women, and female artists in particular, have voluntarily taken on in earnest, regardless of whether their witchcraft is literal or metaphorical.

I've already declared my love of five magic-making visual artists earlier in this book, but there have been many others whose works and wardrobes channeled the witch, such as Ithell Colquhoun, Leonor Fini, Rosaleen Norton, Marjorie Cameron, and Vali Myers (not to mention those still living such as Betye Saar, Judy Chicago, Kiki Smith, and Cindy Sherman to name but a few). And it's a telling development that as women gained more of a voice in general, many female poets came to invoke witches in their writing in order to express something true and specific about themselves as well.

Outspoken feminist Edna St. Vincent Millay wrote these words in her poem "Witch-Wife": "But she was not made for any man / And she will never be all mine." Many, including Millay biographer Nancy Milford, have surmised that she was writing about herself. When we consider that the poem was written in 1917, three years before US women got the right to vote, we see this witchly self-portrait as representing a woman who was ahead of her time in envisioning a life of liberation and self-determination.

Sylvia Plath's well-documented mental health struggles are alluded to in her 1959 poem "Witch Burning." On its surface, it is about a witch who is being put to death on a pyre, but it can also be read as a metaphor for being consumed by the flames of depression: "My ankles brighten. Brightness ascends my thighs. / I am lost, I am lost, in the robes of all this light."

The fact that Plath experimented with Ouija to write poetry, and that she would go on to do a magic spell to hex her husband, Ted Hughes, after he left her for another woman—all before taking her own life—retrospectively adds a shroud of tragic mystique to the poem.

Poet Audre Lorde utilizes the witch as an emblem of her outsider status as a black lesbian in her 1978 poem "A Woman Speaks." She describes herself as ". . . treacherous with old magic" and ends the piece by proclaiming: "I am / woman / and not white."

And in Anne Waldman's Trump-era poem "crepuscular," she directs the reader to engage in witch-tinged activism, and "Practice disobedience as a coven might."

Then there are those poets who more blatantly draw a line between witchcraft and wordsmithery. Anne Sexton wrote about herself as a witch on multiple occasions, most famously in the poem "Her Kind," which begins "I have gone out, a possessed witch, / haunting the black air, braver at night; . . ." A later work, "The Gold Key," opens her book of fairy tale poems, *Transformations*. It reflects a more obvious comparison of witches to writers, stating "The speaker in this case / is a middle-aged witch, me— / . . . ready to tell you a story or two."

And Margaret Atwood's "Spelling" is about the relationship between language and female agency, and it is filled with witch imagery. She begins the poem by describing her daughter playing with plastic letters on the floor in order to learn "how to make spells." Atwood then alludes to the ways in which women have been bound, whether by society, in war, or by actual witch hunts. In her poem, speech and writing are tools of liberation: "A word after a word / after a word is power."

The metaphor of witches and writers is particularly apt when one considers that the words *grammar* and *grimoire* are sprouted from the same etymological seed.

The witch has been a touchstone for female musicians as well, especially women who are automatically freakish by virtue of the fact that they dare to put their own selves and songs front and center. I think about the rock stars throughout the 1970s and '80s who have either beseeched the witch or become her in acts of sonic sorcery: Stevie Nicks swirling in shawls and crooning about night flights and crystal visions. The chronically maligned genius Yoko Ono singing defiantly "Yes, I'm a witch / I'm a bitch / I don't care what you say," and Grace Jones stating she'd "rather be a bitch, just look at me / Bein' a witch is what I'd rather be" in her song "Sinning." Patti Smith pale and spike-haired, looking like "a crow, a gothic crow" per Salvador Dali's description, and yowling about how "Jesus died for somebody's sins but not mine." Chrissie Hynde worshipping "the maid and the mother / and the crone that's grown old" in the Pretenders' goddess ode "Hymn to Her." Siouxsie Sioux with her kohl-lined eyes, turning from a black cat into a woodland wraith in the video for "Spellbound." Kate Bush waking her own witches with a shriek, and being chased by nocturnal "Hounds of Love." In an industry that was so male-dominated, it's no wonder these women felt like outsiders. Fashioning themselves as witches was a means of turning a liability into a strength—not to mention that images of the occult lend themselves well to a medium that thrives on spectacle and shock via album covers, music videos, and live performance.

I discovered my own auditory oracles at the same time that I started experimenting with witchcraft. When I was making my new age shop excursions in the nineties, I was also on the hunt for another sort of magic. Those far-flung towns were where I could get the rarest albums and import CDs from my favorite musicians that I gulped hungrily into my gothling gullet. Pilgrimages to the Rutgers University campus in New Brunswick or, best of all, Tower Records in NYC supplied me with the soundtrack to my burgeoning life of mythological devotion. B-sides and bootlegs by Tori Amos, PJ Harvey, and Björk were tricky to find back then, and happening upon a new song by one of them felt like uncovering a lost spell in a dusty old codex.

Looking back now, it's clear to me that those musicians offered an artistic template for what a modern witch actually was. All three of them were unapologetically outré, weaving references to Paganism and power throughout howling hymns to female sexuality. They wrote their own music, and they played it loud. They wore sparkling makeup, flamboyant outfits, and glamorous grimaces. Though I thought each was breathtaking, none of them was "pretty" in the typical sense. Their beauty was large and forceful and unsettling.

It's no exaggeration to say that the first time I heard Tori Amos, I was terrified. I was in fifth grade at the time, and my best friend, Jenny, played me *Little Earthquakes*, an album she herself got hooked onto by her cool older brother, Travis. At the time, my primary musical intake consisted of hit singles like "Finally" and "The Promise of a New Day," my mom's *Pippin* soundtrack, and whatever easy listening songs the Strathmore Pool Club had played over the loudspeaker that summer.

I was entirely unprepared for the singing banshee with bonfire-red hair who writhed on a piano bench like Babylon incarnate. Tori sent shock waves through my prepubescent circuitry, and I was stunned and repelled, unable to fully compute how she made me feel. I ran quickly back to the comforting arms of CeCe

Peniston and Paula Abdul (whose album of the time was, incidentally, called *Spellbound,* though its witchy connotations were limited to the title track).

Once my more worldly sixth-grade self set in, I found myself drawn to Tori, and I became obsessed, listening to her album on loop. I doodled her lyrics in school notebooks, learned "Silent All These Years" on the piano, and sang to an imaginary listener that he must "Hand me my leather." I wasn't quite clear on what the leather was for, mind you, nor did I understand that the line "So you can make me come / that doesn't make you Jesus" was actually spelled *cum* for a reason. But what I did know was that this was a woman who sang about desire and loss and magic and pain. She was an ingenious composer whose cryptic lyrics flooded my psyche like a potion. Her world was one of denim-wearing mermaids and "black winged roses that safely changed their color." But she also sang candidly about taboo topics like sexual abuse, menstruation, and starting her own religion. She was the High Priestess of Impropriety, and I was her willing disciple.

Other love affairs soon followed. I fell head over heels for Björk's eldritch screech, and her songs about "Venus as a Boy" and being "married to myself." I thrashed around my bedroom to PJ Harvey as she shredded her Fender Telecaster along to vaginal "Sheela-na-gig" goddess anthems and lovesick lunar serenades. Artists like Rasputina, Portishead, and Mazzy Star came shortly thereafter, but it was those three solo artists who first showed me that music could be raucous and ravishing and full of feminine incandescence.

So many of the musicians of the current age feel like next-gen versions of the witchy women who helped craft my own young identity. Florence and the Machine, Grimes, Lana Del Rey, and Chelsea Wolfe have each alluded to the witch archetype via image and song, if not embodied it entirely. Princess Nokia threads witchcraft references through her single "Brujas," and the video for it shows groups of women engaging in rituals from both Yoruba and Wiccan traditions. Lorde has stated, "I am not weirded out by ghosts or spirits. I am basically a witch," and frequently wears glittery black garb. Azealia Banks starts her song "Yung Rapunxel" with the line "Who's cooler than this witch," and the accompanying video shows her rapping in a montage of owls, eyeballs, and crescent moons. Banks has also stated that she practices witchcraft, and she attracted much controversy from animal-rights groups when she posted an Instagram video of herself cleaning up what appears to be the remains of sacrificed chickens from "three years' worth of *brujeria*." Ghanaian artist Azizaa identifies as "A Wild Heart. Songstress. Witch . . ." according to her social media bio, and her singles "Black Magic Woman" and "Voodoo Pussy" are both magic-packed paeans to self-empowerment. And artist Witch Prophet makes hypnotic songs about manifestation and cosmic destiny that live up to her lofty name.

Each of these musicians is certainly gifted and unique on her own terms, and I know that my comparing Bat for Lashes, say, to Tori Amos may make fans defensive, the same way I felt when I was told that Tori was "just another Kate Bush." Still, they all feel cut from a similar cloak. The fact that more witch-affiliated musicians keep emerging shows how effective the archetype is as a symbol for rebellion, creativity, and female autonomy.

And it's no surprise to see pop colossi dip their toes into witchy waters as well. A purple-caped Katy Perry danced in a giant crystal ball and haunted forest set during the performance of her song "Dark Horse" at the 56th Grammy Awards. Her occult theatrics may been a bit too convincing for some, because she later became embroiled in a series of lawsuits when she tried to purchase an LA convent from some Catholic nuns who refused to sell it to her. They said that they disapproved of her lifestyle and videos, citing her attendance at the 2014 Salem Witch Walk as evidence that she was a practitioner of black magic. One of the sisters is quoted as saying, "I'm sorry but I am just not into witchcraft and I am just not into people who are into witchcraft. It disturbs me and that was our mother house and our retreat house and it's sacred ground." Perry assured them that she is not actually a witch, and that she intends to use it as a home for herself, her mother, and her grandmother, as well as to sit in the garden to meditate and drink green tea. As of this writing, the sale is still pending.

Lady Gaga has long associated herself with the dark feminine, referring to her fans as "little monsters" and herself as their "Mother Monster" in turn. She's embraced shocking aesthetics throughout her career and has worn several witch-appropriate outfits both onstage and off. When she met with WikiLeaks founder Julian Assange in October 2012, CNN reported that "[s]he was dressed as a witch, in a black gown and a fitting witch hat"—actually from Hedi Slimane's line for Yves Saint Laurent that season. In May 2016, she posted an Instagram video of herself dancing to the Radiohead song "Burn the Witch," with the caption: "This song speaks to me on a deep spiritual level as a woman thank you. RADIOHEAD [sic]." Later that year, she played the role of an immortal witch in *American Horror Story: Roanoke*, a character that show creator Ryan Murphy considered to be "the Original Supreme" of all of the witches throughout the series.

Beyoncé's 2016 visual album *Lemonade* is filled with imagery of transformation and spiritual healing specific to the black female experience. In the video for "Hold Up," she channels the golden gown–wearing Oshun, who is the Yoruba deity of water, beauty, and sex; and in "Formation," she dons a black wide-brimmed hat and holds her middle fingers up to the sky in a gesture of defiance. Images of black women gathered in groups throughout the film read like a matriarchy and a coven all at once, and painful topics of infidelity, racism, and sexism are enveloped in otherworldly opulence. Though many of us may think of Beyoncé as a powerful witch in the symbolic sense, her actual spiritual beliefs are beside the point. As Omise'eke Natasha Tinsley writes in *Time* magazine, "Beyoncé's vision of black women's divine retribution . . . is not a confession of her occult practices. Her imagination of black women tapping into supernatural powers to right wrongs also continues Africana feminist legacies of protest against social injustice." *Lemonade* is Beyoncé's elevation spell for herself and women like her, metamorphosing wounds into wings.

THERE MAY BE a lot of mixed feelings about witches going mainstream. But I will say this: one very happy result of the growing popularity of the archetype is that it is bringing about an upsurge of inquisitive travelers who feel emboldened to walk in the witch's path without apology or fear. More people waving their preternatural pennants means that we can more easily find each other, and then form meaningful alliances built on our shared values and dissident fascinations. And when more of us celebrate witches, they become less vilified bit by bit. This brings me immense hope for an emerging society that truly honors female power, and that not only praises the sanctity of nature and the body, but actively works to keep both out of harm's way. Whether as transformative spiritual figures, rabble-rousing cultural symbols, or bewitchingly complex characters in stories and histories that we read and watch and reimagine, I know this: witches are the future.

But if our contemporary coven is to last, it must also be a ring of radical honesty and exacting compassion. As with most Western occult systems, modern witchcraft has always been marked by syncretism, or the merging of many cultural influences, which makes it both revolutionary and inherently problematic. It combines and interlinks symbols from many different traditions and attempts to blend them into a universally relevant concoction. "Isis, Astarte, Diana, Hecate, Demeter, Kali, Inanna," begins one popular goddess chant, written by Deena Metzger and Caitlin Mullin in the 1980s. The names are pulled from Egyptian, Greco-Roman, Hindu, and Mesopotamian mythologies. On its surface, the line delivers a moving message of the divine feminine, which has been erased or suppressed in so many spiritual narratives, particularly in the Abrahamic religions. But there are some who criticize this approach as being an example of witches grazing from the spiritual salad bar. There's danger in plucking out only the most attractive bits of an entire body of theology, without going into any depth or knowing the full context in which these deities dwell.

As with the broader cultural conversation happening right now about identity, intersectionality, and representation, the witchcraft community is also undergoing a reassessment about when appreciation of another group's heritage becomes appropriation of it.

For instance, there are many American witches of color who incorporate Yoruba-influenced religious practices, such as Candomblé, Santería, Vodoun, and Hoodoo, into their rituals. When white practitioners of witchcraft "borrow" from these religions willy-nilly, and without acknowledging their long and painful histories, it can feel like a breach. It's also important to bear in mind that religions such as these, as well as the folk-magic traditions of the indigenous people of Ceylon and Borneo that "Father of Wicca" Gerald Gardner was inspired by, have been around for far longer than Wicca and its offshoots, which only began in the mid-twentieth century.

Gardner and the other founders of Wicca were white and British, and likewise, the American-born feminist-driven witchcraft movement was steered by white women. Looked at in the kindest light, they were people who were trying to reach a spiritual truth that transcended the false constructs of separate cultural boundaries. But they can also be considered in a harsher one: further evidence of white imperialism.

To that end, there is currently a great deal of debate about the ways in which twenty-first-century witchcraft sometimes incorporates elements from African Diaspora, Indigenous American, and other non-European traditions. Santería candles, Haitian Vodoun *vèvès*, and "Native American" smudge bundles of white sage are just a few of the elements derived from communities of color that are regularly featured throughout contemporary Pagan covens, altars, and occult shops—not to mention in chain stores currently trying to appeal to a young and spiritually curious demographic. Representation of different cultures is an admirable goal, but not at the expense of the original creators, who are often being erased or exploited in the process. Of course, these infractions occur to varying degrees and with varying consequences. A white American woman trying to connect to her "spirit animal" may be offensive to a member of the Lakota tribe. A luxury wellness company selling a $2,800 spirit-animal ring designed by a white woman, while American Indian reservation residents have a 39 percent poverty rate, is another matter altogether. Likewise, many white owners of hipster-approved witch shops get frequent press coverage as the heralds of the "new" witchcraft movement—not so much the brown and black owners of neighborhood botanicas that have been selling many of the same herbs, candles, and oils for far longer.

No group is a monolith, however, and there are multiple perspectives on the mix-and-match approach to modern witchcraft, with opinions varying from person to person. I've heard from witches of color who welcome the incorporation of their familial traditions into other contexts and who feel proud to have the ways of their ancestors honored by people on the outside, as long as the practices are done with respect and awareness about their origins. I've also been told that Spirit doesn't care what we look like or where we're from, so why should we? As one Dominican Vodoun practitioner said to me, "Vodoun chooses who it wants. The flesh is such an impermanent thing." From this point of view, we have a shared commonality as human beings and spiritual seekers, so the trappings are beside the point. And anyway, aren't a Wiccan banishing spell, a Mexican *curandera*'s *limpia*, and a Cheyenne smudging ceremony all rituals for cleansing unwanted energies?

But there are those who see this kind of thinking as yet another example of racism. To them, it's understandably painful to have their culture further co-opted and exploited at the hands of white supremacy, well-meaning or not. Some have expressed that connecting to ancestral practices and reclaiming their roots has been a large part of their own healing from generations of trauma inflicted by racism and colonization. These traditions were often all their families had when their property, possessions, and liberty were stolen by genocide, enslavement, and forced assimilation. The fact that white people would sometimes try to justify these atrocities by calling native religious customs "devil-worship" or "witchcraft" adds insult to injury. For those who hold this point of view, seeing a Caucasian "witch" cavalierly pray to a nonwhite goddess can feel like a trespass, because their own relationship to that deity is so precious and hard-won.

Finally, there is the matter of cultural mutability to contend with. Whether we like it or not, ideas hybridize and stories cross-pollinate. We see this in cuisine and in music, as spices mix and genres blur. The same can be said of spiritual culture. One might argue that Vodoun, for example, incorporates threads of Catholicism, Freemasonry, and various indigenous African traditions. Likewise, Christianity itself was developed from an amalgam of earlier influences: Zoroastrian, Greco-Alexandrian, Greco-Roman, and, of course, Jewish. This is an oversimplifiction, to be sure, as it doesn't account for the reasons behind shifting power dynamics, nor the countless individuals who have been profited off of or silenced along the way. But there has also been so much wisdom gained, art created, and connection fostered through the interplay of disparate sources. Having a witchcraft practice that does this intentionally, and with humanity, is difficult but not necessarily impossible. As Yoruba priestess and author Luisah Teish has written, "I maintain that the biggest challenge in the new millennium could be a change of habit. We could change from a dominating commodity culture into one of true exchange in which we learn from each other in humility and respect. I do think it's possible. But it's up to us."

These conversations will continue, and it's important that they do. The histories of people of color have been systemically excluded and erased so often and for so long by a dominant white narrative, and it is crucial that those who practice contemporary witchcraft don't perpetuate this pattern. No matter what each of us thinks about a culturally mixed approach to magic, it's imperative that we remain sensitive to one another's perspectives and lived experiences, and open to recalibrating as we listen and learn. This is especially necessary for white practitioners like me, who've benefited from the cultural advantage of white privilege, and who have an obligation to continuously confront and undo our own racism. There is a reason that the archetype of the witch resonates with those who feel different or oppressed: she is an outsider herself, after all. In declaring allegiance to her, one forges a sacred bond with anyone who has been overlooked, underrepresented, pushed aside, or cast out.

It is said that witches do "sympathetic magic," which involves a system of linking correspondences. In a spell, red rose petals are thought to bring about love, and a green candle can conjure up some money. But if we want to move forward as a truly revolutionary community, it's *empathetic* magic that we must practice. Support, compassion, and mutual consideration are the key ingredients to manifesting prosperity and peace for everyone. Lifting each other up whenever possible is how we'll truly take to the skies.

THERE ARE SO many ways to be a witch. Likewise, there are many ways to define what witches are, what they do, and what they do for us. Some people enter the witch's world because they are turning away from something that no longer serves them, such as a religious past that they found insufficient, or a self-image that made them feel diminished or unseen.

For others, *witch* is an additive descriptor. "Catholic witch," "feminist witch," "fashion witch," and "queer witch" are just a few examples of how I've heard people refer to themselves lately. As a modifier, it signals a stance of revision, defiance, and self-direction. It bolsters one's other identities, enhancing them with the power of myth and moxie. As such, *witch* is a magic word in itself.

And there are more of us than ever who call ourselves witches, whether figuratively or literally, poetically or politically. We do it out of a need for rebellion or a sense of belonging. We may say it in a whisper or shout it loud to the moon. We can sing it to the sky, state it on a tote bag, paint it on a protest sign, or write it in a secret grimoire of the heart.

But no matter the how of it, there is a reason why so many of us are reaching out to the witch for gratification and for guidance. She offers us a pitch-black blueprint for building alternative social structures and stronger selves. Hers is an old story that we're retelling in order to get somewhere new. We walk through her forest of marvels and, in doing so, are made to confront our fear, our fantasies, and our faith. The path she sets is personal and different for everyone, but the destination is the same. It leads to a land of liberation, where each of us can be our most complicated and imaginative and troublesome and true.

When we arrive, the witch welcomes us. She opens her door with a shriek and a cackle.

And we greet her in turn, wild and blazing, arms open and eyes wide.

Witches are not only divine, they're diviners. They throw sticks and bones, read cards and stars, and scry in crystal balls. They have night vision and second sight and can see what may come tomorrow.

And so I feel compelled to do my own foretelling:

The redemption of witches and the ascension of women will be forever interlinked. That both are happening at this moment in time is no coincidence. Each is a reflection of the other.

Witch.

Woman.

A word of horror turns into an honorific; disgrace changes into consecration; shame shifts into reclamation.

That the witch has been reconsidered as a positive figure in the West bit by bit since the nineteenth century shows how far we have come, but also how far we still need to go before women's power is no longer debased, suppressed, snuffed out. The witch's mother is Magic, but her father is Fear. She was born from a disdain for the feminine, a hatred of the female body and how it creates and ages and wants and is wanted. To love her is to embrace this tragedy and to turn her trauma into triumph.

The witch is a relative of goddesses and fairies and devils and monsters, yet is wholly her own breed because of one crucial differential: she is usually human. And so we not only relate to her, we can become her. In choosing to take on her mantle, we cloak ourselves in her many associations, both her fictions and her truths. And in bringing our selves to her, we further add to her meaning. This is how she has survived for so long, and why she thrives still. She is a creature of accretion.

Her route to the top of popular consciousness has been riddled with contradiction. She's been dreaded and desired, executed and exalted. She's a murderer and a martyr, a being who honors nature even as she defies it. She's surrounded by beasts and demons and spirits and sisters, and she stands entirely alone.

And that is why those who feel outside or "other" are so drawn to her. She offers an understanding of persecution, a circle of protection, and a promise that what once was lost will be retrieved. Though her story is bound up with the history of women, her archetype has been embodied by people across the spectrum of identity. This, too, brings me hope. Integrating the feminine with the masculine is an alchemical working that benefits all. Dismantling patriarchal oppression throughout both our externalized systems and our internalized thinking is work that belongs to everyone. Elevating the witch helps all of us move forward.

I believe her upsurge of popularity is indicative not of a trend, but rather a sea change. May more of us feel the pull of her nocturnal tide.

But let us also realize that this waxing age of the witch has come at great cost.

The very fact that so many of us can now joyfully speak the witch's name aloud is a glorious thing. But we must remember the many thousands of people who have had their lives threatened or taken in her name as well—and this continues around the world to this day. To call oneself a witch with pride, whether ironically or with full-throated sincerity, is a marker of great privilege. Though it's never an entirely safe thing to do, those of us who use this moniker in public are very fortunate to feel able to take the risk.

And for those who do not consider themselves witches, but who love to watch her and read about her and hear her supernatural song nonetheless, she still has plenty of messages to share. She gives us all an opportunity to consider questions about terror and gender, freedom and restriction, mystery and majesty.

Hers is also a lesson about adaptation and evolution, for the witch is constantly being rewritten and remade—and she'll take on many new shapes, no doubt, as time flies on. She becomes what we need her to be, and she transforms us in turn.

The witch has shown me how to trust myself, to gather up my sharpest parts and turn them into tools. She's taken me by the wrist and twisted me into the best kind of trouble. She's shown me that I am capable of changing my own life.

She talks to me between branches, gleams at me from the mirror, says I'm wondrous and worthy and full of holy fire.

She tells me dirty jokes and buries my secrets in the soil. We plant seeds, eat weeds, and wake old memories. We haunt. We howl. We harvest.

We round up the feared, the forsaken, the forgotten, and let them know they matter, here and now. Together we raise the dead.

I was scared, and she made me brave. I was small, and she made me grand. I was strange, and she made me strong. Evening after evening, she told me she would never leave my side, and she never has.

She took the hallowed dark and formed a hearth.

⋆ *Further Reading* ⋆

The following list is by no means comprehensive, but rather a narrow cross-section of texts that were particularly informative and inspiring for the writing of this book.

Aberth, Susan L. *Leonora Carrington: Surrealism, Alchemy, and Art*. Farnham, Surrey: Lund Humphries, 2004.

Adler, Margot. *Drawing Down the Moon: Witches, Druids, Goddess-Worshippers, and Other Pagans in America*. 4th ed. New York: Penguin Books, 2006.

Braude, Ann. *Radical Spirits: Spiritualism and Women's Rights in Nineteenth-Century America*. 2nd ed. Bloomington, IN: Indiana University Press, 2001.

Callow, John. *Embracing the Darkness: A Cultural History of Witchcraft*. London: I. B. Tauris, 2018.

Chadwick, Whitney. *Women Artists and the Surrealist Movement.* London: Thames & Hudson, 1991.

Grant, Simon, Lars Bang Larsen, and Marco Pasi. *Georgiana Houghton: Spirit Drawings.* London: Courtauld Gallery, 2016.

Hults, Linda C. *The Witch as Muse: Art, Gender, and Power in Early Modern Europe.* Philadelphia: University of Pennsylvania Press, 2005.

Hutton, Ronald. *The Triumph of the Moon: A History of Modern Pagan Witchcraft.* Oxford: Oxford University Press, 1999.

———. *The Witch: A History of Fear, from Ancient Times to the Present.* New Haven, CT: Yale University Press, 2017.

Kaplan, Janet A. *Unexpected Journeys: The Art and Life of Remedios Varo.* New York: Abbeville Press, 1988.

Kaplan, Stuart R. *Pamela Colman Smith: The Untold Story.* Stamford, CT: U.S. Games Systems, 2018.

Michelet, Jules. *Satanism and Witchcraft: The Classic Study in Medieval Superstition*, trans. A. R. Allinson. New York: Citadel Press, 1992.

Müller-Westermann, Iris, and Jo Widoff. *Hilma af Klint: A Pioneer of Abstraction.* Stockholm: Moderna Museet, 2013.

Petherbridge, Deanna. *Witches and Wicked Bodies.* Edinburgh: National Galleries of Scotland, 2013.

Purkiss, Diane. *The Witch in History: Early Modern and Twentieth-Century Representations.* London: Routledge, 1996.

Sollée, Kristen J. *Witches, Sluts, Feminists: Conjuring the Sex Positive*. Berkeley, CA: ThreeL Media, 2017.

Starhawk. *Spiral Dance: A Rebirth of the Ancient Religion of the Great Goddess*. 2nd ed. New York: Harper, 1989.

Acknowledgments

It takes a coven to bring any book into being, and this one is certainly no exception. The following individuals have provided me with many blessings and boons, and without them the preceding words might still be brewing in my brain instead of here on the page.

Thank you first and foremost to Rick Pascocello. I realize that this is not quite the "empowered woman's business book" you were picturing when we first discussed the possibility of working together, and that it exists now anyway is a testament to your wide-open mind and visionary spirit. I'm grateful to have you in my corner, as well as to be supported by Alex Glass and the rest of the team at Glass Literary Management.

I don't know how Gallery Books manages to be full of so many wonderful humans, but I have a feeling that Jennifer Bergstrom's fine leadership has something to do with it. I've been dazzled by each person who has added their magic touch to *Waking the Witch*:

Thank you, Kate Dresser, for providing me with astute guidance, unflagging good cheer, and emergency grilled cheese. You are quite simply a dream editor, and I feel so very lucky that our stars aligned.

Natasha Simons, your early championing of this book is why it found such a happy home, and I am grateful to you for believing in it, and me.

Molly Gregory, your input and kind assistance overall was such a great help. Anna Dorfman, you made sure this book had a cover that is as mesmerizing as the witches I write about. Thank you both for your craft. And many thanks to Aimée Bell, Alexandre Su, Joal Hetherington, Sydney Morris, Tracy Woelfel, Jen Long, Abby Zidle, Diana Velasquez, Mackenzie Hickey, Anabel Jimenez, Lisa Litwack, John Vairo, Jaime Putorti, Monica Oluwek, and Caroline Pallotta for each of your significant contributions.

I owe much to the many witch-centric scholars, creators, activists, and practitioners who came before me, including each and every one cited throughout the text. But two of them merit another mention:

Ronald Hutton, your contribution to the corpus of witch history cannot be overstated (and I'm convinced your swift e-mail replies must be due to some sort of sorcery). Thank you for answering my questions, and for your tremendous scholarship overall.

And while Margot Adler is no longer with us in the material realm, the ways in which she balanced her literary and journalistic career with her magical practice provided a rare template for me. It is my hope that this book in some small way honors her legacy.

Two people in particular have taught me volumes about art, magic, and friendship. Jesse Bransford and Susan Aberth, thank you for gracing me with your generous hearts and brilliant minds throughout this process, and in general. And much gratitude to the Octagon House, where several sections of this book were formulated and/or written.

There have been a number of other witchly luminaries who have helped inform my thinking around many occult topics over the years. Robert Ansell, Christina Oakley Harrington, William Kiesel, Shannon Taggart, and Jon Graham, I'm in awe of each of you, and I look forward to continued collaborations and conversations. Amy Hale, thank you for letting me benefit from your careful eye and boundless knowledge about Pagan history. Cornell University's Witchcraft Collection has been an invaluable resource for me both online and in person, and I thank Laurent Ferri for making it so accessible.

I'm grateful to have had a number of other bright spirits lighting the way for me, particularly when it comes to navigating the world of books. Thank you to Mitch Horowitz, Gary Jansen, Peter Bebergal, Judika Illes, Lauren Cerand, Janaka Stucky, Josh Izzo, and Jason Louv for being so helpful, encouraging, and dear.

Robin Rose Bennett, how happy I am to have conjured you into my life. Thank you for being my teacher, and for showing me that witches really are green. And many thanks to the other women who sat beside me in your circle.

On the subject of teachers, Alice Richter, Kim Thorpe, and John Lach influenced me more than they know. And Lois Hirshkowitz brought me language and so much light. May she rest in poetry.

Much gratitude and deep love to my witch sisters in the Queenright Coven. I'm thankful for your support and continuous presence. Special thanks to Kristen Sollée and Dianca London Potts, whose insights helped make this book better, and to Bri Luna for being such a vocal advocate of my work. Amber King, I appreciate how deftly you wield your cards and clippers. And thank you to the wider community of witches I've met on- and offline, whose commitment to living openly is emboldening to so many, myself included.

Credit must be given also to the people and spaces that allowed me to develop my thinking around witchcraft and culture over the years, including NYU Steinhardt and 80WSE Gallery (with double thanks to Mr. Bransford), Pat Shewchuk and Marek Colek of Tin Can Forest, Elisabeth Krohn of *Sabat Magazine*, Mallory Lance of *Ravenous Zine*, the members and attendees of Observatory, the readers of *Phantasmaphile*, and the listeners and contributors to *The Witch Wave* podcast.

When it became clear that I needed to make a big change and focus on my witchery full-time, my colleagues at Getty Images could not have been more gracious. I thank Jonathan Klein, Dawn Airey, Andy Saunders, Paul Foster, Rebecca Swift, Lindsay Morris, Hannah Meade, and Katie Calhoun, as well as all of the stellar people in the global creative department. (And thank you to Karen Tighe-Izzo for starting this whole chain of events in the first place.)

I am fortunate to have exceptional friends and family members who continue to cheer me on, make me laugh, and show me what love is, despite my periodic disappearence into the author oubliette. Melanie Hawks, Shiwani Srivastava, Lauren Schreibstein, Megha Ramaswamy, Suzannah Murray, Rachel Hansen, Emma Baar-Bittman, the Pomerantzes, the Wilsons, the Freemans, the LeClairs, the Trumbulls, the DelGrossos, and the Baldwin-Ancowitzes, thank you all. To the scintillating Moira Stone: you were an ideal research road-trip buddy, and I'm grateful to you and the debonair Robert Honeywell for gifting me with much-needed respite and writing time at your home. Jess Matlin, thank you forever for rescuing me from Top 40 radio. Extra appreciation goes to those of the above who read early drafts and shared their thoughts with admirable diplomacy.

To my sister, Emily: watching you turn your life into a lesson about bravery and resilience is an inspiration. I love you, and I thank you for allowing me to share parts of our story, and for being a lifelong cheerleader of mine. And for those reading who are struggling with mental health issues themselves or who know someone who is, the National Alliance on Mental Illness is a great resource (nami.org), as is Emily's website (emilygrossman.net).

To my parents, Rich and Nina: I don't know what I did to hit the karmic jackpot of getting to be your daughter, but I am thankful every day that we were brought together in this lifetime. You have always encouraged my creativity and curiosity, even when they took me to far-out places. And you have always made me feel loved. (The feeling is mutual.) I'm grateful for you both.

Matt Freeman: I know it is not easy being married to a person who is writing a book, but you supplied me with a steady stream of tea, understanding, good ideas, and twisted jokes. Thank you for your levity, your artistic audacity, and for being the best Muggle husband a witch could ask for. I love you so, you handsome devil.

To our cat companions, Remedios "Remy" Varo and Albee, you cannot read. But I'm thanking you both anyway for being my furry familiars, darling friends, and the loveliest of office-mates.

This book is written in memory of Grandma Trudy with the healing hands and Grandma Sonya with the painter's wand.

May we all live with the freedom to make our own magic, whatever shape it takes. Blessed be.